G000130250

YEMEN IN CRISIS

ALSO BY HELEN LACKNER

Editor

Yemen and the Gulf States: The Making of A Crisis
(with Daniel Varisco)

Why Yemen Matters: A Society in Transition

Yemen into the Twenty-First Century: Continuity and Change
(with Kamil Mahdi and Anna Wuerth)

Author

PDR Yemen: Outpost of Socialist Development in Arabia

A House Built on Sand: A Political Economy of Saudi Arabia

Helen Lackner

YEMEN
IN CRISIS

Autocracy, Neo-Liberalism and
the Disintegration of a State

SAQI

Published by Saqi Books 2017

Copyright © Helen Lackner 2017

ISBN 978-0-86356-193-1
eISBN 978-0-86356-188-7

Helen Lackner has asserted her right under the Copyright, Designs
and Patents Act, 1988, to be identified as the author of this work.

This book is sold subject to the condition that it shall not, by way of trade or otherwise,
be lent, resold, hired out, or otherwise circulated without the publisher's prior consent in
any form of binding or cover other than that in which it is published and without a similar
condition including this condition being imposed on the subsequent purchaser.

First published in Great Britain in 2017 by

Saqi Books
26 Westbourne Grove
London W2 5RH

www.saqibooks.com

A full CIP record for this book is available from the British Library.

Printed and bound by CPI Group (UK) Ltd, Croydon CR0 4YY

For Jamal

Thanks for being a wonderful human being,

principled, caring, and kind in the face of an unjust world.

And for your children,

Hoping that they will live in a happier Yemen.

Contents

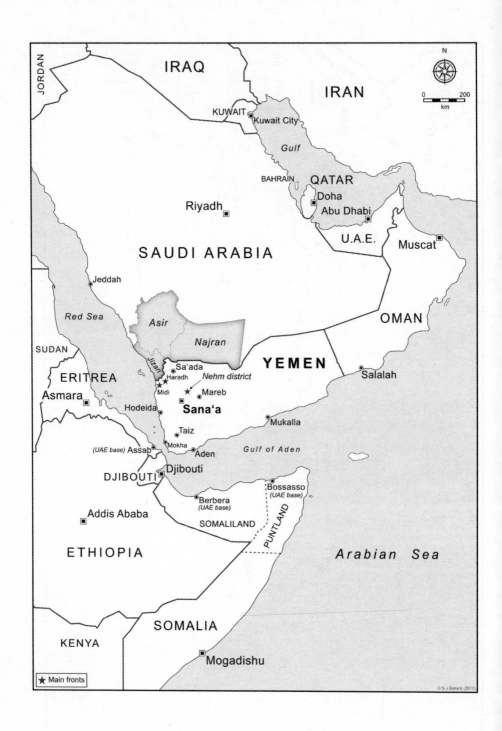

YEMEN IN ITS REGIONAL ENVIRONMENT

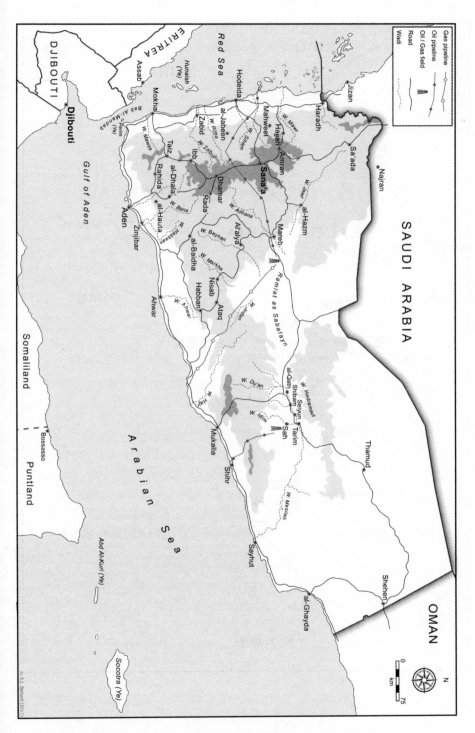

YEMEN'S PRINCIPAL PHYSICAL FEATURES AND INFRASTRUCTURE

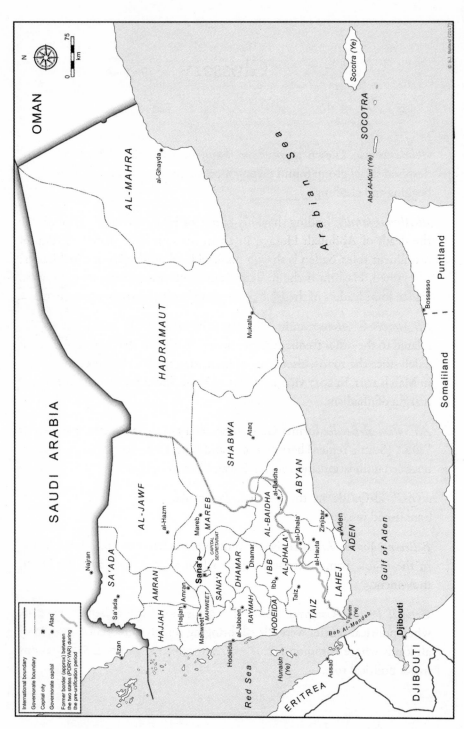

MAP OF YEMEN SHOWING ADMINISTRATIVE ENTITIES

Glossary

Akhdam: also known as *muhamasheen*; status acquired by birth, most despised social group found throughout the country, main occupations are begging and cleaning.

Al-Ahmar family: leading shaykhly family of Hashed confederation. Since the death of Abdullah Husayn in 2007, his sons have shared a group of prominent roles. Sadeq is shaykh mashaykh (chief shaykh or tribal leader) of Hashed, Hashim is the military leader, and Hamid the main political leader. Joint leaders of the Islah party representing its tribal component.

Ali Mohsen al-Ahmar: military leader from same village as Saleh, he is not related to the other frequently mentioned al-Ahmar. Was close associate of Saleh since the 1970s; after years of increasing rivalry, the break took place in March 2011. In 2017 vice president to Hadi, Sunni fundamentalist on the margin of jihadism.

Ali Salem al-Beedh: former General Secretary of the YSP, effective ruler of PDRY (South Yemen) between 1986 and 1990, then vice president of ROY between unification and 1994 civil war. Lives in exile.

AQAP: al-Qa'ida in the Arabian Peninsula, headquartered in Yemen; established in 2009.

Believing Youth: Zaydi revivalist movement started by the Huthi family in the 1990s. Some members went to Iran to study. Became the Huthi movement.

General People's Congress: political organisation, established in 1982, ie. when political parties were illegal, bringing together influential people of all kinds whose common factor was, and remains, ensuring Saleh retains major political role.

Abdu Rabbu Mansur Hadi: President of the internationally recognised government since 2012, Vice President to Saleh from 1994 onwards. Military southerner from Abyan who supported Ali Nasser in 1986 and moved to Sana'a at that time.

Hashed: one of Yemen's major tribal confederations (see Al-Ahmar).

Hiraak: term used to describe the collective southern separatist movement; it is composed of a very large number of entities with very similar names, few of which include more than a few members. Most of them based in Aden, but with origins mainly in al-Dhala', Lahej and Abyan Governorates. Other main base in Hadramaut.

Huthi movement: also known as Ansar Allah; originating in Sa'ada Governorate in the far north of Yemen, it is a family-based movement of Zaydi revivalists whose only ideological characteristic is belief that *sada* [descendants of the prophet] are the only rightful rulers. Involved in six wars against the Saleh regime between 2004 and 2010, now allied with Saleh in fight against the internationally recognised government and the Saudi-led coalition supporting it.

Islah party: officially the Yemeni Congregation for Reform. Political party established in 1990 combining Sunni Islamism of the Muslim Brotherhood variety, a more extremist faction led by al-Zindani, and a third one composed of northern tribesmen, mostly from the Hashed confederation (led by al-Ahmar family).

Joint Meeting Parties: coalition of opposition parties established in 2003, composed of Islah, Yemeni Socialist Party, two *sada* parties (al-Haq and the Union of Popular Forces), the Nasserist Unionist Party and the Baath. Since 2015 most of these are split between the Huthi-Saleh alliance and the internationally recognised government.

Ali Nasser Mohammed: former leader of PDRY from Abyan, led the failed coup in Aden in 1986, then joined Saleh in YAR, living in exile since unification. Occasionally mentioned as a possible interim leader.

Sada [sg *sayyed*]: small social group based on inherited status, claiming descent from the Prophet; there are both Shafi' and Zaydi *sada*.

Salafi: believer in returning to the original roots of Islam, fundamentalist rejecting any interpretation; wants Quranic prescriptions to be implemented literally; a Sunni trend.

Ali Abdullah Saleh: President of YAR from 1978 and then ROY until 2012, head of General People's Congress, military man from Sanhan tribe, a minor component of Hashed federation. In 2017 officially allied with Huthis though rivalry for leadership active.

Shafiʿ: branch of Sunni Islam prevalent throughout Yemen, except the central and northern highlands; main characteristic is tolerance and flexibility.

Wadi: river bed, mostly dry, subject to flash floods.

Waqf (pl. *Awqaf*): religious endowment.

Zaydi: branch of Shiʿi Islam found in the central and northern highlands of Yemen. Theologically far closer to Sunni Islam than to Shiʿi, until the current war there was little to differentiate followers from either creed who prayed together and celebrated the same ceremonies.

Abdul Majeed al-Zindani: prominent Islamist politician in Yemen.

Aydaroos al-Zubeidi: Southern separatist leader, governor of Aden (2015–17) and joint leader of Southern Transitional Council established in May 2017.

Notes on Transliteration
and Abbreviations

Transliteration has been kept as simple as possible. The symbol ' has been used for the letter 'ayn. When an Arabic word or name which has entered the English lexicon appears, its customary English spelling has been retained. With respect to names of people, I use the transliteration individuals use for themselves, which may lead to some inconsistencies.

ACC	Arab Cooperation Council
AQAP	al-Qa'ida in the Arabian Peninsula
CBY	Central Bank of Yemen
CDC	Constitutional Drafting Committee
COCA	Central Organisation for Control and Audit
CSF	Central Security Forces
CTU	Counter Terrorism Unit
EFARP	Economic, Financial and Administrative Reform Programme
FDI	Foreign Direct Investment
FLOSY	Front for the Liberation of Occupied South Yemen
FOY	Friends of Yemen
GARWSP	General Authority for Rural Water Supply Projects
GCC	Gulf Cooperation Council
GPC	General People's Congress
HRP	(UN) Humanitarian Response Plan
HTB	Higher Tender Board
IDA	International Development Association (concessional branch of the World Bank)
IFAD	International Fund for Agricultural Development
IFI	International Financial Institution
ILO	International Labour Organisation
IMF	International Monetary Fund

JMP	Joint Meeting Parties
MAF	Mutual Accountability Framework
MAN	Movement of Arab Nationalists
MTR	Mid-Term Review
NACA	National Anti-Corruption Authority
NDC	National Dialogue Conference
NLF	National Liberation Front
NWSSIP	National Water Sector Strategy and Investment Programme
ODA	Official Development Assistance
OFID	OPEC Fund for International Development
PNPA	Peace and National Partnership Agreement
PDRY	People's Democratic Republic of Yemen (1970–1990)
PRSP	Poverty Reduction Strategy Paper
PRSY	People's Republic of South Yemen (1967–1970)
PWP	Public Works Project
ROY	Republic of Yemen
SFD	Social Fund for Development
SFYP	Second Five-Year Plan
SPC	Supreme Political Council
SRC	Supreme Revolutionary Committee
STC	Southern Transitional Council
SWF	Social Welfare Fund
TPSD	Transitional Programme for Stabilization and Development
UAE	United Arab Emirates
UNHCR	United Nations High Commission for Refugees
UNSC	United Nations Security Council
UNVIM	United Nations Verification and Inspection Mechanism
USAID	United States Agency for International Development
WB	World Bank
WFP	World Food Programme
WTO	World Trade Organisation
YAR	Yemen Arab Republic
YCLU	Yemen Confederation of Labour Unions
YECO	Yemen Economic Corporation
YLNG	Yemen Liquefied Natural Gas
YR	Yemeni Riyal
YSP	Yemeni Socialist Party

Timeline

1839   Britain occupies Aden.

1872   Ottomans occupy Sanaʿa, having ruled parts of the area at various points in the past.

1905   Border established between British Protectorates and Ottoman controlled area.

1918   Muttawakilite Zaydi Imamate re-established in Sanaʿa after Ottoman defeat in World War I.

1934   Britain and Imamate agree on border. War between Saudi Arabia and Imamate won by Saudi Arabia, who take over the provinces of Asir, Najran and Jizan, initially on 20-year agreement.

1948   Assassination of Imam Yahia. After short 'liberal' interlude, Imam Ahmed takes over and his troops sack Sanaʿa. He spends most of his Imamate in Taiz.

1952   Egypt: overthrow of king, Gamal Abdel Nasser becomes leader two years later.

1956   Egypt: Suez Canal nationalised, followed by war against UK, France and Israel.

1958   Yemeni Imamate joins Egypt and Syria to form United Arab Republic.

1959   Establishment of the Federation of Arab Emirates of the South, bringing together most of the Western and one of the Eastern Aden Protectorates under British domination.

1962   26 September: Aden Legislative Council votes for Aden to join the federation which becomes the Federation of South Arabia.

        26 September: Sanaʿa, Imam Badr is overthrown after ten days of reign, following Ahmed's death. Yemen Arab Republic proclaimed, supported by Nasser's Egypt within days.

1962–70 Civil War in the YAR: republicans defeat pro-Imam royalists, but post-war government includes many royalists.

1963   Foundation of the National Liberation Front (NLF) in the south, and beginning of armed struggle against Britain on 14 October.

1967   June: war between Arabs and Israel; closure of Suez Canal; Crater area of Aden taken over by NLF for ten days.

          November: Britain leaves Federation of South Arabia and hands over power to the NLF who establish the People's Republic of South Yemen (PRSY).

1967–8   Siege of Sana'a, fails to oust republicans.

1970s   Migration of Yemeni men to work in Saudi Arabia and other oil-rich states.

1970   PRSY becomes PDRY (People's Democratic Republic of Yemen).

1972   First border war between YAR and PDRY, leads to unity agreement.

1974   YAR President Abdul Rahman al-Iryani overthrown and replaced by Ibrahim al-Hamdi in a bloodless military coup.

1977   al-Hamdi assassinated in Sana'a.

1978   YAR: President al-Ghashmi assassinated, replaced by Ali Abdullah Saleh in July.

          PDRY: Salmeen overthrown and executed in June.

          October: Yemeni Socialist Party established, Abdul Fattah Ismail becomes president as well as Secretary General of the YSP.

          December: new constitution approved by referendum.

1979   Second PDRY-YAR war, followed by Unity Agreement.

1980   PDRY: Ali Nasser Mohammed becomes President and Secretary General of YSP; Abdul Fattah Ismail sent into exile.

1982   YAR: establishment of the General People's Congress (GPC).

1984   YAR: Commercial quantities of oil discovered in Mareb.

1985   PDRY: Abdul Fattah Ismail returns from exile; power struggle, Hayder al-Attas becomes prime minister.

1986   PDRY: 13 January 'events' lead to short civil war and exile of Ali Nasser Mohammed and his supporters to YAR. Ali Salem al-Beedh becomes Secretary General of YSP.

1990   22 May: Unification of PDRY and YAR into the Republic of Yemen (ROY); Ali Abdullah Saleh president, Ali Salem al-Beedh vice president.

1990   Iraq invades Kuwait: ROY votes against use of force at UNSC;

	800,000 Yemenis expelled from Saudi Arabia and other GCC states.
1990s	Growth of Zaydi revival movement in governorate of Sa'ada.
1991	USSR dissolved; Mengistu overthrown in Ethiopia, Siyad Barre overthrown in Somalia and beginning of civil war there.
1991	Commercial quantities of oil discovered in Hadramaut.
	Formation of Islah.
1993	Parliamentary elections.
1994	Civil war leads to attempted secession of South under Ali Salem al-Beedh; defeated on 7 July when Saleh's forces enter Aden.
	Constitution changed to give more power to the president.
1995	Government accepts IMF advice and adopts Structural Adjustment economic policies.
	Yemen-Eritrea conflict over Hunaish islands; International Court decides in Yemen's favour in 1998.
1996	First Five-Year Economic Development Plan issued for 1996-2000.
1997	Parliamentary elections.
1999	Presidential elections: Ali Abdullah Saleh elected president.
2000	Saudi Arabia and ROY sign Jeddah treaty on permanent border agreement.
	USS *Cole* attacked in Aden port by al-Qa'ida.
2001	First elections for local councils.
	Second Five-Year Development Plan 2001-2005.
	Ali Abdullah Saleh rushes to support Bush 'War against Terror' after 9/11.
2002	French super-tanker *Limburg* attacked in Yemeni waters by al-Qa'ida.
	Publication of Poverty Reduction Strategy Paper (PRSP) 2003–5.
2003	Formation of Joint Meeting Parties (JMP) from Islah, Yemeni Socialist Party, Baath, Nasserites, Popular Forces and al Haq.
	Parliamentary elections.
	US invasion of Iraq, overthrows Saddam Hussein's Baathist regime.
2004	First Huthi war: Husayn Badr al-Din al-Huthi killed.

2005   Second Huthi war.

2006   Second Presidential Election.

        Formation of the Southern Military Retirees Organisation.

2007   Third Huthi war, demonstrations for southern secession start.

2008   Fourth Huthi war.

2009   Fifth and sixth Huthi wars, the latter labelled 'Scorched Earth', involves Saudi air and land forces in support of Saleh regime, Saudi losses.

        Merger of Saudi and Yemeni al-Qa'ida to form al-Qa'ida in the Arabian Peninsula (AQAP).

2010   Ceasefire in Huthi wars, Huthis gradually take control of Sa'ada Governorate.

2011   Popular uprisings emerge throughout the country, demanding downfall of Saleh regime, jobs, dignity and end to corruption.

        18 March: 'Friday of Dignity' massacre: over fifty demonstrators shot by snipers.

        3 June: Saleh severely wounded during Friday prayers in his mosque, many killed; Saleh evacuated to Saudi Arabia for medical treatment.

        October: UN Security Council Resolution 2014 supports Gulf Cooperation Council Initiative on transfer of power.

        23 November: GCC Agreement signed in Riyadh.

        December: Government of National Unity formed.

2012   February: Abdu Rabbu Mansur Hadi elected president for two-year transitional period, formally takes over from Saleh.

        21 May: terrorist attack on Sana'a parade, more than 120 military graduates killed.

        UNSC Resolution 2051 establishes Sanctions Committee.

        September: International community pledges USD 8.4 billion for development.

        Government issues Transitional Programme for Stabilization and Development (TPSD).

2013   18 March: National Dialogue Conference (NDC) starts.

        April: Appointment of new leadership and restructuring of military security organisations.

December: Attack on Sana'a military hospital, kills sixty-five people.

2014   January: conclusion of NDC.

February: Hadi-appointed committee decides on six-region Federation for Yemen.

Salafi community expelled from Dammaj, disperse to Sana'a and other sites, including Ma'abar (Dhamar Governorate) and Fiyush (Lahej Governorate).

March: Constitution Drafting Committee starts work.

Huthi-Saleh alliance take over Amran in June and Sana'a in September.

July: Basendwa Government increases fuel prices, leads to demonstrations in support of Huthi anti-corruption claims.

21 September: Peace and National Partnership Agreement signed in Sana'a between transitional regime and Huthis.

Government of National Unity resigns; new government with Khaled Baha as prime minister operates from 9 November.

2015   January: Draft constitution published, to be submitted for discussion.

January: Hadi, Baha and government resign in response to Huthi-Saleh demands, and are put under house arrest.

6 February: Huthi make Constitutional Declaration for two-year transition.

February: Hadi escapes to Aden, declares it temporary capital, Huthi-Saleh attack Aden by air and heavy fighting on the ground.

March: Hadi escapes to Saudi Arabia, via Oman and Arab League Summit in Egypt.

March: Saudi-led coalition launches operation 'Decisive Storm' to restore Hadi to power.

March: World Bank and most international financial institutions suspend activities in Yemen.

June: UN-mediated Geneva peace negotiations last five days; two sides do not sit in same room.

July: UAE land troops in Aden and finally expel Huthi-Saleh forces from the city by the end of the month.

December: UN-mediated Geneva negotiations between Huthi-

Saleh forces and internationally recognised government take place in Biel, Switzerland, no result.

2016   April: Hadi fires Vice President and Prime Minister Baha. Appoints Ali Mohsen as vice president and Ahmed Obeid Bin Daghr as prime minister.

April: Kuwait negotiations start, collapse in August.

April-May: UAE and US arrange departure of AQAP from Mukalla who disperse inland.

July: Huthi-Saleh alliance establish the Supreme Political Council (SPC) to replace the Revolutionary Committee in Sana'a.

September: internationally recognised government issues decree transferring the HQ of the Central Bank of Yemen (CBY) to Aden.

November: SPC announces Government of National Salvation in Sana'a.

UN assesses deep humanitarian needs, with 19 million people food insecure.

2017   January: UAE and other coalition forces launch offensive on Bab al-Mandab and Red Sea coast, take most of Mokha by March.

January: Trump administration launches airborne ground attack on Yakla village in al-Baidha Governorate. Number of drone and air strikes increases significantly in following months.

UN announces prospect of famine in Yemen.

Power struggle in Aden between Hadi and UAE-supported military forces. Focus on position of governor.

UN appeals for US $2.1 billion for humanitarian assistance; US $1.1 billion pledged in April. Financed at 40 per cent end June.

May: Hadi dismisses governor of Aden.

May: Former governor of Aden Aydaroos al-Zubeidi and former minister without portfolio Hani bin Breik form the Southern Transitional Council (STC) alongside other southern leaders from different governorates.

July: UK High Court decides that UK arms sales to Saudi Arabia are legal.

Preface

Hope. Writing well into the third year of Yemen's internationalised war, I hope, first and foremost, that the war has ended when you read this. Second, that the end of the war brings a lasting peace and that Yemen's new leadership joins with its people to solve the country's fundamental social, economic and political problems. Third, that Yemen's unique culture can re-emerge allowing Yemenis of all ages to flourish and develop their talents. Fourth, that reconciliation, rather than revenge, is everyone's priority. Fifth, that the states involved with Yemen focus on helping its people, rather than on pursuing their own geopolitical agendas. Finally that this book helps readers to understand why and how Yemen sank into the war, but also provides the elements needed to contribute to a peaceful and equitable future.

Yemen is in the grip of its most severe crisis: the civil war between forces loyal to the internationally recognised government of President Abdu Rabbu Mansur Hadi and the Saudi-led coalition on the one side and those of the alliance between the Huthi rebel movement and former president Ali Abdullah Saleh on the other has devastated the country. On 12 July 2017, the Special Envoy of the Secretary General of the United Nations told the Security Council that

> the situation in Yemen remains extremely grave. The intensity of the conflict increases day after day ... The humanitarian situation is appalling ... The country is not suffering from a single emergency but a number of complex emergencies, which have affected more than 20 million people and whose scale and effect will be felt long after the end of the war. Fourteen million people are food insecure, of whom almost 7 million are at risk of famine ... There are now over 300 000 suspected cases [of cholera] and over 1,700 have died as a result of the epidemic ... The speed and scale of Yemen's cholera outbreak highlights the consequences of a collapsed public sector system.[1]

This cholera epidemic was declared the worst ever recorded worldwide. At the end of his briefing, the UN's Special Envoy expressed a view shared by many when he reminded the political leadership that

> history will not judge kindly those Yemeni leaders who have used the war to increase their influence or profit from the public finances, and Yemenis' patience will not last. The people need an alternative to politicians who work for their own interests and not for their country, who destroy and do not build, and who use the finances of the people and the state to enrich themselves, rather than serve the people.[2]

Despite this calamitous situation, compared with other crises in the Middle East, Yemen remains the least known and most neglected. In March 2017, a poll found that 51 percent of the UK's population[3] (and 63 percent of 18–24 year olds) did not know about the ongoing war, despite the fact that in previous weeks it had been mentioned daily in the media as one of the four countries where famine was likely to kill many thousands of children, men and women. The nightmare humanitarian crisis had also been subject of a specific appeal from the UK's Disasters Emergency Committee in December 2016, which was covered by all media. In the course of 2016, moreover, Britain's involvement in the war had attracted considerable public attention because of its weapons sales to Saudi Arabia and the latter's role in the many air strikes on civilians in markets, mosques, weddings, funerals and hospitals, among others.

 Why is there such widespread ignorance of a country in such deep crisis? Yemen is most definitely part of the Middle East, yet it has been deprived of the mainstream attention which has for decades focused on the Palestinian-Israeli conflict and more recently the disastrous wars in Iraq and Syria. The Arabian Peninsula is known mostly as the home of the super-wealthy oil exporters, including the new tourist destination of Dubai. In fact, younger readers may be surprised to learn that Aden was a British colony until 1967 and then became the capital of the only socialist country in the region.

 While the current equally devastating crisis in Syria is getting far more attention in the West, this is partly due to the 'threat' of hundreds of thousands Syrians seeking safety and refuge in Europe. Yemenis have even more hurdles to overcome before they reach the borders of fortress Europe: travelling through Saudi Arabia is by no means easy, crossing the Red or

Arabian Seas would then mean travelling through many African countries alongside their desperate colleagues from Eritrea, Somalia and beyond. But even with full-scale war and the many dangers of being in Yemen, more people were still heading towards Yemen than away from it during the first two years of the war.

Geopolitics is frequently stated as the reason for international interest. In this respect Yemen should, in theory, receive considerable attention, given that it controls the strategically vital Bab al-Mandab Strait leading to the Red Sea, which is still a major route for international maritime trade. Yemen is also the poorest country in the Middle East and its living standards, prior to the war, were on a par with those of many African countries. Ranked 160th out of 188 in the UN's human development ranking, Yemen is one of the few non-African countries in the low human development category. A possible explanation for the lack of attention on Yemen is that the situation in the country is complex. The humanitarian emergency which exploded in 2017 has been compounded by war, yet the crisis had roots in a combination of pre-existing factors acting in synergy: climate change, extreme water stress, rapid population growth, internal conflicts, a low-skilled labour force, decades of autocratic rule based on divisive patronage strategies, the existence of three states in the last half century, and neo-liberal development policies which have impoverished the majority. To cap all this, Yemen is all too often described as 'tribal', a blanket term popularly used as an instant simplistic label to condemn a society as backward and reduce the humanity of its people, as if tribal systems were anything other than just one form of social organisation among others.

Why should Yemen be given more attention? The country's position on a major international trading route should be sufficient reason for serious interest by the mainly Asian and European states which depend on it. What little concern this country of 27 million has attracted from the outside world in recent decades has been largely as a result of US counter-terrorism policy, which is focused on the presence of jihadi groups, mainly al-Qa'ida in the Arabian Peninsula, that are given far more attention than they deserve.[*] The

---

[*] According to the Global Terrorism database, between 2000 and 2016, Yemen and the US both accounted for about 2 percent of world deaths due to terrorism, though their populations are 27 and 323 million respectively, while Iraq, Afghanistan, Nigeria and Pakistan combined had suffered 57 percent of deaths. In the case of the US, this includes 9/11.

reality is that this demon is more a creature of Western political propaganda than a real international threat, and Muslims form the vast majority of those killed by jihadis. Moreover, for most Yemenis, jihadism is an insignificant threat in comparison with hunger, disease and other survival-related issues they face on a daily basis.

***

Given its population of more than 27 million people, Yemen deserves our concern and interest simply by virtue of elementary human compassion. The threatened famine affecting 7 million people is an emergency on such a scale that anyone with any sense of human solidarity should want to understand how this came about and help find a solution. Why and how can such a famine happen in the twenty-first century? Part of the answer is that this is largely due to the internationalised war and internal strife which are at the heart of the situation.

Yemen is an extremely beautiful country with fantastic landscapes of mountains, desert and coast. It also has many cultural features, including a unique architectural heritage as well as archaeological and cultural sites dating back to pre-history, which are of major significance in the history of the entire Arabian Peninsula and the broader Middle East. All these could easily make it a top destination for upmarket cultural and 'hiking' tourism as well as research. Yet it has escaped that fate due to limited infrastructure, the prevalence of terrorist incidents in the past three decades, the fact that English is not widely spoken – and, of course, the current war. In addition it is also the home of a people famous for their hospitality and generosity, traits which have somehow survived the worsening impoverishment and international hostility of the past few decades. I remember a friend telling me that in his home area people invited passing strangers to join them for lunch. I initially thought this was a slight exaggeration and that it was his way of saying people back home were friendly and generous, but driving through that very area later, farmers and others we drove past did indeed shout loud invitations to lunch.

***

Like so many others, my interest in Yemen and my sympathy with its people increased as soon as I arrived there. The country has remained my main interest and concern for more than four decades. Initially going to Aden, the capital of the then People's Democratic Republic of Yemen (PDRY), in the 1970s, I intended to improve my Arabic and to understand the reasons why this colonial outpost had become the only socialist state in the Arab world. Living and working under the same conditions as Yemenis, I then did what many of them did, and moved to the Yemen Arab Republic (YAR) to earn some money as my PDRY salary was substantially less than what I would have received from unemployment benefit in the UK. In the YAR, I found employment in a development project and thus started my involvement in the kind of rural work I had always dreamed of, and for which my social anthropology studies were helpful. Since that time, I have worked in most parts of rural Yemen. I thus have seen the changes of living conditions for rural and urban Yemenis throughout the country over much of the past half century.

Returning to analytical work happened both by choice and through the changing circumstances in many of the countries where I have worked. Years of field encounters with rural Yemenis in different regions gave me a good understanding of existing social and cultural differences. I also witnessed the impact of the autocratic regime and the internationally imposed neo-liberal development policies on people's daily lives. I saw how the combination of these two factors contributed to people's impoverishment and increasing frustration, which eventually blew up in the uprisings of 2011. These decades also saw significant changes and here, again, my long-term involvement enabled me to notice the significance of what might at first sight appear to be unique and isolated incidents. Some changes were positive such as improved communications, particularly the now almost universal presence of mobile telecoms and the ability to connect to the world through the internet. Many, however, were perceived as negative, such as the high cost associated with increased availability of medical services. Overall deteriorating living conditions affected the vast majority and were exacerbated by the lack of employment opportunities, including the dramatic reduction in emigration destinations.

This long and intimate experience of most parts of Yemen has given me a unique insight into the social, political and economic transformations which have taken place throughout this period. Without writing a personal memoir, I have tried to reflect some of these experiences in this book. However, its main objectives are to present the country, its people and the socio-economic and political changes which have led to the current crisis. I hope the book informs readers whose involvement and concern for Yemen is new. My insights should also assist others who have been or are currently involved with the country, whether in humanitarian and development work or as diplomats, journalists or even analysts and politicians. For them, my experience of the country and focus on ordinary citizens should improve their understanding and, ideally, assist in developing strategies and policies which will address their challenges. Far too often only the views of the elite are heard at the expense of the majority. Younger Yemenis and many in the diaspora may also learn something new about aspects of their country. Or at least they may benefit from a vantage point based on a broader context.

The book starts with analysis of the country's main political features. Chapter 1 presents events and the situation since the crisis started in 2011 with the popular uprisings, the apparent downfall of President Ali Abdullah Saleh after thirty-three years in power, and the internationally supported transition regime of the period 2012–14. It also addresses the war, which became internationalised in 2015 with the intervention of the Saudi-led coalition and which, by mid-2017, at the time of going to press, shows no sign of ending. Chapter 2 discusses the role of other countries in Yemen's development in the past century, focusing on those which have the greatest influence, Saudi Arabia and other Peninsula states, as well as the permanent five members of the UN Security Council. Chapter 3 addresses the country's recent history, the different social and political environments which prevailed in the two states, the People's Democratic Republic of Yemen (PDRY) which took over from the British Aden Protectorates and became the only socialist state in the Middle East and the different track taken in the Yemen Arab Republic (YAR) after the overthrow of the Imam in 1962 and the civil war which lasted for the next seven years. It also explains the origins of the unification of the two regimes into the Republic of Yemen (ROY) in 1990. The political characteristics of the two regimes and the details of the merger process explain the brief civil war which took place in 1994 and the rest of that chapter describes the nature of the regime till the watershed events of 2011.

Chapters 4 and 5 present the role of political Islamism. Chapter 4 analyses the main formal Sunni Islamist Islah party and the role and nature of the various jihadi groups which have given Yemen a bad reputation, despite their limited significance and far more complex nature and relationships with the regime. Chapter 5 deals with the other major Islamist trend, the Huthi movement; it briefly presents its origins in the Zaydi sect of Shi'i Islam and its emergence from being an obscure regional movement of little national significance in the 1990s into the major ideological and military movement that it has become since 2015. This is followed by my analysis in Chapter 6 of the other main long-term threat to Yemen's unity, the Southern movement, which arose from the bitterness and resentments festering in the former PDRY area during the period after the defeat of the separatist movement in 1994.

These political aspects are related to fundamental social and economic changes in the past half century, which are discussed in the following chapters. Chapter 7 addresses the shibboleth of tribalism and the changing nature of Yemeni society, as modes of production were transformed. Two dominant themes are the emergence of an embryonic class structure, and how the determination of status shifted from acquisition by birth to achievement through wealth. It also examines changes in gender roles with respect to the position of women in relation to other changes in the social structure, although it needs to be emphasised that everything else in this book concerns women as much as it concerns men.

Chapter 8 examines the country's limited natural economic assets, giving particular attention to the two major issues, water and mineral resources. Yemen's well-known water scarcity derives from the coupling of increased demand from a rapidly growing population, with excessive use through irrigated agriculture. Climate change factors play a major role in reducing both aquifer replenishment and cultivable areas, as well as affecting the reliability of rainfall for rain-fed agriculture thus diminishing yields and production. In the long term, water and other climate change factors jeopardise Yemen's future at least as much as the current war. Yemen's limited oil and gas resources remain the mainstay of the economy and chief contributors to state coffers, even though the quantities produced are almost insignificant by comparison with those of neighbouring states. Their predatory management and exploitation have neglected the welfare of the population at large, and the chapter examines the past and the possible future of these essential elements to the very survival of Yemen.

The impact of neo-liberal, structural adjustment policies encouraged by the international financial institutions and the bilateral financiers operating in Yemen is the subject of Chapter 9, which goes into some detail of the extent to which these policies have influenced development and aroused resistance from various quarters, including within state institutions. This chapter also addresses some of the basic problems in the social sectors of health and education, and infrastructure. Finally, Chapter 10 considers the trend of rural-urban population movements, revisits the theme of remittances from Yemeni workers abroad, and looks at the impact of all policies on daily life in rural and urban areas. Following the macro-level overview of earlier chapters, this one turns to a more detailed view of the flavour of life for ordinary Yemenis prior to the war.

In conclusion, I assess the underlying social, political and economic features of the current national and international political situation and their significance for coming decades in anticipation of the post-war phase. In addition to reminding readers of the short- and long-term problems, I also point to elements which could be used to bring about the 'new Yemen' that many hoped would be the outcome of the 2011 uprisings and the transitional regime which started in 2012.

***

My main debt in writing this book is to the hundreds, if not thousands, of ordinary Yemeni women and men who have shared their views, lives and problems with me over the decades. In recent years, many patiently explained things despite having prefaced their words with disbelief that yet another study of their circumstances would lead to a project which would improve their living conditions. In earlier times, people actually believed that these conversations would have a positive practical outcome. They are women and men, landless cultivators and livestock holders, smallholders, fishers, artisans, casual labourers and others, young and older, in most of the country's governorates. Senior, middle-ranking and junior officials at local and central levels have also contributed to my understanding of the constraints imposed by the international financial institutions as well as the ruling regime. Many Yemeni friends and colleagues have helped me develop my analysis over the decades, and will remain anonymous as they would be too numerous to mention and some would prefer it that way. Others might prefer not to see their names next to each other, so I have reluctantly decided not to acknowledge any Yemenis by name. You all know how much you helped, and have my gratitude and hopefully recognise some of our discussions and debates in these pages. I trust that those of you who might have preferred to see your names here will understand and accept my decision.

Drafting the book, I am grateful to the following European friends and colleagues for reading some or all the chapters, and making useful comments, suggestions or corrections of fact and analysis. They are, in alphabetical order, Ramon Blecua, Laurent Bonnefoy, Marieke Brandt, Noel Brehony, John Gittings, Martin Jerrett, Dot Lewis, Peter Salisbury, and James Spencer. At Saqi, I am grateful to Lynn Gaspard who chose to publish this book and to her staff who contributed to different aspects of its publication. Following convention, I claim sole responsibility for the views and interpretations expressed here which I am sure are not shared in full by any of the above mentioned. Equally, any remaining errors are entirely my responsibility.

Helen Lackner,
Oxford, July 2017

CHAPTER ONE

How the 2011 Uprising
and the Transition Led to War

From the mid-2000s, Yemenis and close observers alike considered that President Saleh's regime was on its last legs. All wondered what would finally bring it down. The descent into civil war was predictable. The series of wars in the far north against the Huthi rebels, the increasingly militarised confrontations with Southern separatists, numerous localised military conflicts, increasing tension between the official opposition and the regime, worsening poverty, the water crisis, reduced oil exports, unmeasurable rates of youth unemployment, increasingly open popular anger and frustration, all led to paralysis of the formal political system. The end of the regime and the disintegration of the existing polity were the obvious outcomes of this situation, with the likely fall into fragmentation and multiple military conflicts. What I, alongside many others, failed to predict was, first, what would trigger change; and, second, the fundamental transformation in neighbouring Saudi Arabia from a regime which pulled strings in Yemeni affairs from behind the scenes, to one willing to openly intervene militarily.

By mid-2017 Yemen faced total humanitarian disaster, its first famine since the 1940s and the world's worst cholera epidemic. This situation was unprecedented and avoidable: both were the result of a civil war dramatically worsened by international intervention. Concerning cholera, the collapse of the medical services as well as the long-lasting absence of clean water partly explain the intensity of the epidemic and the speed at which it has been spreading. As pointed out by Stephen O'Brien, the UN's Under-

Secretary General for Humanitarian Affairs, by mid-2017, the country's health system had been devastated and '55 percent of [medical] facilities closed due to damage, destruction or lack of funds. Some 30,000 healthcare workers have not been paid in nearly a year and no funding has been provided to keep basic infrastructure such as hospitals, water pumping and sanitation stations operating ... This cholera scandal is entirely manmade by the conflicting parties and those beyond Yemen's borders who are leading, supplying, fighting and perpetuating the fear and fighting.'[1]

As for the famine, under 'normal' conditions, Yemen imports 90 percent of its main staple, wheat, and 100 percent of its rice, tea, and sugar; overall, 70 percent of its food needs. The prime cause of the situation where almost 21 million of Yemen's 27 million people were in need of humanitarian assistance and 10 million of these were 'in acute need of immediate assistance to save or sustain life',[2] that is, on the verge of starvation, was the war. Specifically, the constraints on its main sea port Hodeida, combined with the economic warfare against the Central Bank, prevented commercial importers from getting the letters of credit necessary to buy grains on the international market. Leaders of the warring factions prioritised military objectives over the needs of Yemeni men, women and children. The international community complacently allowed this situation to persist to the greater benefit of arms traders, fuel and food smugglers and other war profiteers. Stephen O'Brien told the UN Security Council on 10 March 2017 that Yemen 'is already the largest humanitarian crisis in the world and the Yemeni people now face the spectre of famine'.[3] He continued to remind his audience that the Humanitarian Response Plan for 2017 needed US$ 2.1 billion to reach 12 million people, only two-thirds of those in need. By mid-July, into the second half of the year, it was 40 percent funded, receiving less than half the funds needed to help less than two-thirds of desperate Yemenis. A month earlier, in June, US President Trump signed agreements to sell arms worth US $110 billion to Saudi Arabia, some of them likely to be used to kill Yemenis.

So, how did Yemen reach such a sorry state? What role has the international community played? This chapter examines the second decade of the twenty-first century, which started so hopefully with the 2011 uprisings that strove to bring about democratic governance, an equitable economy and an end to elite appropriation of the country's wealth.

The 2011 Popular Uprisings

As the first decade of the century came to an end, the political crisis in Yemen accelerated. Throughout 2010, the frequency and intensity of demonstrations increased and, by the beginning of 2011, there was already a long-term encampment in Sana'a by a group of villagers from Ja'ashin in Ibb Governorate, whose lands had been illegally appropriated by a local shaykh whose poetry was appreciated by Yemen's president, Ali Abdullah Saleh. Among other regular protests in Sana'a, the Women Journalists Without Chains, led by future Nobel laureate Tawakkol Karman, a representative of the more 'progressive' branch of the Islah party, had been demonstrating weekly outside the prime minister's office for many months, demanding freedom of speech and protesting about restrictions and oppression of journalists.

Parliamentary elections scheduled for 2009 had been postponed to 2011 with the reluctant agreement of the Joint Meeting Parties (JMP) opposition which was involved in an ongoing struggle with President Saleh's General People's Congress (GPC) over who would be included in the electoral register.[4] In January 2011 Saleh added fuel to the fire of his tense relations with the opposition by attempting to change the constitution so that he could stand for an unconstitutional third term in the 2013 presidential elections,[5] although he had already been in power for thirty-three years. This move confirmed the widespread suspicion that he intended to remain as president until his eldest son, Ahmed, reached the constitutional age to succeed him.

In addition to demonstrations in the capital and beyond, the latest developments in Parliament triggered protests in Sana'a starting on 17 January 2011; by 27 January, they brought between 15,000 and 20,000 people on the streets calling for Saleh's departure. On 2 February Saleh made a speech meant to defuse the situation: he announced the postponement of the parliamentary elections due that April, increased authority for governorates, i.e. an intensification of decentralisation, the cancellation of the proposed constitutional amendments, the establishment of a government of national unity and salary increases of 33 percent[6] for security and military personnel, the latter move being a frequently used tactic to ensure the loyalty of this essential constituency.

The apparent success of the Tunisian and Egyptian people in ousting their presidents gave a great boost to the demonstrations which immediately increased in size and turned into a 'live-in' on the road crossing at the main entrance of Sana'a University, re-named 'Taghyeer' or 'Change' Square. People had been prevented from following the examples of other countries and taking over Tahrir or Liberation Square by Saleh's skilful pre-emptive installation of large tents full of his supporters including mostly military/security personnel on 2 February. All of Saleh's backers were fed and supplied with daily rations of qat,* thus ensuring that they stayed and came out on pro-Saleh counter-demonstrations during the following months.

The tents set up on Taghyeer Square were very varied in style and activities, and included both smaller 'residential' ones and others devoted to meetings. Within a longer term perspective a number of points need to be noted about the Yemeni Change squares.[7] First, the movement lasted longer and was far more widespread than in other countries: although attendance reduced and was affected by increasing factionalism over time, the demonstrations and tents continued well into 2013, when major thoroughfares were still closed. The capitals of all Yemeni governorates had Change Squares, including large cities such as Hodeida, Aden and Taiz and small towns such as al-Ghayda, al-Jabeen and Zinjibar.

Second, they were sites where all social groups mixed and discussed a wide range of issues, involving many who had previously assumed that they had nothing in common. Given that about 75 percent of Yemen's population are tribespeople, it is unsurprising that they played a major role in the movement. But people joined as citizens, not as members of tribes, professions or occupations like students, farmers, or unemployed graduates. Age was a factor, and youth dominated, but this is to be expected as 70 percent of the population are under twenty-five years old. Participants found themselves mixing with people both from other tribes with whom they might have been in historic conflict, and from other social groups in Yemen's stratified society, including some from low status groups. Women's participation was both noticeable and important, although their numbers

---

*   Qat, *Catha edulis*, a mild euphoric drug which also has an appetite suppressant effect. It is a bush cultivated at altitudes between 1,200m and 2,200m above sea level and its fresh young leaves are chewed for many hours in the afternoons by most Yemeni men and a fair proportion of women. While clearly a drug, its harmful effects are less than those of tobacco, but it is widely blamed by external funders for many of the ills of the country. Yemenis themselves consider it part of their culture. In the PDRY its consumption was restricted to weekends and official holidays.

were far fewer and attracted significant opposition from different quarters. Societal characteristics of the movement will have a long-term influence on Yemeni politics as they contributed to the emergence of new connections and ideas, thus challenging many preconceptions about the nature and type of politics that can take place within Yemen's social structure, as is discussed further in Chapter 7.

While individual members of political parties and other organisations were present in the squares from the beginning, the movement's earliest days were dominated by independent youth who helped initiate a wide range of discussions and cultural events on all aspects of Yemeni life. It was the dynamism of these events, as well as the persistence of the encampments, which rapidly forced the formal opposition of the Joint Meeting Parties (JMP) to join in and take an active role as parties, though they were unable to dominate the situation till the dramatic events of the 'Friday of Dignity' massacre of 18 March 2011 when 'dozens of men wearing civilian clothes and armed with military assault rifles ... opened fire. Over the course of three hours, the gunmen killed at least 45 protestors ... and wounded 200, while state security forces made no serious effort to stop the carnage.'[8] This massacre perpetrated by Saleh's forces outraged the population at large and had a fundamental impact on the nature of the movement.

Not only did it lead to the largest set of defections from Saleh's party (ministers, Members of Parliament, ambassadors, and others) thus seriously weakening his regime, it also triggered a split in the army, when the First Armoured Brigade, led by Ali Mohsen al-Ahmar, changed sides and swore to protect the demonstrators. He was joined by the leadership of the Islah party, the al-Ahmar brothers (unrelated to Ali Mohsen, see glossary); they now followed many of their rank and file members who were already active participants in the movement. The JMP then officially declared its allegiance to the revolution. While this 'protection' limited physical repression by Saleh's forces, it also reduced the independence of the movement. Thereafter, for example, the main speaking platform in Sana'a was largely controlled by the Islah party, which prevented many independents from speaking. Segregation between men and women's areas was strictly enforced and women found themselves under attack from their conservative male colleagues, including physical assaults. Despite the expansion of the movement to include traditional political forces, and despite the movement's insisting on remaining peaceful, violence increased in following weeks with clashes between the two military sides taking place alongside the rival Friday mass demonstrations which were a feature of Sana'a in life during 2011.

By April, the threat of full-scale fighting between elite forces on both sides added to the political crisis. Representatives of the major foreign powers present in Yemen came to the conclusion that Saleh would be unable to control the situation. Internal discussions within the GPC and with the official opposition had produced a proposal for a transition in which Saleh would hand over power to his vice president, new presidential elections would be called within sixty days, a new constitution would be drafted to be approved by referendum, and Saleh and his associates would be immune from prosecution. This agreement became known as the Gulf Cooperation Council (GCC) Initiative and was signed on 21 April by all political parties and witnessed by the GCC secretary general and the UAE foreign minister.[9] Saleh refused to sign it under different pretexts on various occasions, including the farcical performance of 22 May 2011 when foreign ambassadors and emissaries from the GCC were assembled at the UAE embassy in Sana'a waiting to travel to the Presidential Palace for the formal signature. Saleh organised his supporters to besiege the embassy, demanding that he stay in power. The ceremony was cancelled and the emissaries had to be helicoptered out.[10] Needless to say, this move did not endear Saleh to the likes of the GCC Secretary General Abdul Latif Al Zayani and other senior GCC officials.

The following months were marked by a succession of similar manoeuvres, continued mass demonstrations and counter-demonstrations throughout the country, and occasional military clashes in Sana'a and beyond. The crisis merely worsened with the 3 June explosion in Saleh's palace mosque which seriously wounded him, Saleh's evacuation to Saudi Arabia for treatment, and his unexpected return to Yemen on 23 September against the wishes of both his Saudi hosts and the majority of the Yemeni people. Additional pressure was put on him through Resolution 2014 of the United Nations Security Council which called for immediate implementation of the GCC Initiative[11] and regular follow-up reports from the UN Secretary General's Special Envoy for Yemen who had been appointed in April. Pressure from a combination of these forces, the international community, the deteriorating military situation as well as Saleh's very shaky medical condition finally persuaded him to sign the agreement in Riyadh on 23 November 2011. Some people did note that at that ceremony, attended by many senior Yemenis and officials from supporting countries, the GCC and Saudi Arabia, the only smile was to be seen on Saleh's face.

The Transition to Good Democratic Governance[12]

Documents signed on 23 November included the original GCC Initiative Agreement, but also a more comprehensive one titled Implementation Mechanism of the GCC Initiative[13] which outlined the components of the transition process 'to good democratic governance'.[14] In brief, the transition was to last for two years from the formal election of Vice President Abdu Rabbu Mansur Hadi as President as he would stand unopposed. During these two years, while a new governing structure was to be developed, the country would be managed by a government of national unity including equal representation of Saleh's GPC and a partnership between the JMP and the new movements arising from the 2011 popular movements. The process to bring about a new governance system was to include a National Dialogue Conference also addressing issues of transitional justice, a Constitutional Drafting Committee and a committee to reform the military and security sectors.

While most terms of the first phase of the GCC Agreement were formally implemented, in practice the transitional regime was unable to make the fundamental changes essential to bring about a 'new' Yemen and transfer power away from the previous elite groups. In addition to the points discussed below, this was largely because the GCC-sponsored deal remained firmly within the confines of neo-liberalism and did not support a fundamental transformation which would challenge the financial and economic interests of its existing elites.

Throughout, the UN had a double role: first, its Department of Political Affairs supported different elements of the transition, but in practice it acted like yet another faction in the various struggles, alongside the GCC states, the US, EU member states, the European Union and others. The latter operated together as the Group of Ambassadors representing the Friends of Yemen, an informal group established in 2010. The second element was a series of resolutions of the United Nations Security Council (UNSC) designed to strengthen the transition process: UNSC Resolution

2051 in June 2012 and regular reports and discussions of Yemen at the Council initially helped the transitional process.[15] However, their weakness failed to prevent what the UN called 'obstructionists', primarily Saleh and his supporters (but there were others too) from undermining the process – despite Resolution 2140 of February 2014, which agreed sanctions on a number of individuals to be named by a committee.[16]

The early stages of the transition went well. President Abdu Rabbu Mansur Hadi, elected on 21 February 2012, surprised many by not acting as a mere puppet managed by remote control by Saleh. Unfortunately he proved unable to manage the political transition. The Government of National Unity was formed as planned: the mechanism for selection of government members was a formula which seemed to have been designed to produce paralysis and conflict. One party was to determine the distribution of ministries and the other to choose which set they would appoint. A majority of ministers came from the largest existing elite factions (Saleh's GPC and the Islah party) and used their ministries as bases to increase patronage and income. Meanwhile the ministers from minority parties, women, youth and civil society were unable to influence the situation. This government gained the reputation of being the most incompetent and corrupt in the country's history. Islah's influence operated through the aged prime minister Mohammed Basendwah who had been chosen precisely for his weakness and ineffectiveness. He remained in post until September 2014 when Islah had lost influence to the benefit of the Huthis who imposed a change of government.

Security Sector Reform

Most discussions of the transition focus on the National Dialogue Conference, but there is little doubt that the failure to implement effective reform of the military and security services was a far more important element, for two reasons. First, the Saleh regime's control over the country was based on successful creation of a multiplicity of competing security and military institutions, all of whose commanders were loyal to him; thus they 'coup-proofed' his regime. Second, no state can enforce its rules or authority in the absence of loyal and effective security and military institutions.

Although the military/security committee was formed early on, the rest of its responsibilities were never fully implemented. Road blocks and other interferences with daily civilian life by military/security official and unofficial groups were occasionally relaxed, but were never removed anywhere – whether in Sana'a or beyond. From the earliest moments of the transition, President Hadi faced major difficulties in his attempts to address this fundamental element of Saleh's power structure. There were innumerable smaller and larger rebellions against his orders, with troops refusing to follow their leaders, because they either supported or opposed Saleh. There were rebellions by whole units against changes to their leadership. Overall, despite considerable efforts by the new transitional leadership, the security sector's indiscipline and lack of commitment to respect the constitution came to typify the transition period.

Hadi attempted to use a 'salami-slicing' approach, to remove Saleh top appointees one at a time. However, he was unable to replace the middle-ranking officers or the loyalty of the troops, and the majority of units, particularly the well-trained ones, remained faithful to Saleh. In the face of strong resistance Hadi used major terrorist incidents – such as the killing in Sana'a of over a hundred new military graduates on 21 May 2012 – to remove those leaders who had so patently failed to protect their troops and prevent the outrage. In this way, within eighteen months of taking up his post, he transferred Saleh's closest associates and relatives from their leadership positions in the most powerful, best-equipped and best-trained (by the US among others) military/security institutions.

Although in principle the plan was to replace Saleh cronies with individuals loyal to the state and the constitution, in practice most new appointees were from Abyan, Hadi's own home governorate; this in turn led to accusations that he was filling the posts with his own cronies. It is easy to understand that he felt safer with people who might have a close relationship with him, particularly in the context of frequent assassination attempts. However, there was clearly an issue of balance which sapped support for the transition regime. Essentially the new regime seemed to be operating on the same patronage principles as the previous one.

Among the reasons Hadi failed to overcome the entrenched loyalty of the elite military units to Saleh and his close associates was the care and attention they had received in the past, including good salaries and fringe benefits. Moreover, both troops and junior officers from elite units came from Dhamar and Sana'a Governorates and were recruited from tribes whose leaders were close associates and beneficiaries of the Saleh patronage system; hence community loyalty also played a part. This was demonstrated in 2014 and 2015, when these units cooperated with the Huthis, whom they had fought in six wars between 2004 and 2010, in taking control of much of the country from Amran southwards. From late 2014 onwards, the elite units openly defied the transitional authority. The success of Huthi expansion into areas traditionally hostile to them was largely attributable to their unholy alliance with Saleh. In the northern highlands another factor was their ability to mobilise support from all groups in the region which had been unhappy about the dominance of the al-Ahmar leadership of the Hashed tribal confederation. Hadi's ambiguous relationship with his Islah allies was a further contributing factor.

The security sector reform process was closely monitored by the international community; the US had taken the lead on this issue as it had been closely involved in training and equipping the elite forces since Saleh had joined the US in its 'war on terror'. The US officials supporting and monitoring the military/security elements of the transition must have been aware of their strengths and loyalties. US failure to effectively support this reform essential to the success of the transition may be linked to its counter-terrorism agenda and apparent belief that these forces were working against terrorists, such as al-Qa'ida. It certainly suggests an ambiguous attitude regarding a transition towards greater democracy, as well as doubts about abandoning Saleh associates with whom some US agents had developed close and long-lasting relationships. While this may or may not be an adequate explanation for the insufficient support given to Hadi's reforms, there is no doubt that the failure of security sector reform was one of the major causes of the descent into civil war in 2015.

The National Dialogue Conference

The National Dialogue Conference (NDC) was intended to bring together all Yemeni political forces, traditional parties and personalities, the northern Huthi movement, the secessionist Southern movement, as well as the new forces emerging from the 2011 popular uprisings, including women, youth and civil society. Although it started late due to disagreements on the selection of its membership, participants represented most areas, social groups and political tendencies in the country, with the notable and unsurprising exception of the jihadis who were not invited and would presumably have turned down any invitation. Of the 565 members, Saleh's GPC nominated 112, the JMP parties had 129 and new forces and parties the rest. Instead of the planned 30 percent female membership it achieved 28 percent, and 20 percent of members were young people. Southerners took 56 percent of the seats though only eight-five individuals represented Southern separatists. The Huthis had thirty-five seats.

The NDC lasted ten months rather than the planned six. Plenary sessions provided opportunities for position statements rather than debate, but were also the site for final votes. Most action and discussion took place in the nine committees: good governance, the Southern question, Sa'ada (euphemism for the Huthi problem), state building, military and security affairs, development, rights and freedoms, independent entities, and reconciliation and transitional justice. Decisions were either approved by consensus of more than one committee and then endorsed, or else they were put to the vote in plenary session. The NDC completed its tasks in late January 2014 and produced a document of more than 1,800 outcomes or decisions which were supposed to be the basis for the work of the Constitutional Drafting Committee (CDC). These outcomes were not all mutually compatible and left a difficult task for the CDC. Most importantly the NDC failed to agree on some fundamental and contentious issues: details of the future federal state, the Southern issue, military reform, and CDC membership.

Some of the NDC's intended procedures were not implemented, leaving it without an effective internal problem-solving mechanism. Transitional justice was a major unresolved issue, particularly for those who had participated in the 2011 uprisings and seen their colleagues killed by snipers or wounded by regime-inspired thugs. This problem remains unresolved at the time of writing in mid-2017. Disagreements about the scope of the 'transitional justice' law focused on the start date for liability for prosecution. Different groups involved with resentments from various historical periods each supported a different start date. The NDC was unable to make implementable proposals and its recommendations, while worthwhile and praiseworthy, were never translated into action, due to the unravelling of the transition process.

The decision to have six regions in the federal state and the borders they were given marked the final break between the Huthi movement and the transitional process. As put by Mohammed al-Bukhaiti, then spokesman for the Huthis, 'we have rejected it because it divides Yemen into poor

Federalism

The issue of federalism is closely related to that of decentralisation. As discussed later in Chapter 3, at the time of unification, the Southern leadership of the Yemeni Socialist Party had favoured a federal form of unification, with each of the two former states remaining an autonomous entity, yet handing over foreign relations and defence to the unified state. After the 1994 civil war, the debate was transferred to discussion of devolving authority to governorate level. The Local Authority Law was forced through Parliament in 2000 by Saleh's GPC, despite strong opposition during a widespread debate in the previous years which had delayed its processing.

The law was clearly designed to prevent any serious and effective decentralisation. Although it allowed local councils to be elected, executive authority remained with governors appointed by the president who were almost all senior military officers. In addition, while governorates were given increased responsibilities they did not get the right to raise funds to enable them to deliver services, hence they remained dependent on the central budget and the goodwill of the regime. One of the indicators of pressure on the Saleh regime was its concession in 2008 when the law was amended to allow local councils to elect governors.

During the transition period starting in 2012, a federal state was seen as a mechanism to address the problems of decentralisation as well as the issues of Southern separatism, and the demands of the Huthi movement. It was also seen as a mechanism to reduce the influence of both Saleh's and the Islah elites and to transfer some control of resources, particularly oil and gas, to the producing areas. Although NDC participants formally agreed that the future Yemeni state should be federal, disputes over the meaning of federalism and principled opposition to any loss of centralised control only served to worsen the power struggle on the issue. Lively daily debates avoided the fundamental issues by discussing the number and detailed borders of the future regions. The NDC failed to reach agreement, partly because there was strong opposition to any form of reduced control from the capital, particularly from Saleh and his GPC and others.

Immediately after the NDC ended, Hadi appointed a special 'Regions' Committee to decide on the number of regions. Following his advice, it promptly resolved to create six regions. The delimitation of each region took no account of any of the basic issues relevant to the social, political or economic factors essential for viability, such as access to economic resources, water basins, ease of communication, or even tribal membership. As the issue of regions may remain relevant in the coming decade, it is worth noting that the six proposed regions were:

- Aden (including the Governorates of Lahej, al-Dhala' and Abyan)
- Al-Janad (Taiz and Ibb Governorates)
- Azal (Sana'a, Amran, Sa'ada and Dhamar Governorates)
- Hadramaut (Hadramaut, al-Mahra, Shabwa and Socotra Governorates)
- Saba (al-Baidha, Mareb and al-Jawf Governorates)
- Tihama (Hodeida, Raymah, Mahweet and Hajja Governorates).
- The cities of Aden and Sana'a were to have special status outside of their regions.

and wealthy regions'.[17] For instance, the region that included the Huthi heartland had neither access to the Red Sea nor to the natural resources (oil and gas) of al-Jawf and Mareb. It also included areas whose population were by no means Huthi supporters. Nor were the six regions welcomed by the southern separatists, who wanted a single region for all the former PDRY, or South Yemen. The alternative of having two regions (one for the former YAR, or North Yemen, and another for the former PDRY) was rejected by many on the grounds that it was a step towards separation and therefore, if that was the plan, why pretend otherwise and delay the inevitable?

The National Dialogue Conference was an important event in Yemeni political life. Although it failed to solve the country's problems, it provided experience for new forces which should contribute positively to Yemen's future when politics once again takes over from war. It gave a voice to social groups which had previously been ignored and who are unlikely to accept being relegated to insignificance in the future: youth, women, civil society groups, as well as the *muhamasheen* lowest social status group were actively included in political debate to express their concerns and interests. Most importantly, the older generation of traditional male leaders had to treat them with the respect accorded to fully entitled participants. The 2011 uprisings and the NDC created groups of Yemenis who have also developed skills and gained experience in political negotiations.

Given that the NDC is still one of the main 'references' to reach peace, the reasons for its overall failure need to be examined to prevent a repetition. On the one hand, there was a fundamental gap between excessively high expectations and what it could realistically achieve given its mandate. There was, nationally and internationally, a widespread perception that the NDC and the transition were one and the same. This is simply wrong: the NDC was one element of the transition process. Other equally or more important ones were the security sector reform, economic development and the nature of the transitional government. Nor can the NDC be absolved of all responsibility.

First, it was assigned tasks inappropriate to such an assembly. Bringing together a miscellaneous group of people with such a wide range of concerns and priorities was not the best mechanism to decide on a new constitution, determine transitional justice mechanisms or solve the Southern or Huthi problems. There is great value to the open discussions which took place, but these should have been followed by a set of smaller decision-making meetings. A second aspect was the ridiculously short period of time allowed by the international community for the NDC and, indeed, for the transition as whole, which took no account of the time required for any of the complex processes involved. Third, it was also slowed down, and sometimes paralysed, by the rivalry between Saleh's GPC and other forces, particularly Islah. Both sides used delaying tactics throughout. Finally, the NDC took place in the country's only luxury hotel, thus further isolating it from the living conditions of the population and normal Yemeni life; this caused considerable scepticism among those Yemenis who even knew it was happening.

Membership of the NDC could certainly have been more representative of Yemeni society. Rural people and those from many areas were barely represented while Southerners, who number at best 30 percent of the country's population, were vastly overrepresented with 56 percent of seats. While not helping to solve the Southern issue, it enabled Southerners to hold the NDC to ransom. It is also a simple fact of life that the massive amounts of time spent on the Southern issue and the time wasted with their frequent boycotts and other interruptions was not available to discuss other, equally or more important issues for the majority of Yemenis, such as the economy, youth unemployment, inequality, poverty, water and plenty more.

Finally, the UN Department of Political Affairs had a significant role in the management of the NDC, despite claims that the process was entirely Yemeni and that its staff did not interfere. In reality UN personnel attempted to influence nominations and decisions, while denying involvement whenever things went wrong. Among UN responsibilities was the provision of experts on different issues: some of these were committed, serious and extremely competent specialists, others were not. Some requests for expertise were not followed up. On a daily basis, UN advisers and the NDC administration should not have allowed debates to use valuable time on interesting but not crucial issues. The UN should have contributed to setting agendas, focusing discussions and helping reach practical implementable decisions, while thwarting delaying tactics. This would have supported the many participants who were enthusiastic and determined, but lacked experience of such debate and negotiations. Those delegates were increasingly frustrated, as they saw the process drift without guidance or support from the NDC's presiding committees and the UN. That said, whatever it did, the UN was likely to be criticised.

The Constitutional Drafting Committee

Following the NDC, a Constitutional Drafting Committee of seventeen jurists was established with the task of transforming the 1,800 outcomes of the NDC into a draft constitution; it was left with unsolved issues including the Southern problem, whether to have separate national and regional constitutions, the level of women's participation, the justice system and the role of Shari'a law in the constitution. It met for nine months, including a substantial period out of Yemen, mostly in the luxury of facilities put at its disposal by Abu Dhabi. The CDC was also plagued by obstructionism and delaying tactics primarily by Southern members, though the delays did not reduce the daily stipends received by those walking out! Huthi participation was minimal. The CDC finally delivered the draft constitution to Hadi on 3 January 2015, thus triggering the next phase of the crisis.

Collapse of the Transitional Regime

The Economy

While most observers and participants focused their attention on Sana'a, where the political aspects of the transition, the NDC and associated events were taking place, the situation on the ground was characterised by events and, in some cases, non-events of great importance to an understanding of developments in 2014. The main non-event was the lack of improvements in the economic situation. People's living conditions continued to deteriorate throughout the period. The need for development financing was acknowledged by all, and most people expected a more equitable economy, the creation of jobs and income-generating possibilities to emerge from the 2011 uprisings. People had also looked forward to improved infrastructure in the shape of greater availability of electricity and water, as well as easier access to medical services and education. None of these hopes were fulfilled.

In apparent recognition of the importance of economic and social development to the success of the transition, the states supporting the transition held two pledging meetings in September 2012, producing pledges totalling US $7.9 billion (discussed in Chapter 9). Well-planned disbursement of even half this amount could have made a major contribution to the success of the transition. Financiers gave two main justifications for delay: lack of transparency (i.e. corruption) and low absorptive capacity of state institutions. This paralysis ensured that no development investments were made while people's living conditions continued to deteriorate, which in turn led to rising frustration.

From 2011 onwards, while participating in the transition processes, the Huthis had been quietly consolidating their control, first over their home Governorate of Sa'ada, and then expanding their power well into the neighbouring governorates of Hajja, Amran and al-Jawf during 2012 and 2013. After their rejection of the six-region federal plan, they moved further south. Their alliance with Saleh first became openly manifest when in June 2014 they took over the capital and other parts of Amran Governorate, which were the heartland of the Hashed al-Ahmar family leaders of Islah.

In July, the Hadi regime raised diesel prices in compliance with the demands of the IMF, an unpopular but necessary move to ensure disbursement of the pledged development funds. Previous fuel price rises had incurred popular protests which Saleh had skilfully managed. This time, the sudden and overnight increase gave the Huthis the opportunity to claim that they alone represented the interests of the people. Had Yemenis seen any improvements in their living conditions in the previous two years, they would probably have come out in support of the transitional government against the Huthis. Instead, thousands demonstrated with the Huthis issuing calls for reduced prices, dismissal of the government and an end to corruption, thereby further weakening the transitional regime.

The Balance of Power Shifts as the Huthis Reach Sana'a

The Huthi move into Sana'a was assisted by a number of factors: passive support of the population, of forces loyal to Saleh, and Hadi's belief that he could manipulate them to weaken the Islahi element of his government. Neither Saleh's security forces, nor the government's military and security units, attempted to prevent the Huthi militias from taking over the capital, indicating collusion at all levels. There is little doubt that, at that time, the Huthi militias were not a powerful military force able to counter serious resistance. Although the government operating since early 2012 was dominated by Islah, and Ali Mohsen, its main military leader, was a senior adviser to the president, Hadi himself has never supported Islah. Under the influence of the international community, he had hoped to use the Huthis to get rid of Islah in his government, not realising that the Huthis were unlikely to fade back into the background once they had achieved such a success.

The Peace and National Partnership Agreement (PNPA), signed on 21 September, was the final attempt to reach peaceful agreement between the transitional regime and the Huthi movement. UN endorsement of the PNPA has enabled the Huthi leadership to consider it as a reference for peace negotiations alongside the GCC agreement and the NDC outcomes, which it also recognises. The signing of the PNPA led to the immediate resignation of the government. The departure of the prime minister had long been called for by most people in Yemen due to his incompetence and slavish attitude to instructions he received from his Islahi masters.

Indications that the PNPA was not going to enable Hadi (and his supporters in the international community) to consolidate his power at the expense of rivals, whether Islah, Saleh or the Huthis, emerged immediately with the problems he faced over the formation of a new government. Hadi's initial candidate as prime minister was Ahmed Awadh bin Mubarak, a university business administration teacher whose main qualifications appeared to be excellent English and lack of political baggage.[18] A favourite of the international community, which had groomed him for the post since 2012, his political career had started as NDC secretary general and he was then appointed director of the president's office. The mere fact that he had been promoted by the UN and other foreigners ensured that he would be rejected by the Huthis, who eventually agreed on the appointment of Khaled Baha, then Yemen's representative at the UN, who became prime minister in October 2014, leading a government which lasted all of four months.

Early Months of 2015: Finalisation of the Slow Coup

Initially, the Huthis made no attempt to exercise power directly, but instead operated behind the scenes by installing advisers in all government institutions and ministries whose 'advice' ministers and others were expected to accept without debate. The year 2015 first saw the Huthis formalise and finalise their control over Sana'a. With the prospect of the draft constitution including the six-region federal state being submitted for approval by the post-NDC authority,[19] the Huthis kidnapped the director of the president's office on 17 January as he was on his way to deliver it. They then demanded that Hadi accept Huthi nominees as vice president, deputy ministers in most ministries and more than 160 top officials in senior positions in security and other key institutions. At this point the president and prime minister had two options: resign or openly operate as Huthi puppets. They chose the first, and at the very least retained self-respect. On 22 January they stood down within hours of each other and were put under house arrest. The Huthis probably wanted to keep Hadi as a puppet president, in the hope that his presence would ensure continued external political and financial support. However, Saudi Arabia, the main financier, had already stopped payments for anything other than emergency humanitarian aid since the September take-over of Sana'a, while the other partners of the GCC agreement also rejected this illegal move. As a result aid soon dried up.

Over the following days the Huthi leadership tussled with Saleh. The latter wanted Parliament to meet and accept Hadi's resignation, but the former realised that, according to the constitution, this would result in a Saleh ally, the speaker of Parliament, becoming president, and thus the process would hand over power to Saleh. This was a first indication of what has since become the ongoing struggle for power between Saleh and the Huthis within their alliance. Unable to agree a solution on the post-resignation leadership, the Huthis proclaimed a Constitutional Declaration on 6 February, creating a Supreme Revolutionary Committee (SRC) which would run the country for two years. They also ordered the suspension of Parliament and of any aspects of the constitution which contradicted their declaration. The SRC also announced the establishment of various entities, such as a Transitional National Council of 551 members to replace Parliament and a Presidential Council of five members; neither of these ever happened so are not discussed further.

After a month under house arrest in Sana'a, Hadi escaped and arrived in Aden on 21 February where he withdrew his resignation, attempted to establish his government and decreed the city to be the temporary capital of Yemen, although many of his most important ministers were still under house arrest in Sana'a. Huthi and former President Saleh military forces increased their attacks southwards even though the Southern separatists, one of whose main strongholds is Aden, gave Hadi tacit support. Fighting in Aden became heavy in March, including air strikes on Hadi's palace, which prompted him to escape to Riyadh via Oman after attending an Arab League meeting in Sharm al Sheikh in Egypt. On 24 March 2015 he requested military assistance from the GCC to restore himself to power.

Assessment of the Transition

The transition process which started in late 2011 effectively ended in early 2015 when the Huthi movement formally took power in Sana'a and the country was overcome by a civil war. Its failure is relevant to the future, as the pre-conditions set by Hadi's internationally recognised government to participate in negotiations include return to the GCC Agreement and the outcomes of the NDC as two of its three basic references. First and foremost, the fact that Saleh was not only allowed to remain in Yemen but even to retain his position as leader of the most important political organisation jeopardised any chance of the transition succeeding. He still considers himself the saviour of Yemen, the creator of its unity and is determined to take revenge on all those who, in his view, betrayed him, from the perpetrators of the 3 June 2011 explosion in his mosque to anyone who wants to usurp his, and his family's, right to rule. Throughout the transition, he used a range of tactics to undermine the process, including supporting rival factions, forming a discreet alliance with the Huthis, and enabling some terrorist attacks which were claimed or attributed to al-Qa'ida or others.

Second, the government of national unity formula was doomed to fail: a government composed of opposing and competing factions was not a recipe for success in the absence of any effort at reconciliation. The integration of the new forces emerging from 2011 as minor elements of one of the two original rival factions gave them no clout and did not prevent the Islah party from dominating that faction of the transition. This meant that the two main rival groups of the 'old elite' remained the determining elements, ensuring that fundamental political change would not happen.

Third, the international community failed to support a fundamentally transformative process. While outside powers remained largely united, with only minor disagreements between the Western partners and the GCC, their overwhelming priorities of counter terrorism and support for a neo-liberal economic model underpinned their actions. The likelihood of the GCC monarchies supporting the establishment of a truly representative democracy in the Arabian Peninsula was minimal, to say the least. Specifically, under spurious pretexts, the international community provided neither the political impetus nor the finance needed to address the economic and social needs of the majority of the population which would have ensured popular support for the transitional regime. Instead, the people were alienated from a process which did nothing to address their concerns. Further, organisers set an unrealistically short timetable for the transition which prevented the emergence of strong new forces or the sequencing of activities, both of which were essential to success. The NDC, security sector reform and all activities were supposed to take place within two years, and more or less simultaneously; so it was impossible for the transitional regime to adequately address the problems of a complex transition.

Finally, not only was the transitional government paralysed by having an Islah-nominated prime minister who was unable to take any independent decisions, but the entire process was led by a president who clearly demonstrated, over this period, his overall inability to take a long-term view in the interests of his nation. Hadi rapidly (if not initially) adopted the self-centred and self-interested strategy of his predecessor, Saleh, but without the latter's skills and guile. All the decision-makers in this conflict, whether Yemeni or foreign, appeared to be motivated more by personal interests ranging from seeking financial gain to exercising power and control. Further, none of the players involved demonstrated the slightest concern for the welfare of the 27 million Yemenis, most of whom suffered worsening conditions on a daily basis.

Civil War and Internationalisation of the Conflict

By March 2015 Yemen was in a state of civil war with the Huthi-Saleh forces controlling the northern highlands and fast moving beyond them in all directions. Hadi's internationally recognised government had retreated to Aden and lacked military force, other than small groups of 'popular committees' mostly created by local communities to resist advances from jihadi groups. Without the intervention of the Saudi-led coalition, there is little doubt that the Huthi-Saleh troops would have taken control of the whole country in short order. This might have reduced the duration and obviously the extent of destruction of the war, but would probably have kept it at the level of a long-term insurgency with indirect intervention from a range of external parties.

The Saudi-Led Coalition

Saudi Arabia had been the lead state in the GCC Agreement and had intervened indirectly in Yemeni affairs since the kingdom's creation in 1932, as is discussed in detail in Chapter 2. The surprise in 2015 was not its intervention, but the form it took. King Salman succeeded his late brother Abdullah in January and soon initiated a radically new approach to the country's politics. The most surprising move was the appointment of his young son Mohammed as deputy crown prince, thus skipping the older generation of the sons of previous incumbents. To demonstrate his ability and consolidate his position, in the hope of overtaking his uncle as crown prince, Mohammed bin Salman wrongly saw Yemen as an easy opportunity to reach the throne.

Believing in his country's massive military capacity thanks to decades of US training for its forces, let alone the billions spent on advanced weaponry, he presumably assumed that Saudi forces would achieve a rapid and easy victory over the ill-equipped forces of the poorest nation in the Arab world, a country whose citizens most Saudi nationals perceive as lesser beings. For comparison's sake, at constant 1990 prices, Saudi Arabia imported US $17.8 billions' worth of weapons between 2001 and 2016, while Yemen imported US $1.8 billion.[20] Although the official request to the GCC for assistance from Hadi was only issued on 24 March, the intervention had been under preparation during the weeks Hadi was in Aden, when he held regular meetings with the Saudi ambassador, hence its rapid intervention.

The coalition itself is indeed Saudi-led: Saudi Arabia is its main financier and architect. It includes all GCC states with the exception of Oman (Saudi Arabia, UAE, Kuwait, Bahrain and Qatar[*]). Not only does Saudi Arabia cover the costs of most military operations, but it also finances the inducements to the non-GCC allies who have been persuaded to join

---

[*]   Qatar was removed from the coalition in June 2017 when it came under concerted political and diplomatic attack from Saudi Arabia, the UAE, Egypt and Bahrain, as well as Yemen's internationally recognised government.

the coalition (initially Egypt, Jordan, Morocco, Senegal and Sudan) with Somalia and Eritrea joining later, formally or otherwise. The UAE is the other main decision-making and financing partner; it has military forces on the ground including its own nationals as well as men of other nationalities (Australia and Colombia). As discussed below, there are significant differences in policy and aims between these two leading states.

The coalition intervention, initially code-named Decisive Storm, started with air strikes on 26 March 2015 complemented within four months with ground forces. It has fundamentally transformed the nature of the conflict. Saudi Arabia acts primarily through air strikes and logistical and financial support to Yemeni and other troops along its own border and in the neighbouring governorates, as well as in the Red Sea, where it is developing a military base in Djibouti. The UAE concentrated its interventions in the southern part of the country, only becoming actively involved in the former YAR region in 2017 with the offensive to retake the Bab al-Mandab strait and the Red Sea coast. The UAE has significant ground forces in Yemen, though numbers were reduced after the September 2015 Saleh missile strike on Mareb which killed more than fifty of its nationals. Since then it has deployed more contracted foreigners operating under its flag, mainly Colombian.

As of 2017, the UAE behaves in a manner which indicates plans for long-term deep involvement in the internal affairs of the southern part of Yemen and beyond: in Yemen it built air facilities on Perim Island in the Bab al-Mandab strait, in addition to the construction of a large naval base at Assab in Eritrea[21] and others at Berbera and Bossasso in Somalia.[22] Some of these locations were used to train Yemeni and other troops. That year the UAE was also reported to be investing heavily in civilian and military infrastructures on the island of Socotra.

Against the background of divergent views between the UAE and Saudi Arabia on Yemen's future, it is fair to question the long-term objectives of each of these partners. Islah (discussed in detail in Chapter 4) is the main issue on which their positions differ. Composed of separate tribal and Muslim Brother components, this Islamist Yemeni grouping is supported by Saudi Arabia, which has reconciled with the Muslim Brother tendency after a brief period of opposition. By contrast, the UAE is totally hostile and demonises anything which might even hint at a Muslim Brotherhood element. This virulent opposition has led the UAE to deploy in the southern governorates security units composed of local Salafis, who are far more extremist than Islah. Some of the members of these units, including some leaders, may have non-hostile relations with al-Qa'ida. While their activities are systematically reported as being in opposition to al-Qa'ida, in practice they are more active at arresting Islahis than others. These 'Elite Forces' (in Hadramaut and Shabwa) and Security Belts (in Abyan, Aden and Lahej) are all militia-type organisations which lack official status within the Yemeni state structure.

Since late 2016 some Southerners, including Salafi militias, were persuaded to join in the anti-Huthi war in the far north, particularly on the major fronts of Sa'ada and al-Jawf on the Saudi border. Mareb, where Vice President Ali Mohsen is mainly based, is where Islahi supporters participate in military action and are supported by Saudi Arabia and Qatar (while it was part of the coalition). Another topic on which the UAE and Saudi Arabia do not see eye to eye is Iran: while Saudi Arabia demonises it and inflates Iranian involvement in Yemen to justify its 'proxy war' approach, the UAE, particularly Dubai, has a far more sophisticated strategy and maintains reasonable relations with Iran, refusing to accuse it of all evils. In brief the devil is Iran for Saudi Arabia and the Muslim Brothers for the UAE.

Other foreign participants in the coalition are mainly 'boots on the ground', in the air, or at sea. The latter is the case of Egypt which, given the Sisi regime's financial and political dependence on the GCC, could not refuse to join. However, its reluctance to provide ground troops is mostly attributable to institutional memory of the *debacle* of Egypt's involvement in Yemeni affairs in the civil war of the 1960s in the YAR, let alone its current problems at home. Sudan initially sent 1,000 troops[23] under UAE control, but more later, also operating under Saudi orders. In a surprising development Senegal has involved itself in the Yemeni war by sending troops[24] to protect the Saudi border. Interestingly, Pakistan, which had been expected to lead the land war given the quality and experience of its armed forces, refused to participate in the coalition, but in early 2017 agreed to send units to the Saudi side of the border.

US Involvement

While not formally members of the coalition, the US, UK and France support the Saudi-led coalition by providing weapons, intelligence and training to its members. In addition, the US provides targeting advice in the operations room and also in-air refuelling of aircraft bombing Yemen, as well as continuing its war against al-Qaʻida in the Arabian Peninsula (AQAP). When the war started, the US closed its embassy in Sanaʻa and, when the Huthi-Saleh forces approached Aden, it evacuated the al-Anad air base (about fifty kilometres north of Aden) from which it had been operating.[25] Between the beginning of the war and 15 February 2017, the US Air Force logged 1,778 tanker sorties for the in-air refuelling operation, involving 7,564 refuelling 'events' with coalition aircraft, transferring 54 million pounds of fuel.[26] Given that many of the bombing sorties could not happen without this action, the US Air Force must be considered an active participant in the air strikes, most likely including strikes which have killed civilians and destroyed civilian facilities. In its last days, the Obama administration halted the sale of some types of weapons because of the coalition's many breaches of international human rights law, and due to the risk of the US being accused of unlawful killings. This decision, however feeble, has been reversed by the Trump administration which had resumed sales in the first half of 2017.

US air strikes against supposed al-Qaʻida targets, mostly with drones, have increased significantly in the first weeks of the Trump administration, in number, type and scope of attacks, which indicates a more aggressive approach. In short the new leadership in Washington is showing even less concern for either civilian casualties or Yemeni perceptions of the US, let alone any lessons learnt from its Afghanistan or Iraq adventures. January 2017 also saw the first landing since December 2014 of special forces when the US attacked a village in al-Baidha, losing a marine and an aircraft in a botched operation which the US later denied had been targeting senior al-Qaʼida personnel; as with the 2014 attack, US citizens were the most widely publicised casualties, though many more Yemenis were killed, including children. The table below shows that the period of the Hadi government and particularly the years 2012–2014 had the highest number of drone strikes, as there were only twelve strikes prior to 2012.

US Drone Strikes and Casualties (2009–2016)[27]

Year	Number of Strikes	People Killed
2011	11	46
2012	37	205
2013	22	79
2014	17	90
2015	21	75
2016	33	92
Jan–June 2017	90	91
Total	231	668

In addition to the drone and air strikes in Abyan, Shabwa and al-Baidha Governorates, the US also had a small group of commandos in Hadramaut operating with UAE forces from mid-2016 onwards. Their possible involvement in the ill-treatment of detainees was raised in June 2017 when evidence emerged about secret prisons run by the UAE in Aden and Hadramaut. In the latter 'Several US defense officials ... told AP that American forces do participate in interrogations of detainees at locations in Yemen, provide questions for others to ask, and receive transcripts of interrogations from Emirati allies. They said US senior military leaders were aware of allegations of torture at the prisons in Yemen, looked into them, but were satisfied that there had not been any abuse when US forces were present ... None of the dozens of people interviewed by AP contended that American interrogators were involved in the actual abuses. Nevertheless, obtaining intelligence that may have been extracted by torture inflicted by another party would violate the International Convention Against Torture and could qualify as war crimes, said Ryan Goodman, a law professor at New York University who served as special counsel to the Defense Department until last year.'[28]

US weapon sales have, throughout, remained a major form of its cooperation with the Gulf States. Between 2001 and 2016, the US was the largest supplier of weapons to Saudi Arabia, with contracts worth US $8.4 billion, while the UK followed with US $4.6 billion of the total US $17.8 billion. Interestingly, total Saudi purchases were barely more than those of the UAE totalling US $17 billion of purchases with the US dominating (US $9 billion).[29] However, the second supplier to the UAE was France (US $5 billion). All these are reduced to insignificance by the signature of deals totalling US $110 billion during Trump's first overseas visit, to Saudi Arabia, in May 2017.

The Role of the UK

Alongside the US, the UK sells weapons and is also involved in the operations rooms, though not in re-fuelling. The legality of UK arms sales to Saudi Arabia was challenged in the High Court in February 2017, given that the UK is a signatory to the International Arms Trade Treaty. The Campaign Against the Arms Trade challenged the sales on the basis of evidence that Saudi-led coalition strikes against civilian targets were in breach of international humanitarian law.[30] The hearings were held in February 2017 in London; in July the High Court declared the sales legal and that 'the coalition were not deliberately targeting civilians. [It had not been established that] there was a clear risk that the items might be used in the commission of a serious violation of international humanitarian law.' The Campaign Against the Arms Trade appealed against the ruling.

Politically, the UK has a role significantly above its position on the world stage thanks to being the 'pen holder' on the Yemen issue in the UNSC. As of 2017, it remains active on other major UN and EU bodies, where there has been no sign of any public British initiatives or efforts to find a solution to end the war. While it provided £130 million in humanitarian aid to Yemen in 2016, this is a drop in the ocean compared to its arms sales to Saudi Arabia of US $1.6 billion (at 1990 prices) in 2015 and 2016. The contradiction between aid to alleviate the consequences of bombing and financing the bombing itself is something which the UK government fails to address. It has been emphasised by a senior Conservative MP in early 2017. [31] In coming years, a British government preoccupied by the economic implications of Brexit is unlikely to give priority to supporting Yemen and Yemenis over abject compliance with the wishes of potential GCC post-Brexit investors to the UK.

The Military Stalemate

The Yemeni air force, which would have been under the control of the Huthi-Saleh forces, was destroyed in the first hours of Decisive Storm; hence all aerial activities are now conducted by the coalition. In March 2017, then coalition military spokesman, Ahmed al-Asiri, asserted that it had carried out more than 90,000 sorties since the beginning of its intervention. Most of these are by US-made F-15s, carrying two bombs of 2,000 pounds each; hence the damage they can cause is considerable. While the financial cost of the war is difficult to estimate, each sortie costs about US $40,000, and the overall cost is estimated at anything between US $66 million and US $200 million per day. Although much targeting is extremely accurate, many civilian facilities and events have been hit. They include medical facilities, schools, markets, weddings and funerals.[32] One example of accuracy which has been widely publicised concerns the port of Hodeida where the strikes hit the operator cabs of each crane very precisely, and left the rest intact, while by contrast four Médecins Sans Frontières medical facilities have been hit despite being clearly identifiable from the air.

Overall it is notable that the areas where the coalition has been most successful are those where topographical conditions most suit heavy armour, and where the open terrain facilitates both surveillance and movement. Coincidentally, these also happen to be the areas inhabited primarily by the Shafi' population, rather than the Zaydi mountainous highlands under Huthi-Saleh control. Since the autumn of 2015, the situation on the ground has been characterised by stalemate. Although there have been a few changes in early 2017, after the coalition forces made notable advances on the Red Sea Coast, taking part of Mokha town and its port out of Huthi-Saleh control, other fronts had remained almost unchanged for twenty months by the end of June 2017.

The main fronts are located along the Saudi border at all the formal crossing points and beyond, and particularly on the coast where the small port of Midi and its neighbouring larger town of Haradh have been the foci of fighting throughout. Both sites have been taken and lost alternatively by each side too often to count. East of Sana'a, Nehm, in the last chain of mountains separating it from Mareb, is another long-standing front; while in Mareb itself, Sirwah has remained under Huthi-Saleh control and is therefore subjected to almost daily air strikes. Similarly in al-Jawf, the border areas are fronts while all of Sa'ada Governorate has been considered a military zone by the coalition since the Saudi announcement in May 2015.[33] Al-Baidha Governorate is a complex front still mainly under the control of the Huthi and Saleh alliance while some of its districts suffer ongoing regular clashes against coalition supported forces, while US strikes against jihadi groups are frequent. Fighting flares up occasionally elsewhere, usually induced by a conflict between Saleh and Huthi forces, or alternatively between them and forces opposing them, which can mean groups supporting Islah or any other organisation, or simply local people wanting to stay unaligned.

The most dangerous and complex front is found in Taiz, the country's third largest city, where an intricate maze of rival factions and counterfactions are struggling for control. Here attendant massive destruction and abysmal conditions have hit the population who have been living under siege and blockade from one faction or another for two years, depending on who controls their neighbourhood. Given Taiz's reputation as an intellectual and liberal city, it is worth noting that the main rival groups fighting are Salafis, Islahis, Sunni jihadis, as well as more secular forces of Saleh supporters, Nasserites and socialists, and of course Huthi supporters also.

Fighting on the Saudi side of the border has been an important feature of the war since the beginning. Authorities have evacuated a large number of villages there, and there are daily artillery clashes. The Huthi-Saleh forces not only launch missiles into Saudi Arabia but they also send units to fight on the ground within the Saudi provinces of Najran, Jizan and Asir, some of whom have reached 140 km into Saudi territory. The more the coalition bombs or progresses in Yemen, the more the Huthi-Saleh forces focus their attacks within Saudi Arabia. Although they had failed to take over any large Saudi village or town on a permanent basis by July 2017, Saudi military casualties had numbered at least 100 deaths by November 2016[34] while most estimates of civilian deaths, including foreigners, were over 500. All of these were within the Saudi borders.

In 2016, faced with a military stalemate, the Hadi government, with some encouragement from the coalition, which had already integrated punitive economic measures into its military campaign, chose to complement its efforts against the Houthis with economic warfare. An already weak economy had collapsed in the course of the war. That had placed a growing importance on public sector salaries as the sole form of economic stimulus. State jobs are a primary source of income for more than 1.2 million civilian workers and a further 700, 000 security personnel. When their immediate families are included, this income supports about 8 million people. The Central Bank of Yemen (CBY), one of Yemen's few broadly effective institutions, was the main mediating mechanism between sources of funding and payment of salaries. Amazingly, it had managed to stay largely neutral, operating as effectively as the war permitted, paying salaries despite the reduction of its income to practically nothing.

In September 2016, contrary to the advice of the IMF, the US and UK, the Hadi government announced the transfer of CBY headquarters from Sana'a to Aden. It argued that the Huthi-Saleh faction was diverting funds for their own interests. While there is little doubt that the Huthi-Saleh faction were draining funds wherever they could, with respect to the CBY, the reality was that it had simply run out of reserves which, by early 2017, were down to about US $750 million (dropping from US $4.81 billion in late 2014), an insignificant amount creating a major balance of payments crisis in banking terms.[35] The outcome is that financial transactions have almost come to a halt as the Aden CBY lacks data, cash and competent staff, while that in Sana'a is basically unable to operate. Importers struggle to purchase basic foods on the world market, worsening the prospects of famine, and people throughout Yemen are out in the streets demonstrating daily to demand their many months of unpaid salaries. By mid-2017, only some of the billions of riyals printed in Russia had arrived and, at best, some civil servants were paid small percentages of their salary arrears. There was considerable, most likely justified, speculation that much of the new currency had been misappropriated before reaching the unpaid government staff.

Negotiations, Attempts at Peace, Mediators

From the earliest days of the war, efforts were made to negotiate an end to the fighting. The UN's special envoy was involved in two rounds of indirect talks in Switzerland in 2015, followed by the Kuwait negotiations which lasted from April to August 2016. Then came what was described as the 'Kerry Initiative', lasting till the end of the Obama administration, which failed to achieve anything largely because the warring parties hoped that the next US administration might take different positions. Ismail Ould Cheikh Ahmed, a Mauritanian, was appointed in April 2015 as Special Envoy of the UN Secretary-General, replacing Jamal Benomar who had successfully alienated most national and international concerned parties. Ismail's main qualification for the job, other than a year as UN Resident Representative in Yemen, was the fact that he was considered acceptable by Saudi Arabia.

Hadi's internationally recognised government is still largely in exile. Until December 2016, it was based in Riyadh (the capital of Saudi Arabia) with most ministers going on occasional forays to Aden where they rarely stayed for more than a few days. Others spent much time in Mareb, a town in the north-east of Yemen, which has become the de facto capital for Vice President Ali Mohsen, Islahis and their military forces. Of the two years between the liberation of Aden in 2015 and completion of this book, Hadi spent 167 days in Yemen, most of them in Aden. Like Saleh before him, he appears to treat Aden as a winter capital, since he always seems to visit in winter. When in Aden, he spends most of his time ensconced in his mountaintop retreat on the sea front, from which he usually only moves to fly out of the country. Ministers present in Aden complain of their living and working conditions as they are concentrated in a few 'secure' locations, even sharing rooms; maybe this is one reason why they spend so much time in Saudi Arabia.

Repeated ad nauseam, the Hadi regime's position is that negotiations must take place on the basis of the three references: the GCC Agreement of 2011, the outcomes of the National Dialogue Conference, and UNSC Resolution 2216 of April 2015 which established an arms embargo, demanded Huthi-Saleh withdrawal from the cities and the handover of their weapons. This determination to hang on to this particular UNSC Resolution is due to the fact that it explicitly names Hadi as the person whose authority needs to be restored. Therefore it prevents all efforts from all sides to replace him by a compromise candidate who might be more acceptable to the other side. This intransigence is equivalent to a call for surrender from the Huthi-Saleh alliance, which they find unacceptable, whatever their internal problems.

The Huthi-Saleh position is based on the fact that they control about a third of the country's surface and more than half its population. They agree that the outcomes of the NDC should be taken into consideration and political dialogue resumed; they also demand that the draft constitution with the six-regions federation be cancelled or amended, the PNPA be included as one of the references for discussions, the blockade on Hodeida port should be lifted, and Sana'a airport re-opened to civilian traffic. In addition, Saleh frequently demands direct negotiations between himself or his GPC with Saudi Arabia.

The situation in July 2017 is aggravated by uncertainty about the intentions and aims of the new US administration. Its aggressive war-like statements have encouraged Hadi and the Saudis to believe that the US may intervene militarily on their side and therefore that victory is in sight. In March, Trump declared three Yemeni governorates 'areas of active hostilities' where US rules of engagement are looser than normal,[36] though to what extent this is likely to make much difference on the ground is open to debate. As previously mentioned, he had authorised two ground attacks within the first four months of taking power, both of which killed many civilians.

As is often the case in the GCC, Oman has taken an independent line and refused to join the coalition. Having historically good relations with Iran and a stressed relationship with Saudi Arabia, its regime has been particularly careful in recent decades to remain neutral in the numerous internal Yemeni conflicts. This has enabled it to mediate and, at the very least, to provide facilities for the Huthi-Saleh faction to travel for meetings. Oman's senior politicians are actively involved in trying to bring about peace and Muscat is the only mediator appreciated and praised by all sides. Recognition has come with its inclusion since March 2017 in the 'gang of four' established through the Kerry initiative, composed of the foreign ministers of the US, UK, Saudi Arabia and the UAE. This quartet (or quintet with Oman) is intended to solve the Yemeni problem and the UN Special Envoy attends its meetings. Yet it does NOT include a single Yemeni.

Negotiations to date have been limited to two sides: Hadi's internationally recognised government which, as discussed elsewhere, represents little beyond itself, and the other the Huthi-Saleh alliance. This ignores a multitude of participants on the ground, ranging from the various militias (Elite Forces, Security Belts, Islahis, Salafi groups, the formal army, Republican Guards, Special Forces, Huthi militias, local resistance) to political parties, regional representatives, major tribal groups, civil society organisations (trades unions, cooperatives, women's groups, human rights organisations) and youth representatives. While few would argue for the inclusion of jihadis in political dialogue, the absence of representatives of the population at large is a fundamental weakness, and possibly a guarantee of failure in the medium to long term.

As of June 2017, UN-sponsored peace making efforts had failed. Ismail's international travels appeared futile in the absence of any indication of interest in reaching agreement from leaders on either side. Even in the face of cholera, famine and the threatened death of thousands, if not hundreds of thousands, each side stubbornly maintained its position and refused to compromise. Meanwhile the population's suffering has worsened by the day while warlords, smugglers and black marketeers raked in the cash.

The Humanitarian Situation

In 2014, Yemen's humanitarian situation was already grave. At that time 41 percent of the population or 10.6 million people were food insecure, i.e. they 'had limited or no access to sufficient, nutritious food, and were eating less than the minimum required to live a healthy life'.[37] The UN's Humanitarian Response Plan (HRP) for that year targeted fewer than half of the estimated 15 million (or 58 percent of the population) in need of humanitarian aid; in the end it was only 58 percent funded. The 2016 Humanitarian Response Plan was downgraded half way through the year to seeking US $1.6 billion to address the needs of 12.6 million people. That represented a decrease of 7 percent in the number of people targeted and 9.3 percent in financial requirements from the initial assessment.[38] Those targeted represented a mere 59 percent of the ones in need and actual funding that year reached 60 percent of the requested amount.[39] The 2017 HRP requires US$2.1 billion to reach 12 million people, only 60 percent of those estimated to be in need of assistance by the middle of the year, and at that time was only 40 percent funded.

In addition to the problems brought about by the destruction of the road and port infrastructure through air strikes, the humanitarian situation has been dramatically worsened by the blockade imposed by the Saudi-led coalition on air and sea access to the country. Sana'a airport has been closed to commercial traffic since August 2016 and only occasional flights of UN emergency supplies are allowed in. Naval access to the Red Sea ports is constrained under the coalition's pretext of enforcing the arms embargo.

As a result ships carrying basic supplies are delayed while waiting for inspection, thus incurring serious additional costs in insurance and rental charges. And in some cases by the time of docking the food transported is no longer fit for consumption. The UN established a Verification and Inspection Mechanism (UNVIM) which started operating in May 2016 after a year of negotiations with the coalition, but delays at Hodeida and other ports under the control of the Huthi-Saleh alliance continue to be substantial.

The fact that the UN Secretary General needed to describe the situation in Yemen as the largest humanitarian crisis in the world is shocking at a time when famine has been declared in South Sudan and is also threatening Somalia and Kenya, while the situation elsewhere in East Africa is also dire. Yemen has never before joined these other countries, which are sadly known by many for all too frequent famines. In mid-2017, cholera was added to the list of Yemen's performance as worst in the world since records began. The following chapters discuss the many elements, political, social, historical and climatic, which have led to this dire situation.

CHAPTER TWO

Yemen and the World

From Isolation to Integration
in Regional and World Geopolitics

Imamate Yemen was reputed to be isolated from the world, while Aden was as internationalised as a colonial port-city can be. During the YAR and PDRY periods, the situation was reversed with the YAR increasingly involved with the outside world, while the PDRY was isolated. The Republic of Yemen has been integrated into the wider world, economically through the neo-liberal policies imposed on most 'developing' states, and politically with increasingly close relations with its neighbours and beyond. Its national characteristics, whether cultural or political, have been undermined by inclusion in the pervasive influence of social and other international media emerging since the 1990s.

While Yemen has never been as isolated as claimed by some, there is no doubt that the last twenty years have seen it shift away from uniqueness. It has become similar to many other states in what is still described as the Third or Developing World. It is now often compared to Somalia, first as a disintegrating or failing, and now as a failed, state. Blame for this situation is usually simplistically attributed to 'tribalism', corruption and bad governance, ignoring the role of external players in this outcome, particularly that of the more powerful states. The various interventions of the international community in the past quarter century should be taken into consideration and their responsibility for the current disastrous situation examined. There are similarities with the position in Iraq

(US and UK intervention) and many Arab states (GCC intervention). Economic development policies and financial constraints promoted by the International Financial Institutions (IFIs) in support of a neo-liberal agenda are also very influential and discussed in Chapter 9. This chapter examines the roots of the problems faced by the Republic of Yemen in its relations with those states which play the most important role, focusing on political and social developments.

Yemen has been a land of emigration for many centuries. People of Yemeni origin are found throughout the Arabian Peninsula, in east and central Africa, north Africa as far west as Morocco, east in south and south-east Asia, Europe, the US and Australasia. These migrations have taken place in the past three centuries or longer and have had periods of peak movements. Many Yemenis had some knowledge of the world beyond their homes even before the advent of modern media; and other nationals had a minimal awareness of the existence of Yemen and some of its cultural features. In most cases migration had direct and indirect consequences in state-to-state relations. Cultural impact is also noticeable in diet and clothing: prawn crackers are found in the remotest Hadrami general shops, and the wearing of sarong-type *futas* is commonplace throughout the southern part of Yemen, while rice is the basic staple throughout coastal areas even though not a grain of rice is cultivated in the country.

Three Seminal Moments in the Republic of Yemen's Relations with the World

While there are quite a few analyses of Yemen's relations with the outside world prior to unification, of both the YAR and the PDRY, it is surprising how little is available on the quarter century following unification. Before going into a selection of most relevant relationships, let us focus on three seminal moments in the Republic of Yemen's (ROY) relations with the outside world. Curiously, these have taken place a decade apart and each illustrates Yemen's relationship with a major international entity: the UN system, the US and the GCC led by Saudi Arabia. They are the Iraqi invasion of Iraq in 1990, the events of 11 September 2001 in the US and the Gulf Cooperation Council Agreement to solve the internal crisis in 2011.

While the latter and its consequences have been discussed in some detail in the previous chapter, we will briefly examine the other two here.

1990: The Most Expensive Vote at the United Nations Security Council

In November 1990, barely six months after the merger of the YAR and PDRY into the new Republic of Yemen, and four months after Iraq's occupation of Kuwait, came the US-sponsored Resolution 678 at the United Nations Security Council. Thanks to President Saleh's good relations with Saddam Hussein, Yemen cast the only negative vote against this Resolution. In February 1989 Saleh and Hussein had established the Arab Cooperation Council (ACC) with Jordan and Egypt. 'The US Ambassador brazenly threatened him [the Yemeni representative on the UNSC]: "That will be the most expensive vote you ever cast," and the US immediately cut off 70 million dollars in aid to Yemen."[1] Although the link has not been explicitly demonstrated, in the early years of the ROY most bilateral funders stayed away, few projects were financed by the World Bank and no agreement was reached with the IMF till 1995.

The anger of Kuwait and other GCC states cannot be underestimated and led to the expulsion of more than 800,000 Yemeni workers from the GCC states in the following months. This action not only eliminated their vital contribution to the Yemeni economy and to their families through their remittances, but it also added to the already large number of unemployed and dissatisfied men in the country. This also represented a seminal moment in Yemen's economic development. It seriously constrained potential for the country to develop an independent economy based on remittances to finance community level investments. In the previous decades the cash from Yemenis working abroad had funded local development activities dedicated to small productive and service investments in rural areas, both at community-level and as small innovative entrepreneur activities for households. Reduced remittances coupled with the recent discovery of oil shifted economic power from individuals and communities to the central state, thus weakening the former and strengthening the latter.

This moment came to define relations between Yemen and the United Nations political system. It demonstrated the subservience of the UN system to pressure from the US as well as the influence of both on international financial Bretton Woods institutions. While other UN institutions have had more even relations with the ROY the political relationship has remained strained most of the time, with a mutual lack of trust.

11 September 2001

While there is no doubt that Saleh instructed Abdallah al-Ashtal, Yemen's representative to the UNSC, to vote as he did in 1990, he may not have predicted the strength of negative consequences of his ideological stand till later. He certainly had learnt the lesson by the time of the second seminal moment, the terrorist attack on the US eleven years later. Saleh sent a message of full support to President Bush within hours of the event. In November of that year he was one of the first to be invited to Washington where he again expressed support and was rewarded with millions of US dollars of aid, and particularly of military aid to fight al-Qaʻida. While the relationship became strained in the following years, this move certainly endeared Saleh to US decision-makers who provided him with military training, equipment and the kind of support which enabled him to turn the Republican Guards, the unit led by his son Ahmed, into an elite fighting force. In fact after 2015 the elite units ensured Saleh's strong position in his alliance with the Huthis and kept at bay the forces of the Saudi-led coalition and others who opposed him. It can also be argued that the post-2001 relationship between the Saleh regime and the US, targeted against al-Qaʻida, explains the lukewarm US attitude to a change of regime in 2011.

This moment effectively summarises the complex relationship between the Saleh regime and the US. On the one hand it consists of formal support, almost subservience, allowing the US to launch drones and other air attacks on Yemeni citizens at will, targeting al-Qaʻida in the Arabian Peninsula (AQAP) but also killing civilians and generally spreading terror throughout the country, particularly in the rural areas. On the other, it is made up of a mix of cooperation and undeclared resistance, given the relationship between some AQAP elements and the Saleh regime, if not Saleh personally. Beyond subservience and subversion, it also illustrates Saleh's mastery of tactics and his ability to manoeuvre between conflicting forces in order to retain and sometimes strengthen his position.

The 2011 Uprising and the Transition

The third seminal moment is the Gulf Cooperation Council Initiative and Agreement of 2011 which led to Saleh's formal resignation as president. A country's immediate neighbours are the most important and the role of different GCC states illustrates the complexity and ambiguity of their relations with the Saleh regime. Since the Yemeni uprising of 2011, Saudi Arabia has taken the leading role in determining Yemeni affairs; and particularly so after 2015 with the internationalisation of Yemen's civil war thanks to the military intervention of the Saudi-led coalition. The period since 2011 has been the subject of the previous chapter so is not discussed further here.

Yemen and Its Neighbours: The Key Relationships

Saudi Arabia

Saudi Arabia's policy concerning Yemen, until the current war, could be simply summarised as ensuring that Yemen was both weak enough and strong enough not to be a threat to the Saudi regime. Saudi Arabia is by far the most important state among all Yemen's international partners. It is Yemen's immediate neighbour with the longest shared land border, and the only other country in the peninsula with a large population. The contrast between its wealth and Yemen's poverty has two crucial implications: its regime has been a main financier of Yemeni state and non-state actors since the earliest days of its creation; and its labour shortage makes it the most attractive and (in the past century) the main destination for Yemeni migrants. It was easy to reach until the physical and administrative barriers erected after unification in 1990, let alone the current war on the border. Even today there are large numbers of Yemenis living and working in Saudi Arabia, either as labour migrants, war refugees or exiles. Saudi Arabia's foreign minister asserted that there were as many as four million in late 2016,[2] a figure which seems excessively high as it would represent about 15 percent of either country's population. Most estimates put the figure at between 1.5 and 2 million.

Saudi Arabia has been involved in Yemeni affairs since the establishment of the Kingdom in 1932. In the 1934 war, Saudi forces rapidly defeated the ill-organised army of Imam Yahia. It took over the provinces of Najran, Jizan and Asir, on a renewable twenty-year agreement[3] which was indeed renewed in 1954 under Imam Ahmed. After the establishment of the republican regime in Sana'a in 1962, there was regular, if not frequent, talk of Yemen recovering these lands, which maintained tension between the two states. The issue re-emerged actively in 1974 when Sana'a refused to renew the treaty, though it had no complaints about the clause which allowed Yemenis to travel freely to Saudi Arabia without the complex and expensive sponsorship and other regulations applying to migrants from elsewhere. Ending this privilege was the mechanism used by the Saudi regime in 1990 to force hundreds of thousands of Yemenis out of the country.

The toppling of the Yemeni monarchy and the establishment of the Yemen Arab Republic in 1962 was perceived as a major threat by the actively Islamist Wahhabi Saudi regime, which was then in serious competition with Nasser's Arab Socialism throughout the Arab world.[4] During the eight-year civil war which followed, the Kingdom provided material and other support to the Imam's attempts to reconquer power in Sana'a. While this was partly a war against socialist ideology and the deep involvement of Egyptian troops on the republican side, it was also a monarchy fighting a republic. In the context of the situation in 2017, it is worth noting that Wahhabi Saudi Arabia had no qualms about supporting a Zaydi (Shi'i) monarch against a republican regime where Sunnis had some power, though its main leaders were also Zaydi.

Another feature of this war was the Saudi regime's financial and other material support for some of the tribes in the far north of the country. This enabled them to achieve political influence rivalling that of the Yemeni state. The Saudi regime persisted with this policy throughout the following decades, which explains why, well into the twenty-first century, certain tribes were able to challenge central state authority in a manner that was completely unprecedented under the Imamate.[5] Saudi strategy thus contributed to weakening the Yemeni state, a factor that bears serious consequences to this day.

The civil war ended with an acceptable, though not ideal, solution for Saudi Arabia. The post-1970 republican regime was authoritarian and under the influence of senior tribal leaders. The tribes' increased political and financial power thanks to Saudi support prevented the new regime from controlling them. In addition to using these tribes, Saudi Arabia continued undermining republican and other secular or socialist tendencies in the YAR in a number of ways. The deepest long-term impact was its involvement with the national education system: it financed the Yemeni education ministry's importation of Sunni Islamist teachers from Egypt and Sudan and the 'scientific institutes' which were unofficial educational establishments which emphasised religious education. Third, Saudi Arabia also trained Salafis in Saudi Arabia, and in that way created a body of mosque imams and educators who further promoted this ideology throughout Yemen. Today's generation often underestimates the importance of these moves at a time when there were no electronic media, and hence much less access to information. In the 1970s and 1980s, radio and television were only marginally present in remote areas and they promoted similar views. Access to ideas came primarily through formal education, hence the influence of teachers and mosque preachers was far greater. Altogether these policies strengthened Salafism throughout the country at the expense of both traditional sects in Yemen, the vaguely Shi'i Zaydi and the liberal Sunni Shafi'i. The two groups had lived in reasonable harmony for centuries, despite Zaydi political dominance.

Moreover, although largely tamed, by its very nature as a republic the northern regime still posed a challenge to the Saudis' Wahhabi hereditary kingdom; and southern socialism, also largely moderated in the previous decade, was still perceived to be an atheist God-less nemesis by both the Saudi royals and much of the country's population. Nor did Saudi Arabia only concern itself with the YAR. The Kingdom actively undermined the socialist regime of the PDRY. In the early 1970s, this was done through subversion and military interventions.[6] After diplomatic recognition in 1976 relations remained cold until unification. The government had hoped that recognition would lead to economic assistance and investment from Saudis of Yemeni origin. However, they were largely disappointed. Although open hostility ceased, media offensives and anti-socialist programmes continued by radios and other media supported by the Saudi state.

Saudi Arabia did not welcome Yemeni unity in 1990 as it perceived a united Yemen to be a potential threat, because Yemenis had demonstrated their ability to be superior fighters over many decades, and also because the two countries had roughly the same population. Indeed, regardless of official claims, Yemen had a larger total population, overwhelmingly composed of nationals, by compared to that of Saudi Arabia. By contrast with Yemeni military competence, the Saudi army is frequently described as a 'parade army' rather than a serious fighting force.

Although unable to prevent the unification process, the Saudi regime did its best to undermine it. One tactic was support for the creation of the Islah party (discussed in greater detail in Chapter 4). Both of Islah's leaders, the Hashed Shaykh Abdullah Husayn al-Ahmar and the Islamist Abdul Majeed al-Zindani, were on the Saudi payroll. Al-Zindani issued fatwas against unity and declared others accusing southerners of atheism and other sins. Saudi Arabia also encouraged the involvement of leaders competing with the YSP in the south, particularly those from the colonial period in Aden who had been defeated during the fighting between the rival liberation movements, such as al-Asnaj and al-Jifri.

Once unification had happened, it was internally threatened by the struggle between Saleh and the Southern leader al-Beedh. The Saudi leadership encouraged the attempted secession in 1994.[7] As the social anthropologist Paul Dresch put it,

> Saudi support for Ali Salim al-Bid became blatant. Apart from diplomatic moves and control of much Arab media, large shipments of arms were evident, and on 21 May the YSP leader announced secession. Al-Bid is reported to have said later that this was al-Jifri's doing. Their alliance, perhaps formed under Saudi auspices, set aside all considerations of ideology and around them clustered also such figures from the Adeni past as Abdul al-Qawi Makawi and Abdullah al-Asnag. They attracted only scant support.[8]

The very short-lived secessionist regime included ministers from various former Saudi-supported anti-socialist parties, such as Abdul Rahman al-Jifri's South Arabian League. Although Saudi Arabia did not formally recognise the separatist state, it encouraged its leadership to believe it would be recognised and lobbied in favour of recognition in international forums such as the United Nations. The Sana'a regime's position was defended at the UN and in the US by Dr Abdul Karim al-Eryani, a firm believer in Yemeni unity, whose efforts were ultimately successful. However, as soon as the Southern separatist movement re-emerged in 2007, direct relations between Southern leaders and senior Saudi Arabian officials started.[9]

In the following years, Saudi Arabia reluctantly accepted the reality of a single Yemeni state, but it actively supported any incipient dissidence. In 1995 there were border clashes and Saudi Arabia was suspected of having encouraged Eritrea to challenge Yemeni sovereignty over the Hunaish Islands dispute. The Saudi regime's policy was to prevent the emergence of a strong state in Yemen. To do this, within Yemen, it provided simultaneous support for competing groups, the tribes, the Islah party and others, all intended to keep central authority weak, while at the same time financing the central authority, to ensure it was not overtaken by these groups. The al-Ahmar family, leaders of the Hashed confederation and Islah were said to receive YR 3 to 4 billion per month from Saudi Arabia.[10] Payments to the central coffers were also essential to the survival of the Yemeni regime whose revenues were minimal: its oil production peaked at 400,000 b/d in 2001, an insignificant amount compared with Saudi Arabia's total of 10 million b/d. Given similar populations, the differential in income is striking.

Until his death in 2011, Saudi policy on Yemen was under the control of the Minister of Defence Prince Sultan bin Abdul Aziz. He ran the 'Special Office for Yemen Affairs' which 'remained the main locus of Yemen policy and patronage throughout the 1980s and 1990s, a role that was attenuated after the border agreement of 2000. Its annual budget was believed to be US$ 3.5 billion until then, but was reduced following that year's border agreement. In early 2011, the number of people thought to be receiving subsidies still remained in the thousands, but in April recipients were notified that payments were being terminated by order of the royal court.'[11] It is not clear whether this decision was implemented.

Both Sultan and Crown Prince Abdullah were in favour of normalising relations with Yemen. Negotiations after the clashes of the 1990s culminated in the Treaty of Jeddah, signed on 12 June 2000, which comprehensively settled border issues.[12] Among the ROY's gains was an area of some 40,000 square kilometres including oil and gas resources in the eastern sector. The treaty also included a five kilometre demilitarised zone on either side of the border. This agreement certainly marked the high point in cooperation between Saudi Arabia and Yemen. It is only at the height of the conflict starting in 2015 that the Huthi-Saleh faction has raised the issue of the border once again.

Joint demarcation of the Saudi-Yemeni border proceeded in the years after 2000 with various ups and downs, including occasional military confrontations. It was completed in 2006, a year into King Abdullah's formal reign. As the relationship between the two countries deteriorated with the emergence of the Huthi rebellion on its borders, Saudi Arabia started building a fence along its national boundary: in addition to making life difficult for smugglers (of qat, drugs, weapons and other items),* this contravened the clauses of the Jeddah Treaty which allowed for free movement for herders in pursuit of pasture for their livestock. The measure was also designed to stop Somali and other African migrants from reaching Saudi Arabia, thus leaving them stranded in Yemen, which obviously did not provide them with the kind of economic opportunities they were seeking. In 2007, Saudi Arabia repatriated to Yemen 400,000 illegal migrants, though it is unclear how many of these were Yemenis and how many Somalis or other Africans.[13]

Although he only formally became king in 2005, Abdullah bin Abdul Aziz had been in charge of the Kingdom for the previous decade since his brother Fahd's health prevented him from working. His policy on Yemen was more conciliatory and he enjoyed access to vast amounts of cash to finance support of different types. Saudi financing of development investments increased, particularly in the field of infrastructure. Saudi Arabia's role in Yemen took a military turn in November 2009, when the Huthi wars extended into Saudi Arabia. The Saudi army lost about 130 men in addition to many others imprisoned by the Huthis after their attack on a border patrol.[14] This was followed by the evacuation of civilians on the Saudi side of the border.[15] In addition to problems with the Huthis, 2009 also saw AQAP's first major attack on Saudi Arabia after its formation as a joint Saudi-Yemeni organisation, when a suicide attack on Interior Minister Mohammed bin Nayef only failed for technical reasons, slightly wounding him, and the perpetrator died alone.

Since Prince Sultan's death, Yemeni policy in Saudi Arabia has not been clearly managed and none of the current leaders has the knowledge of, or interest in, the intricacies of internal Yemeni politics to develop a

---

* The importance of smuggling can be assessed from the following sample period: between October and December 2007, Saudi border officials arrested 880 smugglers and confiscated 100 kg of explosives, 400 weapons, 50 000 pieces of ammunition, 100 sticks of dynamite, 2,000 kilograms of hashish, 4 kilograms of marijuana and 40,000 pills. See Wikileaks, 'Yemen's big brother: what has Saudi Arabia done', Cable, 18 June 2008, released 2011, para 13.

sophisticated policy. Other than on war issues, until his unceremonious dismissal in June 2017, Prince Mohammed bin Nayef bin Abdul Aziz was minister of the interior and crown prince as well as the main focal point on Yemeni affairs. Saudi relations with Ali Abdullah Saleh have varied considerably over the period. Like most Yemeni rulers, he was initially considered with suspicion in Riyadh. In the first decades of his rule, as YAR president, relations remained strained, particularly as Saleh had been one of the founders of the Arab Cooperation Council.[16] Riyadh saw this, probably correctly, as a direct threat to the regime through a pincer movement against Saudi Arabia also intended to undermine its influence in the Arab world.

Despite his challenges to the Saudi regime, Saleh depended on Saudi Arabian financing for the very survival of his regime. Nor were the Saudis totally hostile until recently. In 2011, both the honour code of King Abdullah, and Prince Sultan's intimate knowledge of Yemen, contributed to Saleh being flown to Saudi Arabia for treatment after the 3 June attack on his palace mosque. Observers may wonder whether he would have been treated with the same generosity under the current king. At the time, many Yemenis and others would have preferred an inferior quality of treatment that would permit nature to take its course, and his return to Yemen for an honourable burial. Instead he was allowed to recover and escape the attention of his protectors to return to to Sana'a via Aden on 23 September, only coming back to Riyadh to sign the GCC Agreement in November, which was his last visit to Saudi Arabia at the time of writing. Although the Saudis worked with Saleh and supported him for decades, albeit reluctantly, there is little doubt that they widely disliked and distrusted him, because of both his duplicity and his refusal to act with servility.

Relations with Other GCC States

While some of the following points are also relevant to Saudi Arabia, this section will focus on Yemen's relationship with the GCC states collectively, as well as with some of its other members individually. Since the 1990s Yemen's ambition has been to join the GCC as a full member which would give it all it requires from the GCC: first, the ability for its labour force to work throughout the Gulf without restriction; and second, obtain financial support through investment in enterprises or as grant aid to the state. Given the extreme reluctance of the GCC on the former and limited achievements on the latter, relations with the GCC states recovered only slowly from the shock of the 1990 situation arising from the Iraqi invasion of Kuwait.

The earlier status of almost free movement and easy access to jobs throughout the GCC was never restored after 1990. This is primarily because the GCC states decided to recruit their expatriate labour in south and south-east Asia; political militancy from Arabic speakers is still perceived by the GCC rulers as a threat even though concern has shifted from fear that migrant workers might bring socialist revolutionary ideas to fear that they might import Islamist jihadi ideas. While living conditions in Yemen deteriorated and poverty increased, the situation was the reverse in the GCC states which in the 2000s joined the wealthiest states on earth, with some of the world's highest per capita incomes: in 2015 Qatar had the world's highest per capita income of US $140,720 double that of Saudi Arabia's (US $70,570), while Yemen's was US $1,300. For Yemen, idealised memories of the late 1970s and 1980s remain vivid in national consciousness, and a return to free movement of labour to the GCC is widely perceived as a realistic target. In 1996, the Republic of Yemen formally applied to join the GCC at the Doha summit. This was rejected.

Faced with the worsening social and economic situation in Yemen, the October 2002 GCC summit allowed Yemen to join four of its institutions: the Health Ministers' Council, the Gulf Education Bureau, the Council of Ministers of Social and Labour Affairs and the GCC football tournament. In Yemen, this was viewed as a first step towards inclusion. The GCC saw it as a palliative measure to silence further demands for Yemeni membership, without giving Yemen either authority in decisionmaking, or the means of achieving its main objective, namely free movement. Outside observers might see this as a simple stalling action intended to fool Yemenis into believing they were making progress.

Prior to the current crisis, the GCC was hostile to the inclusion of Yemen on the basis of a number of concerns: security (read worries that AQAP activists might move into GCC states), the economic gap between the GCC and Yemen (read the risk of mass immigration of Yemenis to the GCC states and resultant increased demands), the risk that a republican spirit might inspire some of their citizens to call for more domestic political participation, and the demographic balance as Yemen's national population outnumbers that of all GCC states put together. Many of these concerns are specious as the actual threats are minimal or non-existent. Nonetheless, perceptions are important and they reflect a basic opposition, and indeed in some cases, racist/ethnic hostility towards Yemenis from the citizens of these wealthy monarchies.

The counter arguments in favour of Yemen's GCC membership basically emphasise the same issues: its labour force could contribute to the GCC economies, and its large population would provide a bigger market and increase consumption. Likewise the ports of Hodeida, Aden and Mukalla could complement those of the Gulf and enable the GCC to avoid potential problems with the Strait of Hormuz, particularly for oil exports. Yemen's strategic location would ensure that the whole peninsula could address security issues collectively and also control the Bab al-Mandab strait at the entrance of the Red Sea. All these arguments have faded into the background since 2015 when the GCC states became the leaders of a military coalition to topple the Huthi-Saleh forces.

Within the GCC, we have already discussed the role of the leading state, Saudi Arabia. A few words about some of the others: the United Arab Emirates (UAE) is, after Saudi Arabia, the state with the most significant relationship with Yemen. Its first ruler, Shaykh Zayed bin Sultan Al Nahyan, invited Yemenis from the Mareb region to move to the UAE and gave them Emirati nationality on the grounds of shared tribal ancestry. Thousands of Socotrans are settled in Ajman, one of the Emirates, and the state has a significant population of Yemeni origin, including some major traders in Dubai. The UAE provided financial support and assistance to the ROY as well as hospitality to numerous political exiles from Yemen. Many wealthy Yemenis have invested their often ill-gotten gains in Dubai and Abu Dhabi, including Saleh and his family.

The UAE's foreign policy has been closely aligned with that of the US, and the country developed its military skills by participating in the US-led coalition in Afghanistan. Its military ambitions have led sympathetic analysts to compare it with Sparta, a small but militarily fearsome state in Greek antiquity. Its recent adoption of military conscription for its youth both serves its military ambitions and contributes to the building of an Emirati national loyalty which extends beyond people's allegiance to each of the seven individual emirates. As discussed in Chapter 1 the Emirates' participation in the Saudi-led coalition goes way beyond the supply of military force and it may be too early to speculate about its long-term aims. It is worth noting that its objectives do not coincide precisely with those of

Saudi Arabia, as discussed further in Chapters 1 and 6.

Qatar's rivalry with Saudi Arabia has been a feature of its politics since it became independent despite its diminutive size and the fact that both states follow the same extreme form of Salafi Islam. In the 2000s, thanks to its massive gas reserves, it became a very wealthy state and successfully strove to develop a strong international presence. One of its strategies was to offer its services as a mediator to a number of Arab conflicts, including the Huthi conflict with Saleh's regime. In 2007, this effort appeared to succeed, leading to a ceasefire in June and a 'peace agreement' in February 2008. However, two main factors ensured the ultimate failure of Qatari mediation: first, resistance from Saleh who objected to the development investments proposed for Sa'ada as well as to the Huthis being treated as a fully-empowered negotiating party; and, second, Saudi Arabia's resentment at any state other than itself meddling so closely in the internal affairs of Yemen. A repeat effort in 2009 also failed. In retrospect, one is also led to wonder whether Saleh's reluctance was connected with early secret cooperation with the Huthis. The long-term problems between Qatar on the one side and Saudi Arabia and the UAE on the other re-emerged in extreme form in mid-2017. With respect to Yemen, it meant the immediate exclusion of Qatar from the Saudi-led coalition. However in the longer term, this breach may have an impact on the position of the Islah party, which is a main element of the internationally recognised government and at the same time at the heart of the tensions between Saudi Arabia and the UAE.

Other GCC states have played a minor role in Yemen since unification. Kuwait has been less involved in Yemen, and indeed had a less active foreign policy, though its Kuwait Fund for the Arab Economic Development continued to invest throughout the developing world. Unsurprisingly, Kuwait took longer than other GCC states to recover from the shock of Yemen's position at the UNSC in 1990, particularly given its generosity in earlier decades. It had been the most supportive (or least hostile) state to the PDRY and had offered considerable financial assistance to both Yemeni states, hence its anger. However, relations gradually recovered and the most recent indicator of forgiveness has been its willingness to host peace negotiations between the Yemeni factions in 2016.

Other than Saudi Arabia, Oman[17] is the only GCC country with a land border with Yemen and thus has direct interests in keeping a good relationship. The border dispute between the two states was settled in 1992 shortly after unification, and long before that with Saudi Arabia. Although Oman had a difficult relationship with the PDRY because of Aden's support for the People's Front for the Liberation of Oman until late into the 1970s, it acted generously with the ROY. Despite the retention of the fence built during the Dhofar insurrection, the Omani regime helped people from across the border in a number of material ways, such as providing a medical clinic on the border and financing the construction of a road to al-Ghayda, the capital of al-Mahra in the 1990s. After the 1994 civil war, it gave refuge to the separatist leader al-Beedh, only asking him to leave when he broke the conditions imposed by Oman to stay out of politics. Its role in the current conflict is discussed elsewhere.

Beyond the GCC

Until the early years of this century, Yemen's relations with **Iran** were considered of limited importance. 2004 was a turning point, In the early years after unification, the two countries had relatively good relations. At the unofficial level, many Zaydis who later became Huthi leaders and others from that community were enticed to go and study in the religious schools in Iran, despite the fact that Zaydism is a very different form of Shi'i ideology from that of the Twelver Iranians, who follow the most widespread Shi'i school. Evidently, the Iranian clergy hoped to convert Yemenis to their beliefs.

In May 2003, Iranian President Khatami led a large delegation on the first high level visit to Sana'a where seven cooperation agreements were signed on subjects ranging from security to agriculture. Once Saleh's conflict with the Huthis worsened a year later, relations with Iran gradually deteriorated, In November 2009, the Yemeni government closed the Iranian hospital in Sana'a, claiming that it was being used to help the Huthis,[18] and the same month it renamed Iran Street after a woman killed by Iranian authorities during demonstrations in Teheran. In his wars against the Huthis, Saleh attempted to persuade the US and Saudi Arabia to increase military aid to his elite troops and to financially support his regime by accusing Iran of assisting the Huthi movement, and of providing them with arms and cash. Initially the US and others were extremely sceptical about these claims, as is clear from Wikileaks cables and other statements.

The situation changed completely in 2015 when it suited Saudi Arabia's purpose to use Iranian intervention as justification for its intervention in

Yemen. By then US priority was to mitigate the negative impact of the nuclear agreement with Iran on its relationship with Saudi Arabia and other GCC states. As a result the US gave uncritical support to Saudi decisions on Yemen. While Yemen is certainly very important for Saudi Arabia, as has been demonstrated above, for the US both Saudi Arabia and Iran are of far greater concern. Although there had been anti-Iranian statements from the US in the late 2000s, these were toned down once serious negotiations were underway between the group of 5+1 and Iran on the nuclear issue. There have been numerous assertions of the capture of marine craft carrying Iranian weapons to the Huthis, and of the capture and killing of Iranians in Yemen since full-scale war started in 2015. As coalition forces have never provided any actual evidence, whether in the form of ID documents, corpses or anything else, it is reasonable to express some doubts about the veracity of these claims.

However, it would be equally naïve to assume a complete absence of Iranian involvement. Some in the Iranian regime are using the Yemeni situation to increase their influence in the Arab world. For example, shortly after the Huthis took over Sana'a in September 2014, 'Member of the Iran parliament, Ali Reza Zakani, who is close to Iran's supreme leader Ayatollah Seyed Ali Khamenei, bragged that Sana'a was the fourth Arab capital in Iran's grasp, joining "the three Arab capitals who are already a subsidiary of the Iranian Islamic revolution," and part of "the greater jihad." ... The other Arab capitals referenced by Zakani are Beirut in Lebanon, Baghdad in Iraq, and Damascus in Syria.'[19] Since then there have been statements from different Iranian officials both claiming and denying involvement in the war in Yemen. The consensus among close observers of the situation is that the Iranian regime is providing some financial assistance to the Huthis, as well as delivering training via Yemenis visiting Iran and Lebanese Hizbollah trainers in Yemen, as well as in Lebanon itself.

Interestingly, there is also evidence of Iranian support for southern separatists, in particular Ali Salem al-Beedh's Yemen Live TV station which operated from Hizbullah facilities in Beirut. Unless al-Beedh was using funds of his own, whose source was unclear, much of the cash distributed to his supporters in Aden was also believed to be of Iranian origin. Thus Iranian support to groups in Yemen includes elements aligned with both sides in the current civil war. As far as Iranian policy makers are concerned, Yemen is of limited intrinsic importance, though its control over the Bab al-Mandab strait gives a strategic edge to any involvement. But the main advantage for Iran is that Yemen provides it with an easy means of annoying Saudi Arabia in the overall context of their regional rivalry.

Throughout its existence the Saleh regime remained close to the **Iraqi** Baathist regime, and this policy was very popular in Yemen. Portraits of Saddam Hussein could be seen throughout the country in vehicles, private sector public places such as restaurants, and in people's homes; people perceived Saddam Hussein as anti-American and a strong supporter of the Palestinian cause. The Yemeni regime opposed the international sanctions against Iraq and the 2003 invasion. After the US occupation of Iraq, Yemen's involvement with Iraq reduced and has not been prominent. Huthi-Saleh delegations to Iraq have resumed since the civil war started, thus strengthening Saudi suspicion of a Shi'i conspiracy against Sunni Islam despite the fact that Iraq has official relations with the internationally recognised government and that its foreign minister met his counterpart in New York in September 2016.

The states on the west of the Red Sea have hardly been more stable than those on the east. **Eritrea**'s illegal occupation of the Hunaish Islands in December 1995 may have been encouraged by Saudi Arabia. Yet it was also probably part of Eritrea's policy of causing maximum instability around its increasingly authoritarian regime, thus distracting its population from major disappointments at the outcome of their long-fought-for independence. The issue was resolved in favour of Yemen by the International Court of Arbitration in The Hague in 1998. In the following years, relations improved, and in 2004 the Eritrean president paid an official visit to Yemen. Eritrea has benefited from the current civil war, with rumours that Iran has rented islands from which it sends weapons to the Huthi-Saleh faction.[20] Meanwhile the UAE was building a major base in 2017 at Assab on the coast. In addition Eritrea allowed the UAE and others to train Yemeni soldiers from the internationally recognised government on its territory.

Since its unification, Yemen has had to deal with the disintegration of **Somalia**, and has even occasionally tried to mediate between factions. The main long-term contact in recent years has been mutual assistance between AQAP and the Somali al-Shabab jihadi groups, while people have continued to travel back and forth across the sea, mainly to Somaliland. In the early years of the current decade many women and men from Somaliland were complaining that travelling to Yemen for trade and labour had become more difficult. Meanwhile the flow of Somali and Ethiopian refugees and labour migrants heading for Saudi Arabia and other GCC states has been reduced by the war, but surprisingly there are still many who take the risks and expense of the crossing in the hope of reaching locations where they could make a living. In the two years between the beginning of the war and end March 2017, 207,000 migrants from the Horn of Africa arrived in Yemen, while only 95,000 travelled in the opposite direction. In recent years, as the situation in Ethiopia has, once again, become more fragile, the number of Ethiopians crossing the Red sea has increased.

The North and the West

The US

Yemen was of strategic importance to the US prior to unification, as both states controlled the Bab al-Mandab, with the YAR serving as an outpost of Western influence in the face of the Soviet-supported PDRY. Unification coincided with the end of the Soviet Union and, by extension, of the Cold War itself. So while dumping Yemen might have been a problem during the Cold War, the nation had lost value to Washington when Saleh made his ill-advised move refusing to bow to US pressure at the UNSC in 1990. Since the establishment of the ROY, its relationship with the US has certainly not been an easy one. In the absence of an alternative superpower and the new regime's lack of commitment to socialism or the welfare of the population, there was no reason why relations with the US should not be good.

The Saleh regime made considerable efforts to improve ties and obtain financial and development support from 1991 onwards though the model adopted was not a straightforward master and servant one. Initial indications of success and of the regime's acceptance of the neo-liberal agenda were seen in the 1995 agreement when the IMF 'executive board met and agreed to extend the Yemenis $193 million loan for a 15-month period ... it shows Washington is turning its attention to Yemen's predicament and has acted to help the country out.'[21] Although it was not implemented as effectively as the IMF and US might have desired, the government did try, and Saleh himself used his usual tactic to strengthen popular support whenever demonstrations against the fuel and other price rises, made as a result of

IMF requirement that subsidies be cut. Recalcitrant implementation of the Structural Adjustment Programme was one of the features of economic development in the following fifteen years, and is discussed in Chapter 9.

Saleh's next important move to increase US support was his prompt statement of support for Bush's war against terror immediately after the 2001 events in the US. Despite Saleh's frequently asserted alignment with US policies, his relationship with the jihadis continued unpublicised, as was wellknown in Sana'a and by most close observers. It is not clear to what extent US advisers and embassy staff were aware of this. On the one hand, they constantly praised the Saleh regime for its support of their counterterrorism agenda and on the other they complained about his, at best, half-hearted cooperation in arrests and interrogation of those it considered responsible for the attack on the USS *Cole* in October 2000. The FBI investigators had 'already revealed troubling connections between the al al-Qaeda operatives who had successfully attacked the USS *Cole* and Yemeni government officials'.[22]

The years of Edmund Hull's tenure as US ambassador to Yemen, 2001 to 2004, clearly demonstrated the roller-coaster nature of relations between the US and the Saleh regime. Starting on a high point, and with considerable increases of aid during the first years of this century, their bumpiness is indicated by events around the Millennium Challenge saga. Funding from this mechanism was allocated to countries which performed well on a set of neo-liberal criteria established by the US. Yemeni officials had been led to believe that Yemen would be included and Saleh was on a visit in Washington in November 2005 when he expected official confirmation of Yemen's inclusion. That would have strengthened his claims to running a well-governed democracy. Instead he was informed that Yemen would not receive any funds due to persistently high levels of corruption.[*][23] He returned to Sana'a furious and dismissed his economic advisers.[24]

US development aid allocations were limited and clearly well below military ones. Development workers were frequently surprised by the many announcements of big funding followed by no visible action on the ground: USAID projects looked suspiciously as if their primary concern was security

---

[*] A month later, the World Bank cut its funding to Yemen by 34 percent, citing bad governance and corruption as the reasons, another indicator of the close relationship in decision making between the US government and the Bretton Woods institutions.

rather than development, given that their geographic target areas were all
the governorates bordering Saudi Arabia. Some of these had a strong jihadi
presence, while others were simply known to be unaligned with the regime.
According to the Congressional Research Service[25] total US foreign aid to
Yemen, including military allocations, was as follows

US Aid to Yemen (current US$ millions)

Item	2006	2007	2008	2009
Economic Support Fund	7.92	12	1.5	19.8
Foreign Military Financing	8.4	8.5	3.9	2.8
Development Assistance	--	--	4.9	11.2
Global Health Child Survival	--	--	2.8	3
International Military Education and Training	0.9	1	0.9	1.1
Total	18.7	25.3	18.2	30.3

The Obama presidency promptly expanded US military involvement
in Yemen against AQAP, increasing both drone strikes and financial
allocations. The first-ever US strike had been in 2002; between 2011 and
September 2016 there were 133 confirmed US drone strikes. The highest
number, thirty-seven, came in 2012, the year in which Hadi gave blanket
authority to the US to launch strikes at will, claiming that he authorised
each one of them individually.[26] Since the beginning of the Trump
administration, the number of strikes has risen dramatically, as can be seen
in the following table.

Confirmed US Air Strikes in Yemen[27]

Confirmed Strike	2002–2016		Jan–March 2017	
	Drones	Other	Drones	Other
Minimum Strikes	143	20	6	70
Maximum Strikes	763	83	8	70
Min. Killed	597	210	10	49
Min. Civilians Killed	65	68	0	27

The year 2010 saw a significant increase in US military involvement, following the 'underpants bomber'* incident. As pointed out by the writer Patrick Cockburn, in a comment on the US upgrading of its military rhetoric, 'There is ominous use by American politicians and commentators of the phrase "failed state" ... The US will get entangled because the Yemeni government will want to manipulate US action in its own interests and to preserve its wilting authority ... In Yemen the US will be intervening on one side in a country which is always in danger of sliding into a civil war ... What it is doing is much to al-Qaʻida's advantage. The real strength of al-Qaʻida is ... that it can provoke an exaggerated US response to every botched attack. Al-Qaʻida leaders openly admitted at the time of 9/11 that the aim of such operations is to provoke the US into direct military intervention in Muslim countries. In Yemen the US is walking into the al-Qaʻida trap.'[28]

Despite the apparent lack of success in the struggle against AQAP, Saleh's positive relationship with the US continued and, in addition to arms supplies, as late as January 2010 he requested that the US 'provide 12 armed helicopters and train and equip three new Republican Guards brigades'. At the same time he rejected the presence of 'USG personnel armed with direct-feed intelligence present inside the area of CT [counter terrorism] operations'.[29] US allocations of aid were higher, at least in the following years, and the data available includes additional sources not mentioned in the previous table. They totalled US $299 million in 2010, 160 million in 2011, 352 million in 2012 and 316 million in 2013.[30]

The US abandoned Saleh in 2011, reluctantly so, given how much it had invested in him as a factor of 'stability' in the country, particularly in training and equipping elite forces which were all led by his close relatives. In 2012, US policy was still defined as follows: 'Brennan goes on to posit four pillars of American policy towards Yemen: supporting the political transition, strengthening governance and institutions, providing humanitarian relief, and improving security and combatting AQAP. The high priority given to assisting the transition, however, at least in Brennan's speech, seemed

---

*   On 25 December 2009, Umar Farouk Abdulmutallab, a Nigerian jihadi, attempted to blow up a US flight to Michigan with explosives hidden in his underwear, hence he became known as the 'underpants bomber'. He claimed to have been trained by AQAP in Yemen where he had spent the months prior to his attempt. This event was the trigger for the establishment by then UK Prime Minister Brown of the Friends of Yemen in January 2010.

limited to calling on President Saleh to step down, advocating a peaceful transition of power, and supporting good governance through USAID projects.'[31] In the transition process, the distribution of responsibilities between the different embassies gave the US the role of guiding the security sector reform process. Its failure to ensure success raises the question of US commitment to the reform, as discussed in Chapter 1.

Overall, as one observer put it neatly some years ago, the US doesn't have a Yemen policy, it only has a counter-terrorism policy. Events since the outbreak of the full-scale internationalised war in 2015 have confirmed this analysis. Since the beginning of this century, a constant problem in the relationship has been the imprisonment of large numbers of Yemenis in Guantanamo, who remained there despite the fact that most of them were cleared by US officials of any crime; 115 out of a total of 770 detainees were Yemenis. In 2016 Yemenis were the most numerous of the remaining detainees. Further, the Obama regime continued to supply weapons and ammunition to Saudi Arabia despite considerable evidence that these were used against civilians and in breach of international humanitarian law. Even cluster munitions which cause untold and long-term damage, death and destruction for decades, are being used, some of them US manufactured.

In September 2016, the US Congress voted a US $1.15 billion shipment of arms and ammunition sale to Saudi Arabia, despite the welcome opposition of twenty-seven or over a quarter of all US senators. Throughout, the US administration has shown that support for the Saudi regime and arms sales, which spell cash for their companies, took priority over human rights and human life in Yemen. Giving a completely free hand to Saudi Arabia and the coalition it led in Yemen was meant as compensation to repair relations in response to GCC anger at the nuclear deal with Iran. It also served the wider US policy strategy of delegating 'policing' to regional states, rather than sending its own troops and taking the risk of having US body bags being flown back home, thus losing the administration popularity domestically. Writing five months into the new administration, the trend is clear. In Yemen, Trump's philosophy can be implemented without complications: Iran is bad and the Huthis are no more than its puppets; Saudi Arabia is a friend which spends billions purchasing US military and other equipment. Yemen has been overrun by very bad al-Qa'ida (and why not Daesh? Who knows the difference?). So the policy fits neatly into a tweet: there will be as many air strikes and drone attacks as necessary to finish off the terrorist

AQAP and Daesh; the Saudi-led coalition will get whatever it asks for to defeat Iran's proxy, particularly as it pays cash. There might well be more US special forces interventions on the ground: the model is the 'successful' Yakla ground attack of 29 January which killed twenty-five or more civilians including young children, achieved no notable victory over AQAP, and caused the loss of a US plane and one of its military. Trump's choice of Saudi Arabia as his first international destination as president confirmed all these, particularly with the signature of deals worth US \$300 billion, a third of this for military sales. So altogether, expecting the US to take a more humanitarian stand regarding the Yemeni people would be an act of naiveté or wild optimism.

The UK

Today a medium-sized economy on the margins of Europe, the UK is no longer the world power it was half a century ago, a fact to which many British officials appear to be impervious. Interestingly, Yemen is a rare example of a country whose leaders share the view that Britain's position still matters. As a result it can punch well above its weight, largely because of its former relationship with Aden which means that many Southerners, forgetting the war of liberation and the socialist period, appeal to the UK to support the Southern separatist cause. For the same reasons, the Saleh regime was concerned about British policy as he considered Britain's possible support for Southern separatism as a threat.

Recent indications of a UK leadership role in Yemen started with the 2006 London donors' conference, where development funds were pledged, most of which failed to materialise. More recently, in January 2010, the British government initiated the Friends of Yemen (FOY) grouping of nations in response to the 'underpants bomber' incident. It was intended to be a 'high level diplomatic coordination mechanism ... to mitigate the regional and international risk posed by the situation in Yemen. International donors agreed to support coordinated state-building measures to encourage better service delivery, good governance and more sustainable economic management.'[32] Staggering along over the following years, it has now petered out.

The UK is the 'pen holder' at the UN Security Council for Yemen, and this role gives it the possibility of taking initiatives to bring about peace. As of

June 2017 it had failed to address the issue of UNSC Resolution 2216 whose wording has been used by the Saudi-led coalition and the Hadi government to resist changes which might bring the war to an end (discussed in Chapter 1). In 2016 public opinion in the UK emerged as a relevant force; British citizens began demanding information on developments in Yemen and, in particular, they raised concern about British arms sales to Saudi Arabia in breach of the International Arms Trade Treaty, as well as the numerous breaches of international humanitarian law. This increased awareness led to a series of debates in the House of Commons, as well as a judicial review of these sales. However, UK government policy-making for the foreseeable future is primarily concerned with the expected problems resulting from its leaving the European Union. As a result it is unlikely to take any action which would irritate, let alone alienate, the GCC states, whether about Yemen or elsewhere, as it hopes for considerable Gulf financial investment and support in coming years. Should a Labour government come to power within this decade, the situation might change.

The European Union

Other European states have lesser roles. France, alongside the UK, is primarily motivated by its economic interests. It needs to balance the conflict of interests between arms sales to Saudi Arabia and the UAE with Total's major investment in Yemen's gas sector. On the whole, it would appear that arms sales are the dominant factor. Germany, which also sells weapons, has taken a greater interest and has attempted to mediate and play a diplomatic role, but little achievement can be reported as of mid-2017.

As an institution, the European Union has a number of advantages over its constituent member states: Yemenis perceive it as a neutral agency and its ambassadors to Yemen have been very active in the past decade, particularly since 2011. The Development Cooperation Agreement signed with the YAR in 1984 was extended to the Republic of Yemen in 1995. In 2004 a Joint Declaration to support stability, security and good governance was launched and formed the basis for including Yemen in the Strategic Partnership with the Mediterranean and Middle East. In addition to considerable political dialogue, the EU has gained real popularity in Yemen through its assistance packages, which are all grant funds and had reached

Euro 242 million by 2012, when EU representation in Yemen was upgraded to ambassadorial level since when its ambassadors have striven hard to bring about peace.

The North and East

Russia

The Soviet Union was the very first state to recognise the Imamate as an independent state as early as 1928; and of course Moscow promptly recognised the YAR shortly after its establishment in 1962, which was an integral part of its then excellent relationship with Nasser's Egypt. Similarly the USSR recognised the independent Southern regime as early as 2 December 1967 and relations remained extremely close during the existence of the PDRY. The Soviets also maintained fairly good relations with the YAR, despite its rivalry and ideological differences with the PDRY, thus preventing the YAR from completely falling into the pro-US Cold War orbit. Coming at a time of deep turmoil and indeed the disintegration of the Soviet Union, Yemeni unification was often compared with that of Germany. The Soviet Union recognised the ROY at its foundation in May 1990 and the ROY recognised its successor, the Russian Federation, in December 1991.

Saleh used his standard tactic of playing different groups against each other in international relations as he did in internal politics. So, although no longer a superpower, Russia featured prominently in his foreign policy and he visited Moscow in 2002, 2004 and 2009. Moreover Russia remained a source of weapons. Yemen purchased more than US $8 billion's worth of armaments by April 2004, including at least thirty MIG 29 fighter jets, bringing the total since 1960 to 200 MIGs of different types.[33] Unlike Russia's other clients, Yemen paid for all these immediately.

There was also tension in the relations between the two states: despite broad agreement on terrorism, Russia complained about the alleged presence of Yemeni jihadis in Chechnya. More problematic were statements of support for Chechen separatists from the Yemeni Islamist leader, al-Zindani, which certainly justified Russian disquiet. Economically, the Soviet Union was actively involved in oil exploration in the PDRY and was equally actively blamed by many Yemenis for not finding any until 1987 when oil was discovered in Shabwa. Joint exploration was renewed in 2002 when a Russian company, Rosneftegazstroe, started exploration in Yemen's al-Mahra Governorate; and Saleh had strongly welcomed Russian involvement in oil and gas exploration in the country during his visit that year.

After Yemen's 2011 uprisings, Russia initially joined other states in supporting the GCC initiative and then agreement. Indeed, it stood alongside the GCC, the US, and the EU as one of four official witnesses to the document. It then participated in the informal group of ambassadors involved in promoting the transition where it initially took the responsibility of supporting the outreach component of the National Dialogue Conference. Up to 2015, Russia supported UNSC Resolutions and contributed to maintaining a united position within the UN political system. Cooperation with other states weakened once the civil war started and in April 2015, Russia abstained in the vote for UNSC Rsolution 2216, for the first time breaking the international consensus. It particularly objected to the fact that the Resolution was one sided, as well as to the arms embargo and sanctions. Alone among the UNSC states, it has kept its embassy in Sana'a open and continued a dialogue with the Huthi-Saleh faction, including some high-level talks. Saleh publicises his frequent visits to the Russian embassy and his meetings with resident and visiting Russian officials.

China Rising

Both the YAR and the PDRY considered relations with China as valuable. Cooperation with Yemen developed continuously despite foreign policy changes in the People's Republic of China. Starting as a form of solidarity with road construction in the YAR and the PDRY, there was a relatively smooth transition since unification to the more commercially based approach operating with the Republic of Yemen. A number of economic and other agreements were made in 1996, and Saleh's visit to China in early 1998 could be seen as a prelude to the much longer one in 2006, when oil exploration and other economic agreements were signed. The Saleh regime's interest in expanding relations with China came at a time when Yemen was under unwelcome pressure from its Western allies to democratise. China's policy throughout the Third World has been to not intervene in the internal dynamics of the states with which it has relations, which probably pleased an autocrat like Saleh. Nor did Hadi markedly change Yemen's stance towards China; during his brief tenure as resident president in Yemen, he visited China in November 2013.

China's ambassador was also part of the group who supported the GCC Agreement and the transition process. Unlikely as it may seem, the People's Republic was tasked with supporting the human rights elements in the national dialogue process, though little seems to have been done in practice during the NDC itself. Since the situation deteriorated after 2014, China has remained fairly silent on Yemeni issues, though it voted in favour of Resolutions at the UNSC, including Resolution 2216. China, like most states, considers its relations with the GCC to be far more important than those with Yemen; this is particularly true with respect to those states who supply it with oil and gas. Hence a Chinese initiative to bring the Yemen war to an end is unlikely.

Other than standard political relations, the south-east Asia connection is really a continuation of the presence of people of Yemeni, mainly Hadrami, descent in Malaysia, Singapore and Indonesia as well as in parts of India. These relationships have continued and focused on trade for many decades. Malaysia is one of the few countries where Yemenis could enter without visas and in the present crisis many who can afford it have moved there for safety, although few can work and make a living there.

Conclusion

The isolation which the rulers of the northern part of the country maintained deliberately until the 1962 revolution, and the very different isolation which affected the PDRY throughout its existence, are both now ancient history. While many welcomed the ROY's engagement with the rest of the world, this has mostly had a negative impact on the Yemeni population, if not its leadership. Unification in 1990 proved to be a difficult birth, largely because of the ostracism brought about by its stand on Iraq's invasion of Kuwait that year. The expulsion of close to a million Yemenis from Saudi Arabia and other Gulf states put an immediate stop to their remittances, in addition to abruptly halting Yemen's receipt of foreign assistance. Recovery from this situation involved submission to the neo-liberal international agenda, which meant further deterioration of living standards. The main positive international economic feature of the 1990s was a limited development of international tourism, though internal strife constrained expansion of this sector.

The late 1990s and the following decade were marked by rehabilitation of Yemen on the international scene thanks to Saleh's explicit support for the war on terror and his willingness to allow the US to carry out covert military operations against jihadis within Yemen itself. This was accompanied by worsening insecurity, something which the regime exploited to increase military support from the US, individual European states and the EU. The phenomenon extended into the development sector as external funding was transferred from economic and social development projects to security-related assistance and, to a lesser extent, to aspects of governance.

The country's formal multi-party democracy helped the regime develop relations both with international institutions and with wealthier Western states. As a result, many of the latter were willing to ignore the worsening repression, uprisings in the north and south, poverty and constraints on freedom of expression. Outsiders from beyond the Gulf were happy to be involved with a democratic regime in the region where autocratic monarchies dominated, and thus tended to ignore the fundamentals of the regime. Despite appearances, some observers saw Yemen increasingly as a failing state – though only those most closely involved in the country and working in daily contact with ordinary Yemenis were unsurprised at the 2011 revolutions.

Throughout, Yemen's relations with the outside world were characterised by the regime's efforts at balancing its own policies, hopes and ambitions with its dependence on others to finance its economic development. The economic crisis and downturn of 1990 were never fully overcome, and Yemen's ambition to join the GCC was thwarted throughout. Although the regime was able to take some interesting initiatives, as, for example, concerning Palestine in 1982, its foreign policy was basically one of trying to use its weakness and dependence to manoeuvre between the competing interests and objectives of others. And for outside parties Yemen was not a priority per se but rather a pawn in a wider game. In this respect, it was perfect territory for Saleh's standard strategy of playing different parties and interests against one another.

US military strikes and the intervention of the Saudi-led coalition since March 2015 have transformed Yemen into a country where external forces are pursuing their own geopolitical struggles, which have little or nothing to do with Yemenis. Their strategy is superimposed on the internal conflicts, making for a situation reminiscent of the long Lebanese civil war, with different groups fighting proxy wars and, in the process, exacerbating social, political and economic internal conflicts. While pretending to seek solutions and solve the conflict, most of the external parties involved are far busier ensuring the profits of arms traders and pursuing their own interests than showing concern for the welfare of Yemenis or the future of their state.

CHAPTER THREE

The Two Yemeni Republics and Unification

1962–2010

Checkpoints provide a great diagnosis of political conditions in Yemen. In the YAR getting through a checkpoint was a completely unpredictable experience: it could take a second and you would just be waved through, or you could end up spending time in local security offices proving your harmlessness; having appropriate paperwork was irrelevant. In the PDRY it was the opposite: with papers in order you got through after a quick check; no papers and you were politely sent back with instructions on how to get the right permit. Since unification, the situation has varied according to circumstances: first being a tourist was great and one was waved on; then being a development worker had the same impact while tourists were compelled to take on security escorts (who had to be paid, fed and supplied with qat). Later, avoiding escorts became increasingly difficult, and finally anything other than air travel became too stressful. Numbers, location and staffing of checkpoints was always complex with personnel from rival entities demanding different authorisations and, amusingly, competing with each other for information. With the crisis, checkpoints multiplied, and now invariably include those whose primary motivation is extracting cash from travellers who are almost exclusively Yemeni.

The establishment of the Republic of Yemen in 1990 took place in the same era as the reunification of Germany, the demise of the Soviet Union and the Iraqi Baathist attempted takeover of Kuwait. All three of these factors had an impact on Yemen. While seen by some as a first step towards the dream of Arab unity promoted by both Nasser and Gaddafi in earlier decades, the unification process in Yemen had a very different rationale and circumstances – all indicators of a higher likelihood of success. It merged two regimes which had both differences and surprising similarities and took place at a time when it was seen by leaders in both 'parts of the homeland' (as the two states were described officially within Yemen) as a response to the crises each of them faced. Moreover, Yemeni unity was the one popular slogan throughout Yemen, while also being part of each state's official propaganda.

The 1960s

In 1960 the southern part of Yemen was known as the Aden Colony and the Eastern and Western Aden Protectorates. These areas fell under British direct and indirect rule respectively. While Britain initially intended to retain Aden as its main base east of Suez, the growing movement towards ending colonialism in Asia and Africa encouraged it to establish the Federation of Arab Emirates of the South in 1959. At first this entailed bringing together under formal independence most of the multiplicity of statelets which composed the protectorates. In 1962 this became the Federation of South Arabia when Aden Colony was included, an event which took place on 26 September, the very day of the overthrow of the Imamate in Sana'a. Had the news filtered to Aden prior to the Legislative Council vote, it would almost certainly have produced a different outcome. The federation was extremely short lived; in practice it barely existed and was largely an irrelevance in the following years when armed struggle both against the British and between rival liberation movements dominated life in that area.

Moreover, the three larger states of the Eastern Aden Protectorate refused to join, as they hoped oil would be discovered and they would achieve independence separately without having to share its income with the poor western statelets. In addition to the distance and remoteness of these areas, they had significantly distinct cultural and historical characteristics from the western areas. Large numbers of their military and other people had origins in the west, particularly Yafi'. Yet for well over a century the area of reference for Hadramis in particular had been south-east Asia and India, and the overall self-perception of the people in the Eastern Protectorate was focused elsewhere than Aden. Given the nature of the states further east and north, they also envisaged a future linking them eastwards. Though the formation of the Federation of South Arabia preceded that of the United Arab Emirates by more than a full decade, its fate was certainly different.

During the five years of the southern Yemeni liberation war, the dominant political and military roles were taken by tribesmen from the mountains of the Western Protectorate, as there was only meaningful Hadrami involvement in the final months. The nature of the struggle was such that the official British-managed armed forces, the Federal Army, played a minor role in the struggle for liberation, either in its official capacity as protector of the Federation, or as an insurgent force with one of the two main anti-colonial fronts. The liberation movements were the Front for the Liberation of Occupied South Yemen (FLOSY) and the National Liberation Front (NLF). On 7 November 1967, when the outcome of the FLOSY-NLF struggle was clear, the Federal Army declared loyalty to the NLF, thus retaining its position in the new republic. Soon afterwards, however, the new regime made fundamental changes in the military structure, depriving the tribal Awlaqi of their dominant position, and replacing them with officers and soldiers from the western highlands, the main areas which had led the anti-colonial struggle.

The Mutawakkilite Imamate in Sana'a had ruled the entire area which became the Yemen Arab Republic from 1918 onwards, after the final withdrawal of the Ottomans following their defeat in the First World War. Its realm was widely described as an isolated and backward state. The three Imams who ruled during this period (Yahia 1918–1948, Ahmed 1948–1962, Badr 19–25 September 1962) had to deal with a series of opposition movements intent on democratising and modernising the state. All were violently and brutally repressed. On 26 September 1962 the newly installed Imam Badr, despite his more modernist and progressive image, was overthrown by a military coup organised by officers who had been exposed to Arab nationalism during their studies in Cairo and Baghdad. They established the Yemen Arab Republic and there followed an eight-year-long civil war between the republicans and the Imam's forces. The republicans were supported by tens of thousands of Egyptian troops sent in by Nasser, until 1967 when the defeat in the Six Day War compelled

Nasser to withdraw his forces. The royalist fighters regrouped alongside the Imam and his senior relatives and received significant open support from Saudi Arabia and secret support from Britain in the form of special military forces, including mercenaries infiltrated through the protectorates, mostly from Bayhan.[1]

The mid-1960s were characterised by a convergence of interests and objectives between the republicans in the YAR and the liberation movement in the Protectorates and Aden. However the situation was complicated by the different political positions of those involved. The republican movement in the YAR had to focus its energies on the civil war within the state, as the vast majority of the population lived in rural areas where alliances were often shifting. Moreover, the republicans' military and financial dependence on Nasser's Egypt largely precluded them from taking positions outside the realm of Nasserism.

On the other hand the liberation movements in the south were split between two groups, FLOSY and the NLF. FLOSY remained Nasserite throughout and included the Aden Trades Union movement, as well as its political representative, the People's Socialist Party. Other than its Nasserist ideology, its main characteristic was its urban base among the (originally rural) working class of port and base workers as well as those in the different nascent industries of Aden. For its part the NLF started as a straightforward nationalist anti-British movement, one that from its early days was influenced by the Movement of Arab Nationalists (MAN)[*]; over time it shifted to the left of the political spectrum alongside sections of the MAN. Although it held its congresses and main meetings in the YAR it was under less pressure from Nasser, largely thanks to its military success: armed struggle against Britain started in the Radfan Mountains in the Western Protectorate on 14 October 1963, led by NLF forces. Between 1965 and 1967, the struggle between the two rival insurgent organisations was almost as violent as the battle each fought against the British. In August 1967 the NLF won decisively, leading Britain to negotiate and hand over the symbols of power on 30 November. Britain's decision was motivated by three main factors: the NLF's actual control of most of the country; Whitehall's almost pathological hatred of anything connected with Nasser,

---

[*] The Movement of Arab Nationalists was created in the American University of Beirut in the late 1950s by mostly Palestinian intellectuals and was the incubator for most of the left-wing movements in the Arab world in the following two decades.

which made it hostile to FLOSY; and, thirdly, Britain's lack of knowledge of the political tendencies within the NLF.

Disagreements and internal struggles continued during the first year of independence of the southern part of Yemen. Most FLOSY leaders had gone into exile in the YAR and beyond, but there remained significant differences between the 'right' and 'left' within the NLF which were 'solved' in June 1969 when the left expelled the right. Meanwhile many NLF military and other cadres had gone to Sana'a immediately after independence to support the republican movement, and particularly its left elements, to protect the city during the seventy days of siege by the Imamate forces. The republican movement lifted that siege in February 1968, thus saving the republic.[2] Given the role of the left from both the YAR's MAN faction and supporters coming from recently liberated Aden, the radical wing expected to strengthen its position thanks to its central contribution in the struggle for Sana'a. The left hoped to reduce the influence of the royalists in a future YAR regime but were disappointed as the left-right struggle in the YAR ended with the defeat of the left faction: the rightist republicans established a regime combining their faction with remnants of the royalist one (excluding only the Mutawakkilite family itself). Among other outcomes, this delayed the possibility of unification between the two Yemeni states as, by contrast, in the south, the left won that struggle and by 1970 had renamed their country the People's Democratic Republic of Yemen.

The Yemen Arab Republic: Instability and the Rise of the Ali Abdullah Saleh Regime

Politics

Egyptian involvement in the northern Yemeni civil war between 1962 and the final departure of its troops in 1967 had positive and negative features and received ambivalent responses from the population. There is little doubt that the Imamate would have been restored without this intervention, so it saved the republic. On the other hand the arrogant attitude of Egyptians, combined with the violence of the conflict, alienated many Yemenis who were otherwise sympathetic to the republic. Neither the left of the revolutionary movement or the suffering population welcomed the Egyptian presence.[3]

The first decade of the regime which emerged from the civil war saw much instability. President Abdul Rahman al-Iryani had replaced Abdullah Sallal when the latter was forced into exile in 1967. He led a succession of short-lived governments as the regime swung between accepting and resisting Saudi Arabian influence in internal policies, and the difficult relationship with the rising left in the 'southern part of the homeland' as the PDRY became known in the YAR. These years were also characterised by attempts at institutionalisation of state structures as well as foreign influence in development and economic policies, mainly from the Bretton Woods institutions.

In 1974, al-Iryani was overthrown in a bloodless coup by Ibrahim al-Hamdi who remains the 'ideal' president in popular lore to this day. He is admired throughout Yemen as a nationalist leader whose ambition was to establish an independent modern Yemen, with good governance and economic policies providing benefits to all, rich and poor alike. While this image may well be far from what might have happened had Hamdi's rule lasted, he didn't have the opportunity to demonstrate either good or bad governance as he was assassinated in October 1977, having ruled for just over three years. His coming to power by a military coup, as well as his ambiguous relationship with Saudi Arabia and, indeed, his efforts to take control over the Local Development Associations (discussed in Chapter 10) are all forgotten in favour of his now mythical position as a hero.

Hamdi's short tenure was followed by the even shorter one of Ahmed al-Ghashmi who was himself assassinated in June 1978, supposedly by an envoy of then-President Salem Ruba'i Ali (known as Salmeen) in Aden, as revenge for the killing of Hamdi. A month later, then Colonel Ali Abdullah Saleh became president after some manoeuvring within the top military ranks. At the time, he was widely expected to follow his predecessors to heaven or hell (depending on one's political views) and bring the qat which Salmeen had forgotten.[4] Contrary to expectation, Saleh demonstrated brilliant skills at political horse-trading in his dealings with tribes, political groups, military rivals, traders and all influential forces in Yemen. He remained in power throughout the remaining years of the YAR and achieved unification with the PDRY.

Saleh's rule in the YAR saw the emergence of a regime based on patronage. From the mid-1980s onwards it also benefited from a shift in the population/ruler balance of power: remittances to Yemeni households dropped significantly while the state was suddenly enriched through income from oil exports. Saleh could thus ensure the loyalty of the different regions and social groups in the country, as they came to depend on state funds which he controlled. Typically Saleh would hand out cash when travelling around the country, when shaykhs or other community leaders came to his court in Sana'a, or through the Department of Tribal Affairs in the Ministry of Local Government.

Remittances continued to play a role at the household level, and current expenditure was financed by state income, while development investments were mostly foreign-financed through projects. Some of them were selected according to technical criteria, but many were extensions of the Saleh patronage system. He also ensured that the increasing number of military/security institutions stayed loyal to him, both by promoting inter-institution rivalry and by selecting close relatives to lead them. Finally he created in 1982 the General People's Congress (GPC), a civil society institution whose only ideology remains to date loyalty to Saleh. Given the absence of political philosophy, it is inappropriate to call it a political party; it is rather a grouping of all influential people, from community leaders to intellectuals, assembled under the banner of supporting Saleh. It was also established at a time when political parties were illegal in the country, hence its name.

The Economy

The financial crises of the early 1970s were solved through foreign aid, and particularly through contributions by Saudi Arabia, thus accentuating the regime's dependence on its richer neighbour. The decade between 1975 and 1985 was particularly unusual as it displayed a rare contrast: a poor state and a wealthier population. State revenues were minimal and came from foreign aid and limited taxation. By contrast, after the oil price rises of 1973, Saudi Arabia and other Gulf states embarked on major investments which required labour. At that time, Yemenis from the YAR benefited from free entry to the country. More than 800,000 Yemeni men were estimated to have migrated towards the end of that decade; while no precise figures are available, they probably also included many from the PDRY who had taken

YAR passports to benefit from easy travel. Most Yemenis abroad worked in unskilled jobs, but their remittances made a massive difference to the situation in their home areas. Remittances rose from US $40 million in 1969-70 to US $1.3 billion in 1978-9 and US $1.6 billion in 1983.

This situation had both immediate and long-term impacts on the political, social and economic structures of the country. First, it meant that the poor state was unable to provide the services expected from it, services which the migrants themselves saw being provided to citizens where they worked, and which were considered to be state responsibilities throughout the Middle East as they were in in Europe.

Second, given that the people had money, they invested in improving family living standards, bringing back new four-wheel drive vehicles, mostly Toyota Landcruisers and pickups. They built good stone houses in their home villages, sometimes also in the cities of Sana'a and Taiz, opened shops, and started small businesses such as electricity generation for the village, car and refrigeration repairs. They invested in agriculture, too, mostly by drilling wells and fitting them with diesel pumps, thus in the long term contributing substantially to the depletion of the aquifers. Third, they contributed significantly to community development investments through the Local Development Associations. The combination of these factors establish this period as a uniquely positive and hopeful time in Yemen's development. It is remembered with nostalgia and is widely attributed to Hamdi's rule and also explains support for Saleh's early years.

Society

Yemeni society during this period also changed considerably, largely as a side-effect of economic transformations. The isolation of the Imamate and the civil war ended, and the 1970s saw a rapid expansion of education, including the arrival in the most remote locations of Egyptian and Sudanese teachers. Other factors were the introduction of TV and the influence of migration. Migrating men returned with the experience of the rapidly changing states[5] elsewhere in the peninsula. They brought back consumer goods and the experience of very different social and cultural living conditions, including the conservative mores imposed in Saudi Arabia. Rural areas witnessed some of the most profound changes, as young men increased their authority and took up new activities beyond agriculture and livestock, also using the new skills they had acquired abroad. Expectations rose and were fulfilled particularly in the 'decade of wealth'. The personalised patronage system of Saleh's rule rapidly led to growing dissatisfaction as the state failed to provide the services expected, and the quality of available services remained well below expectation.

Urban life changed with the rapid increase of population, including the arrival of Adenis after southern independence. The 1970s saw the emergence in the towns and cities of a social group which had previously been almost non-existent, tribesmen turning into shopkeepers. Others returned from Ethiopia when the Mengistu revolution happened after 1977.[6] Rural-urban migration was limited to men coming for seasonal work in construction and casual unskilled tasks. Despite this, cities grew considerably.

The People's Democratic Republic of Yemen

The Economy

Most significant for the future of the PDRY was the abysmal economic situation it inherited at independence. The area covered by the state had never been particularly favoured by nature, with limited natural resources: rain-fed agriculture in the highlands of the western areas, with some meaningful flows into the plains near Aden, around Wadi Tuban (in Lahej Governorate) and Wadi Bana (in Abyan). Both these areas had been developed in the last decades of British rule through the construction of modern spate irrigation structures for the production of irrigated cotton for export. Agriculture also developed in Shabwa, Hadramaut and throughout the country wherever the control of water flows permitted.

One British objective had been to supplement the income of local rulers who were otherwise completely dependent on British subsidies of weapons and cash, and on 'customs' duties for goods travelling through their areas. The cotton schemes also enabled a local peasantry to survive. The other main economic resource in rural areas was fishing, obviously restricted to the coastal populations. Only a few very limited areas inland could take part in the fish trade, as the absence of refrigeration made it impossible to conserve the fresh catch. However, some kinds of fish, shark in particular, were salted, dried and sold inland, particularly in Hadramaut where it could still be bought in the late 1990s. The population outside Aden depended entirely on subsistence agriculture and fisheries, and had to contend with the taxes paid to the local rulers. The latter were landowners of the fields irrigated by the modern spate structures where farmers worked as sharecroppers. In all the main coastal plains, agricultural workers were brought from elsewhere in Yemen, including many from the Tihama coastal plain, hence the term *zubud* (from Zabid) used to describe these groups in Abyan and Tuban.

The limited potential of the southern hinterland explains why the PDRY had expected its economy to rely on Aden port and its associated industrial activities. However, the closure of the Suez Canal during and for many years after the June 1967 Arab-Israeli war ensured that the new state was left with no resources, since the only other main one had been the British naval base and the trade from ship passengers. The agreement with Britain to provide £12 million to the new state collapsed as the regime turned leftwards and only £3 million was ever provided.[7] In 1967 the country had a negative growth rate of 10-15 percent.

The regime's economic policies also contributed to the disaffection of what it called the bourgeoisie, petty or otherwise. About 80-100,000 people left in the early years after British withdrawal[8] mainly from previous ruling families and their economic allies, but they also included ordinary FLOSY supporters. The regime's development focus on previously neglected rural areas, as well as its revolutionary policies, caused further emigration in the following years. It promptly instituted a land reform which handed over the previous rulers' lands to the sharecroppers; this reform was radicalised in 1970 when the government further reduced the size of maximum individual landholdings. But its most important feature was its implementation mechanism involving NLF-sponsored uprisings of peasants against their landowners, forcing them off the land, sometimes violently.

In the areas where most farmers were tribespeople who cultivated their own lands, demands to implement the reform led farmers to exchange lands with neighbours to demonstrate compliance with the new laws. Farmers were encouraged to join cooperatives, something which was greeted with mixed feelings but was useful for the acquisition of inputs. By contrast, the transformation of the larger holdings of the former sultans and emirs into state farms was less successful as few farmers, even sharecroppers, were willing to work as wage earners. The fact that the state managed marketing at pre-determined prices also led to low production in both state farms and cooperatives. But there is no doubt that the land reform reduced the differentials between farm sizes and largely put an end to exploitation of the peasantry by large landowners. Most importantly it had the fundamental social impact of empowering the lower status farmers.

Other revolutionary policies were distinctly more doubtful, in particular the nationalisation of almost all commercial and industrial enterprises including petrol stations and small retail units. Although the regime nationalised the thirty-six foreign-owned economic institutions, it had the wisdom to leave Aden Refinery and the Cable and Wireless telecom to operate privately. The main problem about these nationalisations was not the departure of their owners, most of whom had already left, but the fact that these institutions had been depleting their Adeni assets. Thus the decrees provided no revenue, while alienating people some of whom might otherwise have been persuaded to support the regime.

Development policies concentrated on agriculture, fisheries and infrastructure: the latter had been almost non-existent at the time of independence with only 126 kilometres of asphalted roads mostly in Aden and in the Hadramaut towns. Gradually, asphalted roads were built to link Aden to Mukalla and later to Wadi Hadramaut, connecting Abyan and Shabwa on the way. In the 1980s some of al-Mahra was also reached. Telecoms improved; electricity became more available in Aden and local stations provided it for smaller towns, though few rural areas were connected to networks, mainly because of the low population density and large expanses of uninhabited land between settlements. Larger and smaller water schemes were developed to provide domestic water to the population, mostly in the towns and cities which were all equipped by the mid-1980s. A few similar schemes were also provided in some rural areas where the topography and aquifers were suitable to collective schemes, such as parts of Wadi Hadramaut.

Foreign financing was extremely restricted, given the hostility of the wealthy peninsula neighbours, with the exception of Kuwait which provided significant assistance. British and US hostility precluded their involvement. Despite this, the country joined the IMF and World Bank in 1969 and obtained some development loans in different sectors from these institutions. The Eastern bloc, and particularly the USSR and German Democratic Republic, were major providers of economic aid and financial support. Through the twenty-three-year life of the state, the regime had considerable difficulties in obtaining the external financial support it needed to sustain the level of social services and full employment which it provided to its citizens. The country's population reached 2.345 million people in the 1986 census.[9] In the mid-1980s, oil had been finally discovered but had not reached production and export levels, hence it had no impact on the state's budget by the time of unification. Despite that, in its final years the regime achieved a balance of payments surplus.

Social Policies

The PDRY managed to provide living standards for its population well beyond its financial means, given its reliance on limited agriculture and fisheries, as well as on basic industrial development and the slight revival of Aden port after the re-opening of the Suez Canal in 1975. This was largely due to keeping prices low and providing many basic necessities cheap or free: nationalised housing rents were modest, education and medical services were free. In fact the regime actually benefited from the Cold War atmosphere, as its alignment with the Soviet bloc meant that by 1972 it received as much as £25 million in aid from Russia and China alone (which was quite significant then). Although much assistance was military, this was unfortunately necessary given the hostility of the PDRY's neighbours and the frequent incursions of Yemeni exiled forces supported by Saudi Arabia and other nations. While one may question the regime's strategies in the agricultural or industrial fields, they were no worse than those implemented in other developing countries. At least they reduced, rather than exacerbated, social and economic differentials. By the time of unification, a citizen of the PDRY, whether in the two cities of Aden and Mukalla or in rural areas, had access to good educational standards, medical services including preventative care and an income from his/her labour sufficient to maintain a household.

The education system developed and expanded rapidly, starting from a very low base. By the mid-1980s, Aden University had branches of education colleges training teachers in all governorates, and a quality medical school which had national as well as Cuban and other staff; and all students of the right age group enjoyed access to school, even if not all attended. Moreover a large number of literacy campaigns had significantly reduced adult illiteracy. In view of the limited success of earlier initiatives, in 1984 a massive campaign gave all secondary school students the responsibility for teaching their close and less close relatives, particularly women, which ensured their participation as the classes took place in people's homes. Women's education took off in a big way and by the late 1980s many education colleges gave the mistaken impression of being women-only, as so few men were present. While in the early 1970s most secondary school teachers came from Egypt, the Camp David Accords in 1978 put an end to this as the PDRY expelled all Egyptian teachers. Other foreigners took their place, mostly Sudanese and Palestinians, many of them from leftist parties which were banned or persecuted in their own countries. They were supplemented by secondary school graduates who were sent on national service to teach in the more remote locations for two years. Soon both these groups were replaced by trained Yemeni teachers. With respect to health, medical centres were built even in remote areas and staffed at first by nurses and medical assistants. As the number of qualified doctors increased, first through training abroad and later from the medical college of Aden University, more and more facilities gained fully qualified doctors. Although access was not always easy given the low population density, the services were free and of reasonable quality.

However, the PDRY's social policies went well beyond the provision of services, into realms which clearly differentiated it from its neighbours in the peninsula or beyond. Frequently accused of atheism as it was the only socialist state in the Arab world, the regime was far from that and actually provided a rare situation where there was genuine freedom of religion and belief. Islam was the state religion according to the constitution, and *awqaf* (religious endowment) properties were managed by the Ministry of Justice and *Awqaf*. Contrary to the propaganda promoted by its enemies, Islam was taught in schools but did not take up a disproportionate time in the weekly programmes. The overwhelming majority of the population of the PDRY were Muslim and practised openly, whether with respect to fasting during Ramadan or to daily prayers. Other religions were also tolerated, though their adherents were very few. The regime did not invest in the construction of mosques, and instead used its limited funds to build schools and medical facilities, but it did not prevent mosques from being built.

Indirectly related to the issue of Islam was that of women's position in society. The PDRY's constitution gave men and women equality and the 1974 Family Law was, alongside the Tunisian one, the most progressive in the Arab world. It even stated that 'husband and wife shall share in bearing the costs of their married life.' Furthermore it restricted and almost eliminated polygamy by complex regulations which made it almost impossible, as well as setting a minimum age at marriage of sixteen for women. While legislation is one thing and daily life another, this law had some very fundamental consequences. In areas where traditions were more restrictive towards women, the strict rules concerning marriage and divorce enabled some women to initiate divorce, and others to avoid marriages either due to their youth or their objections to the proposed partners. They could, if sufficiently determined, access support and assistance from their local Women's Union branch, which enabled them to resist family pressures to enter into marriages they did not want, as the law was on their side.

The claim to equality was implemented in a way similar to many East European states at the time, by focusing on women's economic empowerment. First, it increased women's participation in education at all levels, not only in the main cities and towns but also in rural areas. Second, it showed greater respect for women's traditional economic roles in agriculture and encouraged women to take up professions such as teaching and medicine where the numbers of women expanded exponentially. Women's involvement in work and in education grew considerably and their daily life was eased through regulations which officially gave them equality. In this respect the PDRY achieved an impressive female labour participation rate and formal equality.

On the other hand women enjoyed only a limited presence in the higher echelons of power or even in the administration. The PDRY had a few women deputy ministers or serving on the Central Committee of the YSP, but none made it to the Political Bureau. The main promoter of women's issues and concerns was the General Union of Yemeni Women, mentioned above, which had branches throughout the country. These focused on improving the position of women, including addressing family rights issues. The union also provided vocational training and took the lead in literacy campaigns. Of course, regime opponents gleefully asserted that women's equality meant immorality and other ills. Such an attitude did little more than reflect on the standards and attitudes of those making the accusations.

Another unconventional social issue addressed by the PDRY regime was that of tribalism. Alongside other modernist regimes, it considered tribalism to be a social problem. As early as 1968 the regime issued a Tribal Reconciliation Decree which put an immediate formal end to all existing feuds, stating instead that any dispute had to be addressed through the court system. In 1970 it revoked the licences of all clubs and societies based on tribal affiliation. The regime also banned the bearing of weapons in public, which created an immediately visible difference between the PDRY and the YAR to any visitor in the 1980s, as men in the PDRY, even in most rural areas, were not seen to carry weapons, while in the YAR almost every man carried his Kalashnikov (AK47) as casually as women carry their handbags. These measures were aimed at reducing armed conflict between individuals and groups, and they were accompanied by regulations which reduced tribal/regional identification, at least at the formal level. Initially the governorates of the country were given numbers rather than names; when in 1980 names were restored they were not 'tribal' but historical or geographical, and are still in use today. Problems of a tribal nature did occur, but were usually dealt with by negotiations and, if necessary, by force of arms by the national police or army.

Another mechanism used by the regime to reduce tribal allegiances was to ensure that all areas and groups had reasonable representation in party and government structures. Hence there were members of the Central Committee and ministers from all parts of the country. While this distribution of responsibilities was intended to reduce conflict, it also meant that, regardless of intention and policy, some regional/tribal nepotism was possible in the distribution of jobs. At the same time the Ministry of Labour made considerable efforts to ensure that qualifications rather than origin were the prime criteria for selection, and the policy of full-employment ensured broad inclusion on the basis of educational achievements.

The anti-tribal policy was closely linked to the regime's attitude to the nomads or *bedu*. Alongside most world regimes, whether socialist or capitalist, the YSP wanted to settle its small nomadic population. They discouraged nomadism by establishing boarding schools for the young, as well as water points, shops and medical posts which encouraged people to settle within easy reach of these service centres. The regime was particularly concerned with the nomads who moved across the Saudi border, for obvious reasons, given the hostility of the Saudi authorities and its sponsorship of armed opposition to the PDRY. While this policy had some success, a number of provisos need to be mentioned: first, allegiance to expanded family and tribe is not easily abandoned and it certainly takes more than a couple of decades to change such ingrained allegiances. Second, the fact that certain areas provided the bulk of military and security personnel had an impact on the composition of the security forces, and this became evident when political conflicts arose within the leadership, as discussed below.

Politics

Life for ordinary citizens was reasonably good, with jobs and incomes that enabled them to achieve an acceptable standard of living, to eat correctly and to finance basic necessities. By contrast, involvement in politics was inadvisable and a sure way of reducing one's life expectancy rather substantially. For ordinary citizens, the main political issue focused on personal liberties: freedom of movement was officially limited with emigration discouraged and sometimes banned. This policy was motivated on the one hand by the need to retain the labour force, and particularly the skilled labour force, for the construction of the country; and, on the other hand, by fear that migrants might join the numerous opposition groups which were carrying out military attacks on the country's borders. Another concern was limited freedom of expression: again, due to the hostile environment in which the state operated, the regime strictly controlled the media and opposing voices were stifled. It is important to remember here that we are talking of a period when telephone links were rare, the internet did not exist, nor did any of the modern social media.

Politically, the PDRY period was one of violent and frequent upheavals: the NLF changed names as it became more of a party and less of a front. It also gradually integrated other left-wing parties, while early dissenters had left in the years immediately after 1967. The Baath and the Communist parties merged with the National Front in 1975 and in 1978 the Yemeni Socialist Party (YSP) was formed. The senior members of the former small parties were thereafter included in the Political Bureau of the YSP but they generally kept out of the inner struggles which continued to wrack the organisation throughout its existence.

The PDRY survived in a particularly hostile environment. With the exception of the Yemeni republic in the north, it was surrounded by retrograde monarchies who viewed a socialist regime in their midst as a threat. Not only did they support the many exiles from the Federation period, and even former socialists like leaders of the Nasserite People's Socialist Party, they also encouraged armed incursions against the PDRY. In this context, it would have made sense for the country's leaders to develop solidarity, to concentrate on internal socio-economic development and to address these external threats in unity, rather than worsen their weaknesses through internal divisions. This was not to be: although some of these struggles were probably encouraged by the state's foreign enemies, participants cannot be exonerated of considerable responsibility. As mentioned above, the first internecine struggles took place immediately after independence and had brought to power the left of the NLF by mid-1969.[10] Over the following decade the main struggles were between two factions of the organisation, one of which was more populist and believed that the ordinary peasants and workers should lead political action; this faction was perceived to be Maoist and supporting the Chinese Cultural Revolution which had started in 1966. It was led by Salem Ruba'i Ali, known as Salmeen.

The main events associated with this trend were the NLF-sponsored uprisings in the rural areas used to empower tenant farmers and other intended beneficiaries of the land reform. These took place between 1970 and 1973: peasants' involvement in expelling landlords was a powerful mechanism to ensure their support for the new regime and confidence that they would really benefit from the new land tenure systems. In Aden the main event was the 'Seven Days' in August 1972 when mass demonstrations took place demanding reductions in salaries and the nationalisation of housing. Given that these were policies promoted by the recent NLF congress, the government soon agreed and salaries were cut by one third. All urban housing not occupied by owners was nationalised and thereafter rented at low rents to families who needed them. Salmeen was a very popular leader among the rural population and the more militant elements of the urban population, particularly since he tended to address people directly, away from the institutional strata. Moreover, he was a charismatic speaker, and did not talk in abstract slogans, unlike his colleagues.

While Salmeen's policies attracted many ordinary Yemenis, they were not appreciated by other senior politicians within the NLF, due to differences in both ideology and tactics, as he liked to bypass the administrative and party structures that were being built. In short, Salmeen reduced the power and influence of the nascent bureaucracy. From 1973 onwards disagreements increased and eventually blew up in June 1978 when the opposing faction used the excuse of his alleged involvement in the assassination of al-

Ghashmi in Sana'a to arrest and execute him. A few days of fighting ensued and many of his senior supporters were arrested and imprisoned for varying lengths of time. It is worth mentioning here that Salmeen's killing was the only time I saw people openly weeping in the streets of Aden.

Salmeen's downfall was soon followed by the foundation congress of the Yemeni Socialist Party and his absence enabled the remaining leaders to fashion the YSP far more on the model of standard East European parties than would have been possible had he still been leader. By the end of that year, Salmeen's main rival, Abdul Fattah Ismail, had become both secretary general of the YSP and state president. Throughout the decade he had been the organisation's main ideologue and his philosophy was close to the East European and Soviet model. He used to give speeches to the barely literate rural population in remote areas in which he discussed issues of feudalism and scientific socialism, something which did not exactly resonate with people's daily problems. Ismail's tenure was short. By April 1980 he resigned 'for health reasons' and went into exile to the Soviet Union, leaving all three top positions to Ali Nasser Mohammed, who had been prime minister since 1971. The following years were dominated by Ali Nasser who was less ideological and liberalised the economy by relaxing many of the more collectivist policies; he also sought investment and support from the PDRY's neighbours. By 1985, however, Abdul Fattah's allies in the YSP got together with many others who objected to Ali Nasser's monopolising of all three leadership positions, and forced the return of Abdul Fattah and others close to him.

The power struggle intensified and exploded in what became known as the '13 January Events' of 1986 when Ali Nasser attempted to have all his enemies in the Political Bureau assassinated at a stroke during a meeting. While the main historical leaders were indeed killed, a few escaped. This was followed by a 'mini' civil war which lasted a few weeks. Ali Nasser's faction was defeated. He and many of his supporters, military and civilian, went into exile in Sana'a and later formed part of Saleh's army in the 1994 civil war. They included Abdu Rabbu Mansur Hadi and many southerners who have featured as ministers in unified Yemen after 1994. In retrospect, Hadi's role in 1994 as a military leader of Saleh's forces partly explains his unpopularity in the South since 2015; despite being originally a southerner from Abyan, the secessionist Hiraak movement rejects both unity and any potential role for him in the south.

With the main YSP leaders dead, leadership of the PDRY fell to secondary characters: the position of secretary general went to Ali Salem al-Beedh who had been around since the early days, having been minister of defence in 1969–71 and a member of the Political Bureau for some years. Meanwhile the presidency went to Haidar Abu Bakr al-Attas, a Hadrami *sayyed* who had been minister of public works for many years. This group inherited a country which had been traumatised by infighting that had killed over 5,000 people, more or less destroyed Aden and, most importantly, had discredited the regime.

The events of January 1986 traumatised the leadership as well as the population. At the time the Soviet Union was undergoing fundamental change and encouraging its friends to alter their policies and reduce their dependence on Moscow. The PDRY regime faced the additional factor of loss of internal popular credibility. Taken together, these developments led the YSP to reconsider its path. It responded by initiating significant political and economic reforms which, had they been given the opportunity to mature, might have created a sustainable entity. The last four years of the PDRY were marked by the discovery of oil, attempts to diversify the economy through expansion of the private sector, and increased external financial support from its neighbours, particularly from wealthy industrialists of Yemeni origin. Despite an improving economic situation, the final months of 1989 were dominated by negotiations for unification, a process initiated by Saleh and prompted by a number of factors: the weakness of the southern regime, the discovery of oil near their joint borders, and disengagement from the PDRY's East European supporters.

The Road to Unity

Yemeni unity was an extremely popular political slogan everywhere in Yemen throughout the second half of the twentieth century. It resonated well among all sectors of the population. For centuries, population movements between different parts of the country by individuals and households happened for many reasons, including drought and flood-induced hunger, personal and tribal conflicts, and politics. While distinct regional cultures remain strong and some social groups remain extremely homogeneous to this day, many communities adopted individuals and households from other areas through a process of tribal refuge and the relocation of people excluded from their tribes or social strata.

As early as the eighteenth century, Hadrami armed forces had also been recruited from other areas, particularly Yafi'. With the difficulties of survival in Hadramaut during the early part of the twentieth century, many poor and low-status people had migrated to Saudi Arabia after the foundation of the Kingdom. Some individuals became very rich and wealthy over the decades and brought many more of their erstwhile neighbours to join their work force. These include some of the best known business families in Saudi Arabia, such as the bin Laden, bin Mahfouz, Buqshan and Amoudi. After the oil price rises of the 1970s, the Arabian Peninsula oil-exporting states became favoured destinations for a decade or so.

Yemenis left their mountains and made their way to Aden, too, at a time of restrictions on modern economic activities during the Imamate, and in response to the expansion of Aden as an international port under the British. Migration southwards had taken place from the late nineteenth century onwards: significant numbers of people from Hujjiriya, al-Baidha and Ibb came to work in the port and the British base. Most remained in Aden, but a few joined ship crews and built communities in Britain, France and the USA. Marriages between people from the same social group but different parts of the country also took place, thus ensuring that, by the time of unification, a substantial proportion of citizens in either part of Yemen had close relatives in the other.

PDRY independence took place in a context of conflict and social change that led to the immediate migration to the YAR of three main groups: the first two were the Nasserite supporters of FLOSY, and the merchants, traders and industrialists who were driven away by the nationalisation and the perceived threat presented by the regime's socialist policies. The third group was composed of the rulers of the statelets of the Western Aden Protectorate and the larger states of the Eastern Aden Protectorate. Most of these went to the YAR and Saudi Arabia, where they formed a distinct social group in both, and went on to contribute to social and economic life. For Yemenis in both parts of Yemen, although movement was officially restricted in the 1970s and 1980s, there were frequent mutual visits either officially or otherwise. So it is clear that socially there have been longstanding links between the different parts of Yemen, and that the slogan of Yemeni unity was one which was close to the hearts of most citizens throughout the country.

Politically, as early as 1969 the YAR National Assembly reserved seats for southern delegates. Similarly the PDRY regime proclaimed its commitment to Yemeni unity which featured in the daily morning pledge of allegiance in every school. However, after the southern state was renamed PDRY in 1970, politicians in the YAR felt that the new name challenged unity. The differences between the two regimes are sometimes overemphasised: both had significant public and private sectors in agriculture and industry, and shared notable political instability. While the political hue of the regimes were very different, with one wedded to individual leadership based on capitalist ideology, and the other led by a party with a socialist orientation, in both states differences of personality and personal competition played an important role in the state's instability and internal conflicts. Nor could either state be described as a genuine democracy or a totally retrograde autocracy comparable to those elsewhere in the peninsula.

The slogan of Yemeni unity was used to distract people from other problems, but remained a constant theme, the most popular political one at that. This did not prevent two inter-Yemeni wars in 1972 and 1979, each ending with an agreement on unification thanks to the mediation of other Arab states, Libya in 1972 and Kuwait in 1979. In both cases, southern forces had the upper hand because of their greater efficiency and better organisation. The unity agreements were widely seen as cosmetic arrangements which were not taken seriously by leaders intent on retaining control over their states. However, they did result in actions which laid the foundations for unification: after the 1979 war, a number of joint committees were set up to prepare for unification in different sectors, such as education and health, and to draft a constitution for the unified state. They carried on with their work, even in the early 1980s when there was a low-level armed guerrilla conflict in the central region between the PDRY-supported National Democratic Front (NDF) and Saleh's armed forces. In the end Ali Nasser's regime reduced its support for the NDF and Saleh created the GPC which included some NDF cadres, so the conflict was superficially resolved.

From the mid-1980s onwards, incentives for unification were stronger than those for continued division. As we have seen the events of 1986 considerably weakened the southern regime which found it difficult to re-establish credibility among its citizens, despite its belated attempts to introduce political and economic liberalisation. Arguably the suddenly reduced support from Eastern Europe and the USSR played a decisive role in undermining the PDRY. Although the YAR had, by then, started oil exports and thus had more income, the Saleh regime was facing political discontent due to its failure to respond to popular demands for democracy and the social and economic needs of its rapidly growing population. The regime became increasingly autocratic and patronage failed to replace the remittances which had gone directly to households and community development. YAR citizens resented having to 'negotiate' investments with Saleh cronies and supporters. Moreover, both regimes feared that the discovery of oil on their shared border could lead to fighting and give Saudi Arabia the opportunity of taking them over. Faced with such crises, the two regimes chose to negotiate for unification, rather than fight another war.

Surprising Swiftness of the Unification Agreement

As the negotiations were still under debate, few expected the sudden and complete unification which was agreed between Ali Abdullah Saleh and Ali Salem al-Beedh on 13 November 1989. Discussion within the ruling groups on both sides of the border had favoured a federal approach to unification based on a standard formula of allocating responsibility for foreign affairs and overall national security to agencies representing the whole country, while each existing entity would retain autonomy for economic policy and internal administration. Increasingly frequent meetings between the leadership of the two states ended with a *tête à tête* between al-Beedh and Saleh which concluded with a late night announcement of full unification.

Numerous rumours still circulate about Saleh imposing his terms on al-Beedh and the PDRY, including threats of the use of military force; in the absence of open archives, it is difficult to assess exactly what happened. Having signed off on full unification only a few hours after having publicly stated that there would be a federal system giving autonomy to each former state, al-Beedh addressed the objections of the YSP's Political Bureau by the simple expedient of claiming that he had achieved Yemeni unity. This was something the population as a whole longed for and was official YSP policy. It was therefore difficult for his colleagues to force a backtrack, which is worth remembering twenty-five years later when southern politicians, including al-Beedh himself, are clamouring for secession.

Despite its widespread popularity, some powerful forces strongly opposed unity, including fundamentalists in the YAR and the Saudi regime who considered the PDRY to be a hotbed of atheism and immorality. The agreement of November 1989 would have produced a single state within twelve months. To pre-empt any obstruction, the process was accelerated without much warning and the Republic of Yemen (ROY) was proclaimed on 22 May 1990. For a two-year transition period, the government was to be run with half of all senior posts earmarked for officials of each previous state. Parliament would be composed of the two combined parliaments. This was to be followed by national elections which would rationalise the system.

The Republic of Yemen (1990–2010)

When Reality Dashed High Hopes

Yemeni citizens throughout the country welcomed unification with enthusiasm in 1990. Suddenly people could travel anywhere in the country without hindrance, the liberalisation of politics meant that political parties and newspapers mushroomed all over the place, expressing a vast range of views, and everyone was looking forward to a flourishing economy. Socially, women throughout the country were hoping that the PDRY's Family Law would be adopted by the newly formed Republic of Yemen. Most people hoped the PDRY qat laws would also spread everywhere and that the 'free market' economy of the YAR would be the basis for economic development. They also generally favoured the more efficient administrative structure of the PDRY to be the mechanism for managing the country.

These hopes were soon dashed: legally the laws of the YAR extended to the south for women, thus reducing women's rights and re-establishing easy divorce for men. This caused anxiety among southern women of all social statuses and groups, including the least educated farmers. I remember working with farmers in Wadi Hadramaut in 1992: while the men were mostly concerned with the prospect of losing their lands, the women expressed dismay at the new divorce laws and openly stated the fear that their husbands would divorce them. Generally many Yemenis had also hoped for a more efficient administration, based on the principles of administration prevalent in the PDRY. Here again they were disappointed.

As for qat, its use spread throughout the country, even to areas which had previously not known it (Hadramaut and al-Mahra). Inflation was an instant transformation as prices rose dramatically for PDRY citizens who overnight found everything priced in riyals, even though the dinar officially remained legal tender until 1996.[11] Yemen under Saleh had a strong pro-Iraqi bias despite the fact that the PDRY's relationship with Baathist Iraq had been very tense and the Yemeni representative on the Security Council in 1990 was a southerner who had earlier represented the PDRY. Here was an immediate demonstration that the policies of a united Yemen would be unilaterally decided by Saleh.

After a few months of euphoria about the joint government and Parliament, the quality of administration deteriorated and political rivalries emerged. Between 1990 and 1992 more than 150 YSP militants and other influential left-wingers were assassinated in killings[12] attributed to Saleh's security services and his fundamentalist allies, either from the former southern exiles or from 'Afghans', i.e. jihadis (Yemeni and other) who had fought with the Taliban against the Afghan regime. No one was ever arrested or brought to justice to answer for these crimes. Tension was already very high by the time the postponed parliamentary elections took place in 1993. The failure of the YSP to retain a large number of members in the new Parliament weakened the socialist party's position vis à vis Saleh. Al-Beedh, the party's secretary general and now vice president of the ROY, further exacerbated the situation through his political ineptitude which led directly to the civil war in 1994. Saleh's forces won that conflict, supported by northern fundamentalists and 'Afghans' such as Tareq al-Fadhli, as well as other disgruntled southern elements, in particular Ali Nasser's forces, who had been defeated in 1986.

Ali Abdullah Saleh Rules OK

From 1994 to 2010 the Republic of Yemen was ruled according to the principles which had prevailed in the YAR in the 1980s: Saleh operated a system based on personal patronage and distribution of cash and access to economic assets – not only the oil sector but also all profitable trading, industrial and services facilities. He allocated these favours to a small group of cronies who rose through the military/security system thanks to their family or tribal connections to him. No business could succeed without this group's participation as a partner in the profits. Old trading families, either from Taiz and Hodeida, or newly arrived from Aden, simply could not operate unless they included on their boards members of the new military elites who were closely associated with Saleh.

Formal government had little power and was basically the administrative tool of this elite. Ministers and senior civil servants were in the difficult position of being the direct interlocutors of foreign agencies, including the IMF and World Bank. These agencies acted as if the government had the authority to take decisions, yet they faced stiff resistance whenever they threatened the interests of any of the chief kleptocrats. For example, the removal of fuel subsidies, one of the IMF's main demands, could not be implemented effectively as, whenever the government increased the prices, popular uprisings would lead Saleh to announce a slight reduction, and life would go on as usual.

This system operated under a veneer of democracy which was sufficient to ensure support from the northern states, primarily the US and nations of the EU. Officially Yemen is a multi-party state and parliamentary elections were held in 1993, 1997 and in 2003. The country has an elected parliament of 301 members which throughout was dominated by the General People's Congress (GPC). The other main parties present were the Islah, the Yemeni Socialist Party and also a very small representation of Baathist, Nasserist and Zaydi sectarian parties. An unelected upper house, the *Majlis al-Shura*, is composed of 111 members, mostly politicians and community leaders 'kicked upstairs' when dismissed or retired from senior official positions, whether in government or in state institutions. While this superficially democratic system enabled Western states to approve military and other aid to the regime, it was not welcome to Yemen's absolute monarchy neighbours in the peninsula who had formed the Gulf Cooperation Council (GCC) in 1981.

Ali Abdullah Saleh ruled first the YAR from 1978 onwards and then the Republic of Yemen from its foundation until early 2012. During this period of thirty-three continuous years he recycled himself from a military leader to an elected president, first via elections through the Parliament and in 1999 and 2006 by popular direct presidential elections. While in 1999 his 'rival' candidate openly stated that he supported Saleh, in 2006 the opposition parties who had formed the Joint Meeting Parties (JMP) chose a respected independent candidate acceptable to all these parties, despite their vastly divergent politics. His gaining 23 percent of the officially recognised vote was an early indicator of Saleh's seriously reduced popularity and a growing political crisis in the country. Saleh's attempt in early 2011 to change the constitution so that he could stand yet again for re-election was one of the issues which triggered the uprisings that year.

The real democracy and freedom of speech which started at unification in 1990 did not last. Within months, both elements were undermined through the above-mentioned wave of assassinations. In addition, free speech also came under severe stress as regime opponents were attacked in the streets, beaten up and generally harassed. Publications remained available but were increasingly restricted and journalists showing signs of independence also faced difficulties. By the late 1990s, the ROY regime was not significantly different from the earlier autocratic one which had prevailed in the YAR. Social, political and economic aspects of the regime and the many underlying factors which have led to the current crisis are discussed in detail in the following chapters. Of all these, Saleh chose to encourage various Islamists groups throughout the period, whose complex role is discussed in the next chapter.

CHAPTER FOUR

Islamism: Reality and Myth

Islamic fundamentalism is not exclusively aggressive and armed. Sunni Islam has some major 'quietist' fundamentalist movements, including some described as Salafis, the most prominent and best known one being Wahhabism in Saudi Arabia, a term rejected by its adherents. Quietism can simply be defined as obedience to the existing rulers regardless of the quality of their rule, and non-involvement in politics. This interpretation has obviously been rejected by the movements which have taken up arms against the ruling regimes, and by Islamist political parties of whatever hue. In Yemen recent developments have seen 'quietists' changing their spots and taking up arms. This range of positions is not reproduced among militant Zaydis in Yemen who, as distant relatives to Twelver Shi'ism, share a fundamentally political vision of religion. Given its origins, Shi'i Islam is intrinsically political and therefore has no room for 'quietism'.

Basics: Yemeni Islamic Sects

Yemen is a Muslim country. Only a very few people of foreign origin and the even fewer remaining Jews are not Muslims and will not be discussed further here. Yemenis follow two main branches of Islam: first, Zaydism, prevalent in the northern and central highlands including the Governorates of Sa'ada, Amran, Sana'a and Dhamar. Primarily for political reasons over the past century, there are no accurate figures about the numbers of followers of each sect. On the basis of the overall population distribution, Zaydis are estimated to represent between 30 and 35 percent of Yemen's population.[1]

Zaydism is the form of Shi'ism which is closest to Sunni Islam and its followers have very few differences in theology or rituals from Shafi'i Sunnis who form the majority of Yemen's population. Alongside other Shi'i they consider it a duty to rise up against unjust rulers, but unlike Twelver Shi'i they do not believe in the infallibility of their religiously legitimised rulers, whom they call Imams. However, they believe that only the descendants of the Prophet Mohammed through his daughter Fatima can be Imams.

In daily life, Zaydis and Shafi'i Muslims have prayed together and attended the same mosques for centuries and still do so. However, as the rulers of the northern part of Yemen were Zaydi until the 2012 transition, this strengthened the view that contemporary Zaydi movements may be trying to restore the Imamate. Ordinary people in the rest of the country have long resented Zaydi rule, even before unification when they represented about half the total population of the North. A feature of Yemeni republicanism was hostility to *sada* (people who claim descent from Prophet Muhammad) as a group, and few of them were allowed to take up senior positions. Zaydism and its political relevance today are further discussed in Chapter 5, as its association with the Huthi movement is crucial. There are also a few thousand Ismailis, another Shi'i group, who live in Haraz in the highlands west of Sana'a. They have a close relationship with other Ismailis, mainly in India, but also in the border region in Saudi Arabia, and benefit from considerable material and spiritual support from their community at the international level. They are accepted and only play a minimal role in Yemeni politics.

The majority of Yemen's population, however, is Sunni Shafi'i, following one of the major schools of Islamic jurisprudence, which prevails in and around the Indian Ocean rim. Unlike the Zaydis, who are not mainstream Shi'i, Shafi'is adhere to normative Sunni beliefs. In Yemen they live in the mid- and lowlands and basically surround the Zaydi areas on the west coast up to the Saudi border and east into al-Jawf and Mareb.

Members of all Yemeni sects include people holding the widest range of political views, from support for secularist parties to the most aggressive forms of fundamentalism. Many consider their religious beliefs as social and personal issues separate from their political positions. This chapter specifically examines political Islamism. At the outset it is important to realise that Islamist politics are unrelated to the issue of religious sects as discussed in detail by French analyst François Burgat whose conclusions can be summarised crudely as 'Islamism is politics as usual'.[2] While the Huthi movement is almost exclusively Zaydi, the main political Islamist movement discussed here, the Islah party, includes Zaydis and Shafi'is both as ordinary members and in its leadership.

Quietist Salafis: Dar Al Hadith and Its Successors

The far north of the Yemeni highlands, the Sa'ada area, has been the heartland of Zaydism in Yemen for centuries, even when rulers were based in Sana'a. Establishing a fundamentalist Sunni institute there was perceived as a provocation by Zaydi leaders, but Muqbil al-Wadi''s decision in 1980 to set up his Salafi Dar al-Hadith in Dammaj, near Sa'ada city, was due both to his resentment at the discrimination he had suffered from *sada* Zaydi scholars and because Dammaj was his home village. Wadi' was a tribesman of modest origins, not a *sayyed*. In the course of decades studying in Saudi Arabia he had converted from Zaydism to Salafism, but he also rejected political links to the Muslim Brotherhood.

Al-Wadi' maintained this faith despite the fact that his relationship with the Saudi authorities had deteriorated to the point where they expelled him from the country in 1979. Officials accused him of being a mentor to Juhayman al-Utaybi, the leader of the fundamentalist assault on the Mecca mosque that year. Despite this, financial support for his school later came from Saudi charitable institutions and wealthy Saudis.[3] In the following decades, the school flourished and its influence expanded throughout Yemen and beyond, with local as well as foreign disciples, who settled in the village and turned the area into a large community, reaching over 1,000 students in the late 1990s. Additional Salafi centres were established by his followers in Ibb, Mareb, Ma'bar (in Dhamar Governorate), Sana'a, Shihr and Fiyush, near Aden.

Initially, the main ideological position of his school was total rejection of political action and 'a claim of loyalty to the political ruler, even when that ruler is corrupt and unjust, as well as a firm intention to transcend local and national contexts by delivering a universalist message based exclusively on the Qur'an and the hadith, the sayings of the Prophet. This dominant branch of Yemeni Salafism aimed to preserve Muslims from strife by not engaging in politics, including abstaining from voting in elections, and certainly rejecting participation in demonstrations or revolutions. Yet its clerics believed they could play a role in orienting state policies through advice given in private to the ruler.'[4] By default this approach, alongside that of Wahhabis, the official form of Salafism in Saudi Arabia, supports whatever political regime controls the state. This position was maintained throughout the 1990s and the first decade of this century, though al-Wadi' himself made some explicitly political statements. After his death in 2001, his followers first continued to follow the same policies of loyalty to the regime and non-intervention in politics. This only changed with the rise of the Huthi movement and the disintegration of state institutions a decade later. Such a stance clearly set the movement apart from political Islamists, whether of the peaceful or the aggressive variety, despite the fact that the US and others often chose to treat all these organisations as identical.

With the wars between the Zaydi Huthi movement and the Saleh regime from 2004 onwards, Dar al-Hadith was, rightly or wrongly, seen as a base for anti-Huthi activities and the Huthi movement worked hard to get it and its followers expelled from Dammaj. After the Huthis took control of the entire Sa'ada Governorate in 2011, and their influence increased in the following years, their efforts were successful. There had been military clashes between Huthis and the Salafi community in Dammaj in October 2011, when Husayn al-Ahmar mediated and placed groups of tribal fighters between the two factions as part of a ceasefire agreement.[5] As tensions between the Huthis and their then official allies in the Joint Meeting Parties (JMP) worsened during the NDC (and secretly the Huthis were developing their alliance with Saleh), one of the foci of the conflict was Dammaj. Fighting flared up there again in October 2013 when the Huthis were actively expanding the territory and populations under their control. In early 2014, Huthi strength forced the Hadi government to agree to the evacuation of the entire community of students, followers and their families. Interestingly, the transitional government had considerable difficulty in finding somewhere to relocate the community, thus demonstrating the widespread unpopularity of Salafism in the country. Finally most of its members settled in a suburb of Sana'a while others relocated to the other Salafi schools. None went to the Tihama plain where they were first supposed to go as the authorities there refused to host them.

The movement's claim to being non- or even anti-political is clearly contradicted by the facts. According to any logic, a movement which claims to be loyal to a regime, regardless of its politics, is political in that it supports the status quo. Besides Wadiʿ's occasional political statements, some politically motivated Kuwaiti Salafis financed the establishment of the charitable organisations al-Hikma and al-Ihsan, thereby stretching the anti-political concept given that their services substitute those expected from a state. The lack of sustainability of the quietist position has been clear for a while: after the 2011 uprising the Salafis gradually found that they needed institutions to represent their interests and they formed the Rashad party, the first explicit Salafi political party to support political rather than military action.

Political Islam

Islah

The main Islamist political party is the Yemeni Congregation for Reform, known as Islah, the term that will be used hereafter.[6] It was founded in 1990 and comprises three main constituencies whose influence within the party has varied over the period, depending mostly on factors unrelated to its policies:

- a tribal element representing the northern Hashed federation and – to a lesser extent – Bakil tribes which are led, formally at least, by the al-Ahmar shaykhly family, and in particular by its founder Abdullah. This group is composed of Zaydis, though some are said to have been 'Sunni-ised'.
- the Yemeni version of the Muslim Brothers, previously known as the Islamic Front, which existed in the 1980s despite the illegality of political parties, hence its name; this group includes both Shafiʿi and Zaydi members and is strongest in the Taiz region where it originated.
- a more hard-line Islamist faction led by Abdul Majeed al-Zindani, which is frequently believed to be involved in some jihadi[*] activities which also includes members of both sects.

---

[*]   The term jihadi will be used here to refer to unofficial armed actions including assaults and attacks on individuals, groups and facilities – whether military or civilian – the use of IEDs, kidnappings and assassinations (actual or attempted), carried out in the name of Islam by individuals or groups.

Established shortly after unification, when political parties were first allowed to operate, Islah was simultaneously complementary and rival to Saleh's GPC, from which its leadership split. It was mainly intended to compete with the Yemeni Socialist Party (YSP) and free Saleh from the obligation to work with the YSP as specified by the unification agreement. In the 1993 parliamentary elections Islah won more seats than the YSP, and this result allowed Saleh to reduce the participation of the YSP in government to the advantage of Islah. Shaykh Abdullah remained speaker of the Parliament until his death in December 2007, head of the Islah party and, of course, also shaykh mashaykh (or chief shaykh) of the Hashed tribal confederation, which includes Saleh's small Sanhan tribe. This complex hierarchical relationship partly explains why Saleh and Shaykh Abdullah successfully maintained a reasonable relationship.

Given its long institutional history, the best organised section of the party are the heirs to the Muslim Brotherhood. They have therefore influenced the party's organisation, and held most administrative posts. Through their management of the party's paper, al-Sahwa, they effectively determine its political positions and intended image. This has helped them increase support for the party throughout the country and ensure that new members are also aligned with their policies.

Although Islah has more ideological coherence than the GPC, given its three constituent elements it had difficulty in establishing a common programme to which all would adhere. Its basic programmatic principles[7] can be summarised as follows:

- Islam is the fundamental basis of rule and underlying principle of all aspects of life
- Justice must be based on Shari'a (interpreted as Muslim legal principles)
- Freedom of individuals must be respected within the limits imposed by Shari'a
- All citizens are equal regardless of race, sex, colour, profession or social status
- Shura (or consultation) is the basis of the political and constitutional system
- Yemen is a republic and its unity must be maintained

- The state should operate on a multi-party system, based on fair elections and the rejection of violence.

Interestingly this programme has remained unchanged since 1990 when it was first made public. In view of the social diversity and range of political positions represented by its three constituencies, internal tensions are unsurprising. The broad scope of acceptable views on a range of topics contributes to increasing the number of supporters, as each chooses to focus on the elements of policy with which s/he agrees. Democracy and the role of women are two prominent issues on which tensions are palpable. Despite supporting the principle of pluralism, there is doubt about the commitment to peaceful democratic principles among some strong elements within the party. There is evidence both from current and former members that its internal practices are undemocratic, and that obedience overrides discussion and negotiations in decision-making within the organisation. In any case, democratic approaches are only claimed by the Muslim Brother element; the other two have little interest in the matter, or even oppose it. The tribal al-Ahmar leadership runs private militias and prisons, as do the more fundamentalist elements associated with al-Zindani.

The second main issue on which there is substantial disagreement within Islah is the role of women. Equality between the sexes is included in the text concerning social equality, yet most of the rest of the programme stresses that Shari'a should be the basis for all legislation and procedures. The document also fails to use the word 'woman' throughout, focusing on families instead, and thus avoids addressing the issue of women's rights. The Muslim Brotherhood element of Islah encourages women's participation and women are active in that branch of the party. In the 2007 internal party elections the leader of the women's section received the fourth highest number of votes,[8] and the 2011 Nobel Peace Prize laureate Tawakkol Karman is a leading member. Yet, al-Zindani and his followers claim that women should not participate in politics or public life in general. Similarly, while the tribal element formally allows women to participate, there are no women among its leadership team. In the NDC of 2013-14, Islah strongly opposed the 30 percent quota for women's participation in political and administrative bodies.

The party is held together thanks to two fundamental elements essential to maintaining organisational unity:

- *Finance*: The stronger elements have remained those with the greatest access to financing from Saudi Arabia and through the patronage system, i.e. the tribal and al-Zindani groups. In this context, it is worth remembering that, until 2011, the Saudi Arabian regime was the main sponsor and supporter of the Islah party, and earlier under the YAR the Saudis had supported the Islamic Front, the Yemeni branch of the Muslim Brotherhood.

- *The changed relationship between the Islah leadership and Saleh*: Islah rivalry with Saleh's regime increased with the impending shift to a second generation. Shaykh Abdullah's death initiated the collapse of this relationship, as the rivalry between his and Saleh's sons and nephews emerged as the major problem within elite Yemeni politics. Since then, the Saleh family actively worked to undermine the al-Ahmar sons' financial resources and to restrict their access to already diminishing patronage resources. The strategy included strengthening the military and security institutions under Saleh family control through a range of mechanisms, including US help in training and supporting the elite 'anti-terrorist' forces led by Saleh's son and nephew. In response, the al-Ahmar brothers both expanded[9] their own local militias and developed their relationship with Ali Mohsen al-Ahmar and his First Armoured Brigade. In short, they were capitalising on Ali Mohsen's Islamist politics and his position as a founding member of the Islah.

Islah's influence and strength increased since the beginning of the Saleh regime, particularly for the Muslim Brotherhood element. Support came in response to worsening socio-economic conditions and thanks to its claims to promote justice and equality for all, and Islah's rejection of social differentiation based on birth status. After unification, Islamists also rapidly gained strength in the former PDRY. Their political influence grew among younger people who were disappointed with the performance of a regime which had failed to respond to any of their practical problems or ideological hopes. Islamist programmes promised solutions to the worsening economic situation as well as to ethical disappointments.

The YAR Ministry of Education was the site of a struggle between Islamists and the GPC-led regime. Islah, and in particularly its Muslim Brother elements, had established and retained considerable influence in the ministry through its permanent staff (the turnover in education ministers is impressive, with twenty holding the post between 1962 and 1990 in Sana'a, including a single incumbent who stayed in position for five years). They influenced syllabus changes which gave increased time and concentration to Islamic studies in schools at the expense of sciences and other secular subjects. This was implemented by Islamic Front supporters in the 1980s when Saudi funding facilitated the employment of teachers from Egypt and Sudan. These imported educators promoted Islamist philosophy throughout the country, including in remote rural areas. By stark contrast, education in the PDRY had focused on science and humanities with religion as one of a number of minor subjects. So, until unification, most formal education in the YAR was under Islamist control.

In addition in 1980 the Muslim Brotherhood established independent 'scientific institutes' (*ma'ahid al-'ilmi*) with ideological and financial support from Saudi Arabia's extremely conservative religious authorities. Fifty in 1980, their number rose to a peak of 1,200 in 1996, but dropped thereafter due to the emergence of differences between Saleh and the Islah. These institutes were a parallel educational system directly under Islahi control after unification and the Islamic Front prior to that. They provided free education to boys and (fewer) girls throughout the country and their programmes concentrated on religious education, giving little attention to other subjects. Like the rest of the education system, they were mostly staffed by Egyptian and Sudanese teachers selected for beliefs consistent with those of Islah and Saudi Salafism. After unification, they spread to the southern governorates. They were abolished in 2001, when they were integrated into the mainstream education system, and had to teach the official government syllabus. Saleh took action against them as a result both of his concern at the success of Islah in local elections of that year, and under pressure from the US after he had joined its 'war against terror'. Closing them was an easy way to gain 'brownie points' with the US administration, particularly since it conveniently suited his internal political objectives.

Mosques are the other main mechanism for achieving the intellectual 'awakening' of the population. In the conservative Muslim social environment of Yemen, this is unsurprising in view of the following factors which prevailed until the arrival of electronic media in the past decade: high levels of illiteracy, absence of printed media, 'politically correct' repetitive and uninformative radio and TV political reports, and high attendance at

Friday prayers. In such a context most political ideas and social norms are transmitted through mosque preaching, increasing the influence of imams. Yemen had over 570,000 mosques in 2008, for a total of 37,000 settlements. However, only a small minority of them were supervised by the Ministry of *Awqaf* so it is difficult to assess how many imams were Islamists.[10] About 70 percent of the country's population are still rural and close to 50 percent are illiterate, even today. So at community level, the Friday sermon remains the most influential discourse reaching the vast majority of men.

The close relationship between the GPC and Islah to oppose southern socialists and, in 1994, its support for the war against the separatist faction, reflected their common conservative views, based on a retrograde interpretation of Islam and belief in obedience to traditional rulers. After the four-year Islah-GPC coalition government when formal collaboration between the two was strongest, the YSP's diminished importance reduced Saleh's dependence on Islah and the alliance weakened after the 1997 elections. Cooperation between them was only seriously challenged when the 2001 local elections demonstrated unexpectedly high support for Islah, making it a real rival to Saleh's GPC, and suggesting that the GPC might lose genuinely free elections. Saleh then encouraged the different tendencies within Islah to flourish, applying his usual divide and rule tactics. Until the death of Shaykh Abdullah, the situation remained under control as Saleh continued to show respect to the elder statesman who was also his senior in his tribal hierarchy. Although Saleh's alignment with the US following 11 September took the form of mild measures against the more extremist sections of the party, he did not interfere with the political activities of al-Zindani, the most prominent fundamentalist, at the extremist end of the Islamist spectrum within Islah, despite pressure from the US to extradite him. This strengthened Saleh internally as he could claim independence from US influence.

Until 2007 the relationship between Islah and the Saleh regime was more cooperative than competitive, though Saleh was certainly nervous about signs of Islah's increasing popularity. The death of Shaykh Abdullah triggered a crisis between the two families: competition between the second generations turned into active rivalry. Worsening relations between Islah and the GPC became public when the al-Ahmar economic empire was landed with sudden demands for large payments of 'tax arrears' and other punitive financial demands. By the time of the 2011 uprisings, the breach was complete. Young Islah supporters were active in the street demonstrations from the earliest days of the movement, and the rest of the party followed suit after the 18 March 'Day of Dignity' massacre. Within hours, both Ali Mohsen's First Armoured Brigade and the tribal leadership of the al-Ahmar shaykhs formally aligned with the revolutionary movement.

Islah was initially the main beneficiary of the 2011 uprisings as it dominated the Joint Meeting Parties (JMP) – a coalition that included most opposition parties established in 2003. The Gulf Cooperation Council (GCC) Agreement of November 2011 explicitly recognised the JMP and the new forces of youth, women and civil society as entities which were to share power equally with Saleh's GPC in the transitional government. This mandate gave Islah considerable influence as it controlled the formal government through the prime minister it had selected. This firmly set Islah against Saleh's GPC, as well as reversing the earlier convergence with the Huthis in the 2011 uprisings. Both groups had their roots in the northern Zaydi highlands, though Islah was dominated by tribal elements and the Huthis by *sada*.

Islah's Muslim Brother Image in the National and International Political Spectrum

Since 2014, Islah has faced serious setbacks. Having largely controlled the transitional regime, or at least what passed off as such, all branches of Islah suffered from the rise of the Huthi movement. Regardless of the will of the hundreds of thousands who demonstrated for better governance in 2011, the main political elements determining the new struggles remain on one side the Huthis, Saleh and his close associates, and on the other the internationally recognised government including Islah and various local leaders. Islah was seriously weakened by a number of factors: its many compromises with Saleh over the years lost it much support from committed militants who were attracted by the competition from rising extremist groups, including jihadis and Salafis of all hues. Militarily, Islah's tribal supporters were humiliated when the Huthis destroyed the al-Ahmar family home and defeated its militia in the Hashed stronghold of Amran. On 21 September 2011 its main military leader, Ali Mohsen al-Ahmar, was forced to escape from Sana'a in the face of advancing Huthi-Saleh forces and later moved to Saudi Arabia. The abysmal and corrupt performance of the Islah-dominated transitional government had also significantly dented its popularity by the time Prime Minister Basendwa finally handed in his long-awaited resignation.

After the completion of the NDC process in January 2014, earlier tensions re-emerged, and the overall situation prior to the major upheavals of that year can be summarised as follows: the Huthis administered their Governorate of Sa'ada, and had taken control of significant parts of the neighbouring Governorates of Hajja, Amran and al-Jawf. They were poised to expand further south. Saleh and his elite military forces had not been significantly weakened, despite some cosmetic changes at the top and the shifting of units here and there. His close relatives had been removed from leadership positions but middle-ranking officers and the troops remained loyal to him. Southern separatists were divided as usual. As the saying goes, while the elephants fight, the grass gets trampled: most Yemenis' living standards dropped dramatically, and people saw no prospects of improvement. They had no jobs, inflation was rampant, and infrastructure services were collapsing or non-existent. Most foreign-funded development and other investments were frozen, and the people saw no reason to support a transitional regime dominated by Islah and its JMP associates which had done nothing for them.

Two years into the war, the Saudi-led military coalition supporting Hadi's internationally recognised government since 2015 also affected the position of Islah as a result of the vagaries of Gulf attitudes towards the Muslim Brotherhood everywhere. Saudi Arabia soon revived its support for Islahi elements, including hosting members of the al-Ahmar family. Ali Mohsen's appointment as vice president of the Hadi government suggests a re-assertion of Islahi military power and influence, but this applies mainly in the areas east of Sana'a, Mareb, where they make up the main coalition ground forces. One side-effect of this development has been a systematic arrest campaign against Islah in the Huthi-Saleh controlled areas.

By contrast, the pathologically anti-Muslim Brotherhood stand of the United Arab Emirates has eroded Islah's position in the southern part of Yemen, including Taiz; this contributes significantly to the ongoing stalemate in the fighting there. The UAE's differences with Saudi Arabia on Islah are relevant not only to the military situation, but also to Islah's political prospects. Islah has systematically tried to improve its relations with the UAE and demonstrate its value and potential in solving the problems in

Yemen. As of June 2017, this has not proved fruitful. Under the influence of the UAE, in Hadramaut for example, Islahis are arrested and repressed under the label al-Qa'ida in an area where its influence expanded rapidly after 1990. Its ideology of equality between all social strata attracted many lower-status members of groups which had lost influence with unification; this was demonstrated in the 2003 elections when four Islahi candidates were elected to the Parliament in Wadi Hadramaut (out of a total of ten).

The future of the Islah party in Yemen will be determined not only by its ability to be a relevant institution in a post-war situation, but also on how it copes with the competition from jihadis and whether it can restore its position not only with Saudi Arabia but also with the UAE. In June 2017 with the ostracism of Qatar, this appears somewhat doubtful. In summary, ideologically the Islah party has a greater degree of internal coherence than the GPC, though it cannot be described as a political party based on a specific ideology, beyond being broadly Islamist. Its importance in the country's politics is rooted in the influence it has on the formal and informal educational systems and through the mosques. Islah has also benefited from the disaffection shown towards other parties, for example, the reduced support for the YSP in the Southern governorates after unification. Much support also derives from its very influential charitable organisation, the Islah Foundation. Alongside similar organisations in other countries, it distributes assistance to the poor and gives the organisation a high and positive profile. Its power base is largely popular, but its former active participation in Saleh's patronage system provided the financial basis for both its political and charitable activities.

Other Islamist Parties

There is one other Islamist party, the Rashad Union, established in July 2012 in Sana'a. It brought together members of the above-mentioned Salafi charitable organisations, and was the first explicit departure of Salafis from quietism, other than jihadi organisations. It had 170 founding members and was established so that it could participate in the National Dialogue Conference and thus play a role in determining the direction of Yemen's future political institutions. Its philosophy is to ensure that Shari'a law determines the governing system, though it also asserts allegiance to democratic practices and respect for human rights, as well as calling for professionalism in state institutions. Even its establishment was challenged by other Salafis who issued a fatwa against its formation. Its main achievement has been the inclusion of one of its members as minister in the internationally recognised government.

The Jihadis

The borderline between quietist fundamentalist Islam and active jihadism is neither clear nor permanent. While the movements discussed below have been militarily active since their creation, others have shifted from a quietist to a militant position over time and under the influence of political events. So while Islah has been political from day one, some of its factions have militias. Similarly the Rashad Union emerged from the quietist Dar al-Hadith but operates within the spectrum of political debate rather than military action. As discussed elsewhere far more radical Salafi elements also emerged from this group and are militarily active, mainly in the south. However, in 2016 some of them joined the Saudi-led coalition to fight the Huthi-Saleh alliance in areas adjoining the Saudi Arabian border.

Jihadism has removed Yemen from its previous obscurity in Western consciousness, something which says more about the attitude of Western media than about its significance in Yemen. Throughout recent decades and up to now, most Yemenis daily face far more urgent preoccupations and jihadism features low on their list of priorities. Jihadis first appeared in the early 1990s when Yemeni 'Afghans' returned home from having supported the anti-communist Islamist forces there, most of them operating in the mujahideen organisations coordinated by Osama bin Laden whose Yemeni origins are rarely omitted from any mention of his name. Some fighters from other countries who feared the reception they would get at home also came to Yemen intending to fight the 'communist' PDRY regime. Their arrival coincided with Yemeni unification, thus in principle reducing the need for 'anti-communist' actions, although Islamist leaders in Yemen encouraged the belief that there was still work to be done. In the first two years of the ROY, they were undermining what remained of the socialist regime in the southern governorates.

Jihadis provided vital support to Saleh's forces in the 1994 war against the separatists in the south, and thus contributed to his victory. They included 'Afghans' and militants from both northern and southern Yemen.[11] Encouraged by fatwas issued by al-Zindani they ransacked Aden in the summer of 1994. After that they also controlled public life in Aden and imposed many restrictions on the lifestyles of Adenis, particularly women.

The Saleh regime provided good cause for disaffection: it presided over worsening poverty, low educational standards, lack of employment opportunities and other legitimate income-generating mechanisms, plus high levels of youth unemployment. In these conditions, many came to see corruption and ostentatious displays of wealth by the small elite as further insults and reasons to actively oppose the regime by any means. The official opposition also appeared unable to provide alternatives and was perceived as being little different. US actions in other parts of the Arab world encouraged support for jihadism. First and foremost, the increasingly publicised festering situation in Guantanamo directly affected Yemenis who were (and still are in June 2017) the majority of a shrinking number of detainees. For many decades, its pro-Israeli policies had caused the US to be highly unpopular. The 2003 invasion of Iraq worsened the situation given that many Yemenis thought highly of Saddam Hussein. The revelations of the humiliating ill-treatment of prisoners in the Abu Ghuraib prison outside Baghdad was one among many examples of events which encouraged support for jihadism. Potential recruits were also encouraged by the perceived success of the Afghan Taliban in fighting US troops and a US-friendly government, let alone their mujahedeen predecessors' victory over the previous Soviet communist-supported regime.

The Rise, Fall and Rise Again of the Jihadis

As early as 1992, bin Laden claimed responsibility for two attacks on hotels in Aden on 29 December that targeted US Marines on their way to Somalia. This was one of the very first actions taking place under the name al-Qa'ida. The group claimed two other spectacular attacks, first in December 1998 in which four tourists were killed in crossfire during a rescue mission by Saleh forces in Abyan; and second, on the USS *Cole* military ship in Aden port in September 2000, which killed seventeen US naval staff.[12] Despite these incidents, in the 1990s and 2000s, Yemen-based jihadis were fairly weak. In addition to 'Afghans', they included many whose motivations were simply criminal, as well as youth sensitised by their political arguments.

Some may well have participated simply in the hope of being recruited into the security organisations, given the prevailing practice of the Saleh regime at that time, rather than intending to promote an ideology or bring down the regime.

Jihadism re-emerged after 2005 when its forces strengthened after the assisted escapes of its leaders from prison, first in Aden in 2003 and later in Sana'a in February 2006,[13] when twenty-three of the most notorious al-Qa'ida figures got away and proceeded to rebuild the organisation. The link between the latter escape and the humiliation felt by Saleh at being rejected from the US Millennium Challenge funding may be coincidental.[14] The al-Qa'ida which revived in 2006 had new policies: not only was it active against the US and other Western interests perceived to be anti-Muslim, it also now stood against those elements in the Yemeni regime which opposed them, in particular security staff who had mistreated them. In June 2007, al-Qa'ida demanded that 'Saleh should release all al-Qaeda members from prison, lift restrictions on travel to Iraq, stop cooperating with the enemies of Islam, especially the US, and return to Shari'a law.'[15] Attacks increased in frequency and in geographical spread within the country. A few examples: in July 2007 eight tourists were killed in Mareb; in January 2008 two Belgians and two Yemenis were assassinated in Wadi Hadramaut;[16] in March 2008 al-Qa'ida carried out a missile attack on the US embassy. There were many more incidents in the first half of 2008.[17]

Having restored al-Qa'ida as an effective organisation throughout Yemen at a time when it had been weakened, if not destroyed, in Saudi Arabia,[18] the remaining active Saudi al-Qa'ida members moved to Yemen and in January 2009 the two organisations formally merged to form al-Qa'ida in the Arabian Peninsula (AQAP). The merger was followed by some of the most notorious attacks of 2009. The first was a fight in Mareb in which AQAP completely outwitted Saleh's forces (or else they were complicit). Next came the attack by Abdullah al-Asiri on then Saudi Deputy Minister of the Interior Mohammed bin Nayef bin Abdul Aziz,[19] which almost succeeded on 27 August, and the failed attempt by a Nigerian trained in Yemen to blow up a US airliner on 25 December, frequently described as the 'underpants' bomber.

Relationship with the Saleh Regime

Numerous serious attacks have taken place, mostly in Sana'a but also elsewhere, killing hundreds of Yemenis between 2011 and 2015. In view of the increased instability in the country and the conflict between the Huthi-Saleh forces and Hadi's transitional regime, the claims by AQAP for responsibility for these as well as earlier attacks have to be taken with some caution. While the perpetrators were probably AQAP-trained individuals, it is likely that Saleh supported at least some of these attacks as part of his campaign to discredit the transitional regime. By so doing he sought to prove to all internal and international parties that he was the only one who could keep Yemen under control, and that without him chaos would prevail. Having been ousted from the presidency, he was out to prove his point and ensure chaos, as the examples below will show. Many incidents in Sana'a, in Hadramaut and in Aden after the coalition forces had liberated the city in July 2015 are also likely to have some connection with Saleh.

As pointed out by the academic Sarah Phillips 'in Yemen it is always difficult – probably impossible – to know precisely where to draw the line between autonomous acts by AQAP and its affiliates, and those that could, at least conceivably, be attached to power struggles within the regime.'[20] There is considerable evidence to prove the very close association of some of Saleh's security organisations, in particular Political Security, with the various jihadi organisations. Despite the apparent belief by many US officials that Saleh was actively opposing AQAP and jihadism and cooperating with them, even Ambassador Edmund Hull recognised that there was collusion.[21] There were also well-known cases such as the release from Yemeni jails of jihadi Fahd al-Quso and Jamal al-Badawi, both of whom the US considered to be behind the USS *Cole* bombing.[22]

A particularly blatant example of Saleh's attempts at manipulating the 'terrorist' menace to his advantage dates from 2011. The leader of the Aden-Abyan Army, also known as Islamic Jihad, was Tariq al-Fadhli, himself an ex-'Afghan', heir to one of the sultanates of the pre-independence South and a member of the General Committee of the GPC. Al-Fadhli was also a member of the Shura Council in Sana'a, and was brother-in-law of Ali Mohsen al-Ahmar (his sister is one of Ali Mohsen's wives).[23] In addition to his role in the 1994 civil war, al-Fadhli also ran an armed jihadi group in the 1990s near Ja'ar which participated in a number of terrorist actions. When pressed by the US, Saleh put him under very comfortable 'house arrest' but he continued to be a member of the country's leading institutions. In May 2011 Saleh appointed him governor of Abyan; on his refusal to take up the post, Saleh ordered his elite troops to leave their military camps in Zinjibar and Ja'ar, and informed AQAP of the fact. Under the name Ansar al-Shariah, AQAP took over and administered the area from May 2011 to June 2012. Under pressure from Hadi's military forces, they moved on and regrouped in remote, mountainous and inaccessible areas. Despite being dispersed and having been defeated a few times since 2012, they have clearly not disappeared, and returned to action in the Ja'ar area in 2016 and 2017.

However, Saleh also tried to reduce the ideological influence of the jihadis by re-integrating their members into society, particularly when this would strengthen his control over dissident social groups. In 2002, he initiated a policy to empty his prisons of jihadis by involving Muslim clerics in their re-education and promoting a quietist interpretation of Islam. Judge Hamoud al-Hitar set up the Committee for Religious Dialogue whose work attempted to demonstrate to jihadi prisoners that their interpretation of Islam was misguided and that they should not oppose Saleh's rule. In the three years during which it operated, the programme claimed a 60 percent success rate, i.e. six out of every ten graduates did not re-join a jihadi group during that period, and prisoners were released on formally accepting the credo of the programme. Between 360 and 500 men were released through this scheme.[24] Similar projects were put in place in Saudi Arabia and other countries. The Yemeni programme was closed in 2005.

Saleh's Half-Hearted Support for the US War on Terror

The 11 September attacks in the US in 2001 marked a significant change insofar as Saleh then explicitly joined the US 'war against terror'.[25] However this did not change his ambiguous positions on al-Qa'ida operations within Yemen, and he often obstructed US investigations by denying US access to Yemeni or other suspects living in Yemen. Cooperation between the US and the Saleh regime was kept low key. In particular the first ever drone strike outside Afghanistan took place on 3 November 2002, killing Abu Ali al-Harithi, a senior Yemeni al-Qa'ida operative wanted by the US; Saleh had promised to hand him over a year earlier. At the time, the regime tried to keep the strike secret and claim it as a success for Yemeni forces, something which failed as Paul Wolfowitz,[26] then US Deputy Secretary for Defence, boasted about the US achievement a few days before elections there.[27]

At the time of Saleh's visit to the US in 2005, there had been no terrorist attack against Western interests since that on the Limburg French oil tanker in 2002.[28] Saleh was angry when Millennium Challenge Funding was refused, precisely at a time when oil revenues were dropping, thus affecting his ability to finance his patronage system. The American excuse for Yemen's exclusion was the high level of corruption and the inadequate democratisation of his regime. The reality was that the terrorist threat appeared to have gone and Yemen was no longer seen as a major security concern in the US. Saleh learned the lesson. Thereafter he ensured that terrorist incidents would continue sufficiently regularly to guarantee US financial and military support for his regime.[29]

From 2006 onwards, the relationship between al-Qa'ida and Saleh's security forces, particularly Political Security, was revived. Not only did he take little action against jihadis, but he made sure they were available to initiate military attacks to remind the US that Yemen was a hotbed of terrorism and therefore needed its support. So he operated his standard tactics: for example, under pressure from the US, he arrested and 'imprisoned' Jamal al-Badawi, who was on the FBI's most wanted list, but transferred him to comfortable home arrest as soon as US officials had seen him in prison; his freedom to move was barely affected.

Drones and Direct US Strikes

Since 2009, the US multiplied drone and missile attacks against alleged jihadis with a remarkable lack of discrimination. Having considered the 2002 airstrike a unique event, a repetition of direct US attacks aroused considerable anger throughout Yemen due to the large number of civilians killed. The missile attack on 17 December 2009 against the al-Majalla village in Abyan governorate killed fifty-eight people including thirty-five women and children.[30] The number of strikes increased considerably in the following years. But in the US, the killing of two US citizens, first Anwar al-Awlaqi, an AQAP ideologue and, a few weeks later, his 16-year-old son on 30 September 2011, caused the greatest international outcry as the US was killing its own citizens without any recourse to due judicial process.

By 2010, Saleh had agreed to let the US run air operations over Yemen against AQAP, though he insisted that Yemen would claim the credit for any successes. Minister of the Interior Rashad al-Alimi publicly admitted to lying 'to parliament, telling them that the bombs in al Majalla strike had been American-made but deployed by Yemenis'.[31] US policy was changed to designate all adult males killed as combatants unless proven otherwise! The US implemented a strategy that targeted unnamed suspected elements, i.e. anyone. Such pronouncements significantly contributed to the expansion of AQAP and served as very effective recruiting agents. In 2009, Foreign Minister Abu Baker al-Qirbi estimated Yemen had about 300 AQAP members; within three years the number had reached more than 1,000.[32]

The ebb and flow of US direct strikes on Yemen reflect both the level of activity of jihadis and the changes in relationship between the regime and the US. So the gap of seven years between the first and second strike is indicative of the extent of cooperation during that period. From the earliest days of his presidency, Hadi declared that the US was welcome to attack AQAP; his claim that he personally approved each strike was widely disbelieved, given their frequency and his other priorities.[33] Details of the strikes are in Chapter 1.

Jihadis and Tribes

Yemen has about 18 million tribespeople so it is clear that a fair proportion of the Yemeni members of AQAP and Daesh, also known as ISIL (Islamic State of Iraq and the Levant) are tribesmen. Evidence also suggests that low-status groups are attracted to these organisations due to their rejection of inherited status categories. When Ja'ar was under the control of AQAP in 2011–12, the tribespeople left town, but low-status people stayed around to enjoy the benefits of their new power.[34] AQAP's withdrawal in 2012 took place largely thanks to tribal mediation, rather than military action by the transitional regime.

Simplistic interpretations of the role of tribes in Yemen are widespread and discussed in greater detail in Chapter 7. Distortion of the relationship between tribes and extremists has been a far too broadly sustained theme. It is often claimed that jihadis operate in alliance with tribes, something which largely derives from the complete (and often deliberate, some might say racist) misunderstanding of the nature and dynamics of Yemeni tribes. Tribes are one of two major elements of social and administrative organisations in rural areas. Tribes have armed forces and effective community level administrative mechanisms. The other element, the state administration and bureaucracy, depends on government salaries, and is therefore weaker because salaries are so low. Indeed, in recent years government workers have rarely been paid on time. Moreover, there is considerable overlap between the two forms of administration. One of the side-effects of the 2011 uprisings was the increased power and influence of jihadis, particularly in the rural areas, thus facilitating the insulting equation of jihadi with tribe.

Among recent examples of, presumably deliberate, distortion of reality is the following quote from Yahia Saleh, nephew of ex-President Saleh, who commanded the Central Security Forces (CSF) until 2012. 'The coalition between extremist groups and tribal units made it difficult to fight the terrorists, some tribes sympathized with the terrorists.'[35] This statement needs to be taken with a large dose of salt, given that he presumably knows better. The reason why it is mentioned here is to note that such a view is taken seriously by an authoritative publication such as *Foreign Policy*, a journal which also fails to critically address Yahia's role in the Saleh regime.

Once the full-scale civil war started in 2015, jihadis concentrated their attempts to control areas in the Southern governorates as well as in al-Baidha Governorate where skirmishes have been frequent. For almost a year (2015–16), according to international media and the jihadi industry, they were in full control of Hadramaut Governorate. This is misleading. While AQAP certainly was present in coastal Hadramaut, most of the governorate (the wadi, or valley, and the northern and southern plateaux) remained loyal to the internationally recognised regime. Similarly the coast between Mukalla and Aden is only populated by a series of small isolated fishing settlements, so AQAP certainly did not control all of it. The area around Ahwar in Abyan is the home of the Ba Kazem, a tribe notorious for its rebelliousness: equating the actions of its members with support for AQAP distorts reality and plays into the jihadi propaganda discourse.

In Hadramaut, the dominant social group are the *sada* rather than the tribes, hence anti-'establishment' groups include both low-status people and some tribes. This characteristic may explain the willingness of some tribespeople to join jihadis in managing their limited control over Mukalla. Tribes in Hadramaut are mostly on the plateau and they are not as significant a demographic force as elsewhere in Yemen. The same rejection of *sada* domination explains why many individuals from low-status groups shifted allegiance from the YSP to Islah after unification, because that party treated them as citizens: some of their youth may well have chosen to join more extremist forms of Islamism. With respect to support for AQAP, Hadramis of all social categories are extremely attached to the tombs of their saints, and the AQAP practice of destroying them was certainly not welcome. Nor indeed are the Hadramis pleased that jihadis seemed determined to forbid any manifestation of Southern separatism, another strong tendency in coastal Hadramaut.

In reality AQAP's influence in the coastal areas, including Mukalla, was limited. What did exist was achieved through a number of factors: force and threats, cooperation with local bases of Saleh loyalists in the Republican Guards, and local leaders' wish to avoid military confrontation. AQAP left Mukalla in April 2016 and that allowed the internationally recognised government, the UAE forces and the world media to claim a great victory at its expulsion. In fact its members dispersed into rural areas following negotiations which allowed them to keep their weapons and spread their threats elsewhere, including returning to parts of Abyan and Shabwa.

The fact that individual tribespeople have joined the jihadis does not mean that their tribe as a cohesive group supports jihadism. A good example is the situation in al-Baidha. Here is a straightforward case of both jihadis and tribes opposing the Huthi-Saleh alliance, hence they fight together against their common enemy. This does not mean, as is often said, that al-Baidha's tribes are all supporters of AQAP: of about fifteen tribes present in the governorate only small sections of four of them are committed jihadis. Even the leading families who have become notorious as a result of this association are internally divided between supporters and opponents.

Tribes as cohesive institutions also fight against the jihadis. For example, Mareb[36] tribes are reputed to be among the most independent who have least allegiance to Sana'ani authorities, whoever they might be at any time. They have fought AQAP as well as central authority forces. In 2010, in Shabwa, the United States hired a tribe to fight al-Qa'ida: 'Hassan Bannan, a leader of one of the Awalik branches in Shabwa and an opponent of the policy, told The Associated Press that more than 2,500 tribesmen have been divided into small groups to carry out daily searches. Another tribesman, Awad al-Awlaki, said 180 of his fellow tribesmen in the Shabwa town of al-Said each received 100 automatic rifle bullets and a daily stipend of US $50.'[37] However, it is worth noting that the Awlaqi are also the tribe of

Anwar al-Awlaqi, the US citizen and AQAP propagandist, who was killed by a US drone strike in 2011; he was living among his tribespeople when he was killed.

At the time of writing, AQAP is the main jihadi group operating in Yemen. In the course of 2015, Daesh claimed a number of attacks, but it is unclear whether these actions were anything more than the use of a more fashionable 'label' by some AQAP members, perpetrated by rival splits, or by allies of Saleh's security elements. In the first two years of the war, despite occasional claims of interventions, it is clear that Daesh has not become a significant force in Yemen where it is in no position to compete with AQAP. Whether this situation changes when it is expelled from its strongholds in Syria and Iraq may be clearer to readers.

Conclusion

While al-Qaʻida in its various incarnations is systematically described as a phenomenon directly linked to Islam, it is nothing of the sort. It is simply a political movement expressing conflict with Western-influenced politics, using the language of religion to express its views. Its claim to promote pure Islam by contrast with the corruption and politics of local regimes is a political message designed to acquire followers. Nor is Islamism in conflict with the prevailing neo-liberal extremist form of capitalism. Islah's programme does not challenge capitalism, nor does it promote a more equitable distribution of economic resources. It accepts the Washington Consensus policies of the International Financial Institutions (IFIs). Jihadis, insofar as they offer any programmes, also fail to address people's fundamental economic problems. Instead, they promote programmes which ignore economic issues, and their proposed political strategies will not reduce inequality. While AQAP is widely described as a major threat to civilization as we know it, however awful, occasional terrorist incidents do not constitute an existential threat.

In Yemen, a jihadi presence does not demonstrate control over the population; what it does show is that communities and their leaders are currently choosing to tolerate it, although some young people may be supporters or even members. Whenever a region benefits from effective governance by state authorities, this is likely to cease, provided the tribal and community leaders are given the respect and authority they consider to be their entitlement as well as act justly and honourably. In particular, communities must have the means to achieve economic development and improved living conditions for all their members. Without that, there will be no security in Yemen. Unless these issues are addressed, some community leaders will take advantage of the aggressive potential of these groups to continue challenging the state.

As I was told frequently in the field in recent decades, another major factor encouraging support for Islamism has been the weakening authority of older male household heads and tribal leaders resulting from the changed socio-economic relationships within households and communities. Younger men challenge the authority of their elders, as a form of protest, to assert their adulthood, or strengthen their own status within the community. In some cases, particularly where influential figures encouraged it, this has taken the form of joining AQAP or Daesh. That does not mean that the families, let alone the communities of those involved, support these organisations. However, tribal hospitality rules have sometimes forced people to host the comrades of their own 'dissidents' for short periods of time.

There are also numerous cases of tribal leaders mediating between AQAP and the authorities or official military forces to ensure the safety of their communities. Often they have assisted the peaceful withdrawal of AQAP forces, as mentioned above, in Zinjibar in Abyan, Azzan in Shabwa, and coastal Hadramaut. The fact that both sides are willing to benefit from the mediation of the tribes does not mean that either of them has the tribes' support, but simply that tribal leaders, and indeed all community leaders, want to ensure the maximum safety and minimum fighting for their people. This may mean opposing the jihadis with arms, or it may mean tolerating them for one reason or another.

The myth of AQAP-tribal collusion is one which conveniently enables outside observers to claim expertise, rather than admit the complexity of situations and the need for detailed information and knowledge. Dealing with reality would lead to better decisions, which might avoid exacerbating the conflicts and popular disaffection in Yemen and beyond. There is no doubt that accurate decision-making requires committed and long-term knowledge of specific circumstances in each area. In Yemen the fashionable reductionist approach has avoided addressing the underlying social, political and economic causes of the problem and has led to counterproductive policy recipes. In the case of jihadism in particular, these strategies have in the past been proven to be demonstrably inappropriate and unsuccessful elsewhere. The international community's prioritisation of counter-terrorism at the expense of so many other more urgent issues for Yemenis (such as good governance, and equitable economic development) has contributed to the deterioration of the overall political, economic and social conditions and the worsening of the very problem which they purported to solve.

Meanwhile presenting jihadism as a threatening monster only serves the interests of these movements, providing them with the propaganda and media exposure they relish. It also serves the interests of those who need jihadism as a bogeyman, to spread fear among ordinary people everywhere so as to keep the 'security' business going and expanding. Jihadism is an easy demon. The media and the counter-terrorism think-tank experts have produced simplistic analyses while staying comfortably in business in the process. They use it to maintain an ideological grip on populations at home who turn to populist politicians, while the 'security' industry and arms dealers profit. Political and military short-termism have also contributed to pushing policy makers to adopt short-term solutions that fit into their existing political programmes.

Having discussed mainstream Islamism and its more militant off-shoots, the next chapter examines another Islamist fundamentalist movement, one that is opposed to those discussed here, but which has achieved far greater power in the country in the past decade, the Huthi movement.

CHAPTER FIVE

The Huthi Movement

From Nowhere To Centre-Stage

In 1990, when the Republic of Yemen was established, the Huthi movement simply did not exist. It started as a religious revivalist movement in the early 1990s, objecting to Zaydi marginalisation in the power structure. Its relationship with the Saleh regime must be examined as part of a triangular power game between Saleh, Islah and the Huthis: the latter two share the same home area and therefore potential base of supporters among the Zaydi population. Islah, however, relies more on tribal leaders while the Huthis' leadership is exclusively from the sada social category. Saleh's tactic was to encourage the Huthis when he wanted to weaken Islah and vice versa. Hostility between the Huthi movement and the Saleh regime reached its peak in the series of wars between 2004 and 2010 when they confronted each other. This was followed by Huthi participation alongside its previous enemies in Islah during the 2011 uprisings. Yet another reversal of alliances brought the Huthis together with Saleh against the transitional regime from 2012 onwards, culminating in their open alliance during the current war. Thus the Huthis emerged from complete obscurity to being an unavoidable major element of the Yemeni political landscape and the prime focus of international attention within less than a decade. Not only are they at the heart of the current conflict, but they will need to be included in any solution, one way or another. It is therefore important to understand this movement and its development over the past few decades.

Social Cohesion in Sa'ada: Zaydis and the Rise of Salafism

Sa'ada Governorate in northern Yemen is the heart of Zaydism, a form of Shi'i Islam with few theological or practical differences from Shafi' Sunni Islam, which is dominant in most of the rest of Yemen. Their beliefs and rituals are so close that people of both groups pray together in the same mosques. Although the Saudi regime had supported the Zaydi Imam in the civil war of the 1960s in his failed efforts to regain political power, the Saudis consider Zaydism as a threat primarily because of its belief that *sada* have an inherent right to be both political and religious leaders. This characteristic differentiates Zaydis from other groups in Yemen. In Saudi Arabia political leadership is held by a tribal family whose claim to legitimacy is based on its role as the guardian of Islam's two holiest sites, Mecca and Medina, and who also claim a monopoly on religious correctness. Thus, by its mere existence, a group who believe that non-*sada* are illegitimate rulers is a challenge to the al-Saud rulers' claim to legitimacy. In addition, as the Saudi regime has actively promoted Salafism throughout the world,[1] it would have been surprising if it had neglected an area so close geographically and so important politically, which explains its encouragement for Muqbil al-Wadi'i's Salafi Dar al-Hadith school in the Zaydi heartland.

Contrary to the widespread belief that everyone in the far north of Yemen supports the Huthi movement, in reality the area has social divisions. It is also home to a number of long-standing non-Zaydi socio-religious groups, including Sunnis and Ismailis. Hence the Zaydi presence, while dominant, is not exclusive. In addition, most tribes initially opposed the Huthi movement, though this changed in the course of the wars opposing the Huthi movement and the Saleh regime. Broadly speaking, the Huthis are supported by those tribes and other groups which backed the Imam during the civil war of the 1960s, and are opposed by those groups which supported the republicans at that time. While some allegiances changed over time, this generalisation is sufficiently reflected in reality to stand.

The Huthis are generally unwelcome in areas primarily inhabited by Sunni communities (whether Salafi or otherwise). Tribal leaders who had long-standing kin and financial relationships with the Saudi regime, and with their relatives on the Saudi side of the border, were also generally opposed to the Zaydi revivalist movement and the Huthi movement in particular. Others were aware that Huthi propaganda, spread through cassettes and in the mosques, was designed to undermine the authority they had achieved as tribal shaykhs in recent decades, thanks to the importance that the Yemeni and Saudi authorities were giving them. In addition, in areas where Badr al-Din al-Huthi's family settled, 'long-established shaykhs viewed him as an "immigrant" interfering in their areas of prerogative and responsibility'[2] and were thus hostile to the movement when it emerged.

Who Are the Huthis? Ideology and Popularity

Originally set up in 1992 as the 'Believing Youth' Zaydi revivalist movement, the faction's initial objective was to re-activate the main tenets of Zaydi belief among youth in Sa'ada Governorate. It is important to remember that Huthi does not equal Zaydi: there are many Zaydi who don't support the Huthis, just as there are some non-Zaydis who support them. This movement was one of a number of responses to what was perceived as active and hostile Salafi proselytising in the heart of the Zaydi homeland. Initially the Huthis operated within Saleh's political framework and Husayn al-Huthi was elected to Parliament in the 1993 election but lost his seat in 1997. He was killed by Saleh's forces in September 2004 at the end of the first bout of fighting. The movement nonetheless grew in strength despite, or maybe thanks to, increasingly violent repression through six wars which killed thousands, displaced more, and destroyed the local economy and infrastructure.

Scholar Marieke Brandt explains how 'the Zaydi revival movement became a catalyst which could unite the interests of all those in Sa'dah and beyond who felt economically neglected, politically ostracized and religiously marginalized.'[3] By its actions, the Saleh regime encouraged most Yemenis to believe that their areas were being neglected. As discussed below, Southerners make the same claim; many in the South systematically refuse to believe that anyone in the area within the borders of the former YAR is suffering discrimination, while millions living in central Yemen have the same experience and perceptions of neglect, but have not developed major internationally noticed movements.

The Huthi movement is political and was initiated by a family of *sada* living in an environment where the majority of the population are tribesmen. Although in northern Yemen *sada* often bear arms and have been involved in military activity, the movement could not have developed into a major political and military force without the involvement of tribesmen. So the relationship of the Huthis with local tribes and the extent to which tribes have supported or opposed them is relevant. This requires some understanding of the details of relations between *sada* and tribes in general, as well as those between specific tribes and the Huthi movement. What emerges clearly is that at the beginning of the Huthi wars, the movement had far less support than later. Sympathy came from the areas where *sada* represented a higher proportion of the population and where the Believing Youth movement had held frequent summer camps to raise support for its beliefs. It also enjoyed support from friends and relatives of the Huthi family.

Ideologically, the Huthis share the social characteristics of other fundamentalist groups, including claims to theological correctness. Although a Shi'i group, their main distinguishing characteristic is the belief in the innate right of *sada* to rule. This is also the reason why some *sada* from other parts of the country support them. Like all political organisations, the Huthis include people who hold a wide range of political views. That said, changes in political and military circumstances have transformed both Huthi policies and diversified their support base. The range of views was wider and there were more opportunities for internal debate in the early period. This has narrowed over the past decade, very much to the benefit of the hard-line military groups and in support of a more autocratic approach. Hussayn al-Huthi was also a more progressive and democratically inclined leader than his successor. Nowadays, there are few, if any, reports of the leader holding consultation meetings with senior thinkers or indeed military leaders, despite the existence of a political bureau which includes one woman and is headed by Saleh Sumad. The current leader, Abdul Malik al-Huthi, is only ever seen alone on the media, as he never appears in public in person, and his only references are religious. He officially calls himself the Leader of the Revolution, while his religious title is Leader of the Quranic March.

Contrary to what is sometimes claimed, the Huthis and Sunni jihadi movements are in complete opposition to each other, with each side promoting rival and conflicting beliefs and regarding the other as little more than unbelievers; of course, each claims to be the holder of absolute truth. However, there is little difference in terms of the social norms they try impose. In November 2010, AQAP claimed two attacks against the Huthis in al-Jawf which killed twenty-five people[4] and were justified as a response to 'the failure of the apostate governments of Sanaʻa and Riyadh to confront the Houthi Rawafidh'.[5]*

Unlike Sunni quietist fundamentalism, Zaydism is intrinsically and explicitly political; hence it is unsurprising that there are Zaydi-based political parties. The al-Haq party and the Union of Popular Forces were initially the mechanisms for Zaydi revivalist political expression. Al-Haq's 1993 manifesto 'arguing that the ruler or imam no longer needed to be a Hashemite'[6]** was an attempt to reconcile Zaydism with republicanism that caused friction between some leading Zaydis. The Believing Youth movement, by contrast, operated at a grassroots level of Zaydi revivalism and tried to steer clear of party politics. When the Huthis emerged as a political movement through an internal schism in 2001, *sada* supremacy became an issue once again.

In June 2012, Zaydi figures associated with the Huthi movement set up the Hizb al-Umma[7] which is an offshoot of Al-Haq, though its creation was not due to ideological differences but rather represented a tactical move to reduce the influence of some individuals as well as increase the number of Huthi political organisations. It has not emerged as a meaningful force and little is known about it, although its president, Mohammed Ahmed Muftah, is a member of the Huthi's Revolutionary Committee set up when they took control of power in Sanaʻa in September 2014, and Lutf al-Jarmouzi, the head of its politics department has, since early 2017, been minister of electricity in the Sanaʻa government.

The Huthi Wars (2004–2010)

According to Marieke Brandt, the Saʻada wars were 'all at once: social, political, sectarian, economic, tribal and personal ... '[8]

Many causes led to the enormous proliferation of the conflict

---

* Rawafidh is a derogatory term for Shiʻi that some Sunnis use, literally meaning 'rejectionists'.
** Hashemite is an alternative word for *sada* (sg *sayyed*) or Shurafa (sg *sharif*) meaning descendant of the prophet.

throughout Yemen's north though two were particularly noteworthy. First, the government's armed forces carried out the wars with such brutality that the Houthi movement continuously grew in size and fighting ability, gaining sympathy from people who were suffering ... Second, prevalent tribal feuds and rivalries began to merge with those of the Houthi conflict as these tribes allied themselves either with the Houthis or the government. These dynamics allowed distinctions to become gradually blurred over time, playing into the common social overlap of ideological, political, sectarian, tribal, and personal interests. In particular, the involvement of the tribes, with their strong norms of collective honour and vengeance, unleashed an entirely new dynamic on an already complex and multi-layered conflict.'[9]

Chronology of the Fighting and Local Implications (2004–2010)

Six bouts of fighting took place between 2004 and 2010. The first lasted from 22 June to 10 September 2004 and was effectively won by the Saleh regime as its troops were facing a small group of dissidents. At the time, support for the Huthi movement was limited to their immediate geographic and social environment. This conflict ended without a formal agreement, and the possibility of a second conflagration was implicit due to the outstanding problems which had caused it. Six months later the second bout started; although fighting lasted less than a month (19 March to 11 April 2005), it expanded beyond the Huthis' stronghold and involved a wider range of tribal support for the Huthi movement.

Seven months later the third war started, lasting two months (30 November 2005 – 23 February 2006) and expanding further geographically. It was characterised by a media blackout as the regime prevented journalists from visiting the area. For the first time, fighting spread beyond Sa'ada Governorate into two neighbouring ones. The nature of the struggle also turned from an ideological to a more tribal basis: 'By 2006 thousands of men were fighting for the Houthis, but not all of them shared the Houthi ideology. Rather, they were "coasting the wave" of the rebellion in order to fight for their tribe, or against their rivals, the government, or a hated shaykh. Thus many supporters of the Houthi movement had no "real" loyalty to it; they switched sides based on immediate private interests.'[10] This war also saw a formalisation of involvement by Hashed tribal irregular troops against the Huthis, leading to considerable hostility from local tribes and hence increased support for the Huthis for two main reasons: first, the Hashed tribe were seen as tribal invaders in this mainly non-Hashed tribal territory; and second, people were very concerned about the prospect of looting.

The fourth bout of fighting lasted four months (16 February – 17 June 2007) and resulted in further disaffection of regime supporters who were increasingly concerned by their side's disastrous management of the conflict. It ended thanks to Qatari mediation which eventually failed, thus leading to the next phase. The Yemeni regime prevented Qatar from implementing its commitments to finance reconstruction as Saleh was apparently determined to prevent the region from benefiting from significant economic investment. Another reason for its failure may well have been the Saudi regime's resentment at a successful and popular intervention by its Wahhabi rivals from Qatar.[11]

The fifth war (2 May 2008 – 17 July 2008) saw fighting reach further still, this time into the Bani Hushaysh area near Sana'a. It also involved more realignment by previously pro-Saleh tribes. The sixth and final war was the longest (11 August 2009 – 11 February 2010) and started over a year after the previous one ended. The intervening period had enabled the Huthis to establish administrative control over Sa'ada Governorate and those parts of the neighbouring governorates of Amran and al-Jawf where they had influence. They also used the period to consolidate their military capacity. By the time Saleh unilaterally declared it over, there was no sign that his forces might win. The last war was also the most violent and destructive, when the regime implemented a scorched earth policy. It also demonstrated the military superiority of the Huthis over ill-trained Saudi forces who were, for the first time, involved in ground fighting when the Huthis crossed into Saudi Arabia.

One widely remembered incident clearly demonstrated Saleh's duplicity. By that time the rivalry between Saleh and Ali Mohsen over the succession to the presidency had reached breaking point. Saleh is reported to have given the Saudi Air Force the coordinates of Ali Mohsen's base as a target for an air strike, telling them it was a Huthi stronghold. This only failed because the pilots recognised the site before dropping their bombs.[12] While there is some controversy about this incident, there is none about the failure of government troops to achieve their goals. Saleh had denied Ali Mohsen's forces equipment and ammunition. Even when under attack, they got no reinforcements from the Republican Guards or other elite units, which explains why they performed so badly in the face of the Huthi-tribal alliances. A 'joke' circulating in Yemen was that the Huthi wars would end when Ali Mohsen was killed and that the entire purpose of the war was for Saleh to get rid of Ali Mohsen, thus leaving the field clear for his eldest son, Ahmed Ali, to succeed him as president.

In brief, the wars saw worsening violence and destruction, as well as increased support for the Huthis from the tribes, not necessarily because of ideological agreement but more as a reaction to the indiscriminate violence of regime forces. Moreover, the introduction of irregulars from rival tribes transformed the struggle into one based on retaliation and revenge and created a perception that the tribal groups' territories were being invaded by enemies. It ended in a stalemate, with few predicting that the ceasefire would last. The struggle's expected resumption was only prevented by the emergence of other major political developments, namely the 2011 popular uprising, and the intensification of rivalry between Saleh on one side and the al-Ahmar clan and Ali Mohsen on the other over succession to the presidency. Throughout the wars, there were constant sub-conflicts between tribal groups who allied alternately with the Huthis and the Sana'a regime, according to local circumstances. Obviously both the government and Huthis were 'deliberately working at recruitment of local tribes to capitalize on their combat experience and local knowledge and sheer manpower'.[13]

War Profiteers and the International Dimension

As is always the case with conflict, the Huthi wars provided wonderful opportunities for some: arms manufacturers and national and international arms dealers selling weapons to all sides, smugglers of everything from food to consumer goods and drugs, traffickers of human beings and, last but not least, military leaders who pocketed the salaries and food allowances of their troops. The earlier limited border controls with Saudi Arabia completely collapsed on the Yemeni side, and profit maximisation became the operational principle for what controls remained. The notorious Faris Mana, a denizen of Sa'ada, achieved international fame in the arms trade, selling weapons to both Saleh and his enemies. In 2011 the Huthis appointed him governor of Sa'ada Governorate, raising early doubts about their claims of being a new clean anti-corruption force in the country. In 2017 he is a minister in the Huthi-Saleh Government of National Salvation.

Another characteristic of this war which differentiates it enormously from the later situation was the issue of Iranian involvement. Throughout the 2000s, the Saleh regime was actively 'trying to portray the Shi'i rebels in north Yemen as Iranian cats-paws in order to secure American and Saudi support'.[14] Washington interpreted allegations that the Huthis were receiving aid and weapons from Iran as the Yemeni government's 'latest disingenuous attempt to garner Western and Sunni Arab support by casting the Huthis as terrorists, religious extremists, and allied with a hostile power.'[15] Moreover, at that time the US expressed considerable dissatisfaction at Saleh for diverting the support intended to strengthen Yemen's counterterrorism capability to his war against the Huthis; 'the CTU [Counter Terrorism Unit] has been derailed from its principal mission: to combat genuine terrorist target like AQAP while it has been tied down in Sa'dah.'[16] In 2010 US analyst Christopher Boucek wrote, 'There is no evidence that Operation Scorched Earth is a proxy conflict between Sunni Saudi Arabia and Shi'i Iran. There are more than enough grievances in Yemen and Sa'ada to perpetuate the fighting without drawing in regional dynamics. The Yemeni government has never produced any evidence to support its allegations that Tehran is supporting the Houthis; in fact, some Yemeni officials have confided that such assertions are unfounded.'[17]

By contrast, in the second decade of this century the US accepts the Hadi regime's claims that the Huthi-Saleh alliance receives strong support from Iran with cash, weapons and training. While Saleh's tactic had originally failed with the US, it may well, even then, have resonated more positively in Saudi Arabia and this may explain why, to Saleh's great satisfaction, the kingdom got involved in the fighting in 2009. For Saudi Arabia, the issues raised by the Huthi wars went beyond Saudi-Iranian rivalry. Under King Faysal, the informal agreement that Yemenis act as 'border guards' had as its counterpart the idea that 'King Faysal in turn acknowledged the religious and cultural diversity of the Saudi borderlands and their interdependences and tribal affiliations with some Yemeni tribes.'[18] According to Brandt, by expelling from the border areas those shaykhs who had kept the balance of power and economic relations with Saudi Arabia, 'the Houthi conflict generated a crisis serious enough to destabilize the entire system of bilateral border protection which evolved since the 1934 Saudi-Yemeni war, which depended on the cooperation and co-optation of the local tribes.'[19] As early as 2010, Boucek predicted with considerable foresight that the Huthis, seeing their success against Saleh and the Saudis in 2009, might 'encourage some rebel elements to expand military operations with the aim of overthrowing the regime.'[20] As we will see in the following pages, this has now come to pass.

The 2011 Uprisings, the Transition and the Discreet Rise of the Huthis

By the time the anti-Saleh revolutionary uprisings overwhelmed the country in 2011, the Huthis had already gained control over considerable territory beyond their original home governorate. During 2010 they gradually worked their way westwards to militarily take over the northern part of Hajja Governorate. They coveted this specific area for three main reasons: first, to get access to the sea via the small port of Midi and thus avoid being landlocked; second, to gain control over the full length of the border with Saudi Arabia west of Sa'ada; and third, they would also win highly productive agricultural lands in the foothills as well as in the Tihama plain. The Huthis' successful takeover demonstrated their coercive force, especially given that the population of those areas are largely Sunni and, indeed, included a fairly strong Salafi element.

Similarly they had taken over the northern parts of Amran Governorate and the west of al-Jawf; the former was part of their struggle against the al-Ahmar shaykhs, and the latter was to achieve the prospect of greater economic autonomy. There were claims of the discovery of considerable reserves of oil in al-Jawf, which far surpassed its other main asset, namely some important archaeological sites. While extreme violence and destruction by the Saleh regime were widely and rightly condemned at the time, the Huthis also learnt from the regime's tactics. Their actions against their opponents, both within Sa'ada Governorate and beyond, were unforgiving. Once they defeated any group, they promptly blew up the homes of their leaders, whether shaykhs or others.

In 2011, the Huthis participated in the uprisings against the Saleh regime. Throughout the period of the 'live-ins', in Change Square, the Huthis kept separate tents, and held meetings separately from most other groups, though they coordinated and sometimes acted with others; after 2013 Huthi militants occupied most of the remaining tents. The uprisings involved people from everywhere in Yemen who held a broad range of views. The 18 March 'Friday of Dignity' massacre led to a dramatic overturning of old alliances and the establishment of new, apparently contradictory ones. This event brought together Huthis and some of their earlier main enemies, including Ali Mohsen al-Ahmar and all sections of the Islah party. It was an unlikely alliance if ever there was one, and even more so in retrospect when some evidence has emerged that the Huthis were already cooperating with Saleh elsewhere in the country. While everyone's eyes were focused on the popular uprisings and their possible outcome, the Huthis took the opportunity to complete their control over their home governorate of Sa'ada.

In Sana'a and elsewhere the Huthis actively promoted their positions and recruited supporters, mostly clandestinely during the early months of the uprising and the struggle over the GCC Initiative. They participated indirectly[21] in the Government of National Unity established by the transitional regime, and in the discussions leading to the preparation of the National Dialogue Conference (NDC). In September 2012, the Huthi presence in Sana'a emerged with the sudden appearance of its slogan painted on walls throughout the city, but particularly in the Old City: 'God is great, Death to America, Death to Israel, Curse on the Jews, Victory for Islam.'[22]

The Huthis and the National Dialogue Conference (NDC)

When the Huthi movement agreed to participate in the NDC, it adopted the new name of Ansar Allah, so when discussing their activities from 2012 onwards, the two titles are used interchangeably. Some of its leaders actively participated in the NDC committee devoted to the Sa'ada issue, even though they failed to achieve the aims of the group or reach a solution. However, a number of Huthi leaders were assassinated during and after the NDC. As usual, no suspects for these murders were ever arrested or even identified. Given the secret alliance between the Huthis and Saleh by that time, one is led to wonder whether Saleh's faction and security forces might have been involved. Saleh's interests were a) to disrupt the NDC and ensure its failure, and b) to strengthen the Huthi hardliners so as to ensure that they would pursue an aggressive military strategy against the Hadi regime. For the same reasons, Huthi hardliners and various Salafi movements are also likely suspects of the assassinations.

For the record, it is worth remembering that, as pointed out by Brandt, 'the movement's delegation to the NDC was dominated by moderate and consensus-oriented doves, notably 'Ali al-Bukhayti, Ahmad Sharaf al-Din, and 'Abdulkarim Jadban. Around the negotiating table, they met Sunni Islamists with whom the Houthi hardliners were at that very moment engaged in deadly battle. In the NDC, the moderate Houthi delegates dusted off Hussein al-Huthi's social revolutionary agenda ... [calling] for equality of all groups and sects and for the end of patronage and corruption ... They demanded the establishment of a "participatory state" (*dawlat al-sharakah al-wataniyyah*) or – in the words of 'Ali al-Bukhayti – a "second republic" (*al-jumhuriyyah al-thaniyyah*): a state which was neither the imamate of the *sadah*, nor the shaykhs' republic that governed Sa'dah in recent decades, but one that ensured participation and representation of all people and groups. In political terms the Houthi delegates were largely in line with youth groups and the Southern Movement, who also called for a "civil state" and opted for fundamental change and disempowerment of the old elites. The Houthi delegates to the NDC managed to see their vision of statehood included in full in the NDC's final report.'[23] In future, such policies may re-emerge should there be a leadership change within that movement.

End of Cooperation and the Undermining of the Transitional Regime

Cooperation with the transitional regime broke down immediately after the end of the NDC. The assassination of Huthi leaders, particularly that of Ahmed Sharaf al-Din on the very last day of the conference, put the movement under extreme stress. So did the failure of the NDC's Sa'ada Committee. The final breaking point was the issue of the six regions. Throughout the NDC there had been discussions over the establishment of a federal state to replace the extremely centralised one managed so autocratically by the Saleh regime. With the exception of Saleh, there was little disagreement about the concept of a federal state as such; yet the issue of the number of regions within that state was extremely controversial. In the course of the nine months of the NDC a multiplicity of proposals and maps had been circulated. No agreement was reached. Immediately after the completion of the NDC, the Hadi-appointed Regions Committee followed his advice and opted for six regions, a decision immediately rejected by the Huthis who argued that delimiting Azal, the region that includes Sa'ada, on the basis of existing governorates, meant excluding Hajja (hence access to the coastal plain and the port of Midi) and al-Jawf (hence access to its anticipated petroleum resources).

An early sign of increasing Huthi strength in 2014 was manifested clearly in the fate of the Salafi Dar al-Hadith in Dammaj. This community was a thorn in their midst and an obvious target for the Huthis who had until then, unsuccessfully, tried to get rid of it for many years. By January 2014, as the NDC was closing, the Hadi regime had to give in and organise a rushed evacuation of the Dar al-Hadith community who ended up in a suburb of Sana'a. In the following months, the Huthi movement's opposition to the transition regime assumed an increasingly military nature and was no longer discreet. However, its cooperation with Saleh and his Republican Guards and other elite security forces remained secret and deniable. This enabled many Yemen observers to remain blind to this alliance and therefore fail to recognise the serious danger it presented to the transitional regime.

While Huthi advances in Hajja and in al-Jawf received little attention, their moves into Amran caused more of a stir nationally and internationally. They gradually took over the central and southern parts of Amran Governorate, basically expelling the al-Ahmar shaykhs from their dominance in this area. The particularly humiliating destruction of the al-Ahmar ancestral home in Khamer in February did not mark the end of the Islah party or of the al-Ahmar family as a political force, yet certainly symbolised their strategically weakened position. In April the Huthis demanded and obtained the replacement of the governor and of all Islahi political and military leaders in Amran. General al-Qushaybi, the leader of the 310th Brigade and a close ally of Ali Mohsen's, was a particular target. He was killed in early July, just after the Huthis' takeover of the governorate capital. These events took place through complex double-crossing involving the Republican Guards and other forces supposedly loyal to the regime whose main loyalty was to Saleh. Hadi also hoped to use the Huthi movement to weaken Ali Mohsen and Islah so made little effort to oppose them. As events demonstrated, he miscalculated. It is also likely that, yet again, the main strings were being pulled by Saleh, who retained actual control over most of the military.

Popular Support for the Huthis and Their Takeover of Sana'a

The summer of 2014 saw the transitional regime's popularity plummet as it had failed to live up to its promises. Popular anger grew at the government's complete failure to re-establish functioning social and economic services. In addition, as discussed in Chapter 9, no funds were available for development investments as a result of the unwillingness of the international and bilateral funding agencies to fulfil the pledges of the September 2012 Riyadh pledging conference, under the justifiable excuse of corruption and the less justifiable one of lack of capacity.

In August the Huthi movement successfully profited from the unpopular rise in fuel prices, which the Hadi regime had announced to comply with the demands of international financial institutions. Thousands came out into the streets of Sana'a to demonstrate against price rises and in support of the Huthis who also claimed to oppose corruption and promote good governance. Support for the Huthis increased, possibly to its highest level ever, as they presented themselves as popular, clean and untainted by involvement with the previous or even current regime. The Huthis also claimed to promote the interests of the anti-Saleh regime protesters of 2011. They appeared, to some at least, to be acting alone and to incarnate a new political force.

Following days of popular demonstrations, the Huthis effectively took over Sana'a. For those people who wondered how the Huthis managed to achieve this without firing a shot, the answer is that neither the army nor any other security forces made any move to defend the Hadi regime. In September, the Huthis' other main enemy, General Ali Mohsen, escaped to Saudi Arabia, as Hadi made no attempt to rescue him when he was trapped with his forces in the First Armoured Brigade HQ. Although this indicated collusion of the official security forces with the Huthi-Saleh takeover, it also demonstrated the failure of Hadi's strategy to weaken Islah and Ali Mohsen by using the Huthi movement against them. This strategy could only have succeeded in the absence of the Huthi-Saleh alliance, an alliance which had clearly escaped the notice of Hadi and his intelligence service. In the following days, the Huthis organised tours of Ali Mohsen's 'house' in Sana'a, and they also ransacked the homes of absent al-Ahmar leaders.

Having physically lost control over the capital, on 21 September 2014 the transition government attempted a last-ditch effort at compromise and, with UN support, got the Huthis to sign the Peace and National Partnership Agreement (PNPA). In 2017 the Huthi leadership still considers it to be a basic reference for peace negotiations. While never actually implemented, it gave more power to their movement and had some praiseworthy points, such as increasing payments from the Social Welfare Fund (without stating where the cash would come from) and calling for clean government. In practice the Huthis then installed supervisory committees in every ministry, whose arbitrary power was characterised by a combination of bigotry and technical incompetence. According to the then UN Special Envoy Jamal Benomar, 'Ansar Allah is acting as though it were a replacement of the state.' The date of the PNPA signature was later selected by Abdul Malik al-Huthi as the revolutionary anniversary which they have celebrated annually since then.

The Final Straw

While these events were taking place on the ground, the Constitutional Drafting Committee met between March to December 2014 in various locations. The committee included one Ansar Allah sympathiser who refused to sign the draft constitution. The committee's return to Yemen in December and its attempt to submit its draft to the government signalled the final breaking point between the Huthi movement and the transitional regime. When, on 17 January 2015, the head of the president's office tried to take the draft constitution to the National Authority for Monitoring the Implementation of the NDC Outcomes, the Huthis kidnapped him. A few days later they released him to the care of his tribal leaders. Their next step was to besiege various military units, attack Hadi's personal guards and make further demands on the new government. Faced with the prospect of being no more than mere clerks to the Huthi movement, Prime Minister Khaled Baha and his entire government resigned on 21 January, followed within minutes by Hadi himself. A month later, with Hadi attempting to re-establish a government in Aden, the Huthi-Saleh military offensive in and around Aden triggered the launching of the Saudi-led 'Decisive Storm' offensive.

On 6 February 2015, the Huthi movement proclaimed a Constitutional Declaration which cancelled any constitutional provision which might contradict it. It replaced the government by a Supreme Revolutionary

Committee (SRC) with branches throughout the country; it also replaced Parliament with a Transitional National Council of 551 members; and it created a Presidential Council of five members to establish a transitional government. Nothing more was ever heard from either of these last two institutions, which were obviously not created. The SRC was also due to implement the outcomes of the NDC and the PNPA within two years. Saleh's influence prevented the replacement of Parliament and the creation of the Presidential Council, largely because the legislature needed to be recalled to confirm Hadi's resignation: this would have served Saleh's objectives rather than the Huthis', for the simple reason that, constitutionally, the president would have been replaced by the speaker of the Parliament, who was a firm Saleh ally.

The Perfidious Huthi-Saleh Pact

Earlier in this decade, the Huthi movement traded its alliance with Ali Mohsen and Islah for another equally unlikely and unsavoury partnership with Saleh and his military/security forces. This latest unholy alliance enabled them to conquer much of the country in 2014 and during the first months of 2015. It certainly demonstrates that political/military alliances have little to do with shared beliefs or ideological commitment. How did the Huthis rise from being a minority regional politico-military movement to taking almost complete control over the formal state in barely one year? Long suspected by most Yemenis, but ignored by the international community, and denied by both concerned parties, the alliance between the Huthis and Saleh was the main factor behind their success. According to Brandt, 'there had been indications of secret cooperation between the president and the rebels even before the conclusion of the GCC deal: collusion had begun to surface as early as in late autumn 2011 in Hajjah and in al-Jawf, when Houthis fought against Salafis and Islah supporters with Republican Guard weapons.'[24]

In 2014 and 2015, the majority of supposedly Huthi armed forces were military and security units loyal to Saleh. Moreover, even senior Huthi leaders took orders from Saleh, as revealed by a leaked telephone conversation[25] between Saleh and Abdul Wahed Abu Ras (a Huthi representative at the NDC) where the former ordered the latter to coordinate activities with Saleh loyalists, to ensure that they controlled the country's borders. They even discussed the appointment of the next prime minister and Abu Ras is heard meekly acquiescing to Saleh's orders. In early 2015 it also emerged that the military refused to obey the defence minister's order to protect the presidential palace and other strategic locations in Sana'a: the only group who attempted to protect Hadi was his personal guard, who suffered heavy casualties in the process.[26] On 12 May 2015, a day after one of Saleh's private palaces in Sana'a had been bombed by the coalition, he stood in the midst of the ruins and declared to his Yemen al-Yawm television station reporters: 'Earlier I was not an ally of Ansar Allah, but today I declare that the Yemeni people will be an ally of anyone who protects national interests in the face of the Saudi aggression.'[27] Thereafter the alliance was made public, though, beyond their shared enemies, it is clear that there is neither trust nor common objectives between the two parties.

Since then the alliance, although explicit, has encountered difficulties and considerable internal stress. In mid-2016, the establishment of the Supreme Political Council (SPC) to replace the Supreme Revolutionary Committee (SRC) appeared initially to mark the supremacy of Saleh over Ansar Allah, but in practice it would appear that the balance of forces is fairly even. The SPC is formed of ten men,[28] five each from the Huthi's Ansar Allah and Saleh's GPC, and its creation was to be accompanied by the dissolution of the SRC at central level and that of the Revolutionary Committees in local institutions. Despite considerable and regular protests by the SPC about the continued presence and actions of Revolutionary Committees in the ministries and the demand that their overall leader, Mohammed Ali al-Huthi, cease interfering, committees continue to operate in all ministries; and Mohammed Ali al Huthi continues to make statements and issue orders which are obeyed. Moreover, the SPC itself is not operating according to its regulations and up until mid-2017 the presidency, which is supposed to rotate between the two groups every four months, has not been passed on to the Saleh GPC man even once.

It took a full four months to establish the Government of National Salvation which had been promised within days of the formation of the SPC, which again indicates the difficulties of getting the two rival yet allied groups to agree on anything. While on the one hand this is providing what may look like a government in Sana'a, and some institutions have been said to operate better since the formation of the government, frequent events reveal the dysfunctional relationship between the allies. In 2017, the conflicts

between rival top-level appointments at three major institutions provide
tragi-comic entertainment to close observers: the minister and deputy
minister of higher education alternately send troops to evict each other
from the ministry. Meanwhile the Huthi- and Saleh-appointed presidents
of the National Pension Fund do the same. Prime Minister Abdel-Aziz bin
Habtoor, appointed to that post on 4 October 2016, named the minister of
foreign affairs as acting minister of planning and international cooperation;
in April 2017. After an incident when the minister spurned his Huthi
deputy, the latter called in military units and, within hours, the president
of the SPC ordered the prime minister to cancel the appointment, and
was obeyed.[29] A new minister, apparently acceptable to both sides, was
appointed in June.

Militarily, on numerous occasions in the past two years, there have been
armed clashes between Republican Guards loyal to Saleh and Huthi forces,
including the rejection of Huthi-appointed senior officers. In addition, elite
Saleh troops refused to implement Huthi orders, particularly with respect
to going to some frontlines. Saleh also frequently threatens to withdraw
his Republican Guards from active military fronts whenever the Huthis
do something he particularly disagrees with. Certainly in this period, the
Huthi military forces have strengthened, while Saleh's are weaker, though
the balance between them may still be even.

Conclusion

Within ten years, the Huthi movement emerged from being a small family-
based political-military faction to becoming a major determinant of Yemen's
political scene. Although its place at the very front of the stage is largely
due to its alliance with Saleh, even without him, it would be a significant
political and military force in Yemen's landscape today. Although the Huthis
may, once again, be eclipsed by Saleh in the foreseeable future, they are very
unlikely to return to their earlier obscurity and insignificance. While there
is little doubt that the Saudi-led coalition is doing its best to sow dissention
in the Huthi-Saleh camp, and has even achieved the defection of some
Republican Guard units, overall the alliance is likely to continue simply
because its collapse would ensure a rapid victory for their foes.

Quite a lot of the support for the Huthis could disappear almost as fast as it arose, as it is not based on ideology and a positive sharing of views and objectives but simply on common enmities, even within their stronghold in the far northern governorates of Sa'ada, Hajja, Amran and al-Jawf. History has shown that in Yemen there is no systematic and principled support for any one group, whether on a sectarian or tribal basis, as the change in fortunes of the al-Ahmar leaders of the Hashed tribal confederation has demonstrated. Similar principles apply beyond these areas. In addition, the Huthis can claim more support among *sada*, whether Zaydi or Shafi'i, simply on the basis that they are privileging this group as 'natural rulers'. Again, this is not universally applicable, and while there are *sada* villages and groups which support them in Shafi' Sunni heartlands, such as Ibb and Taiz, the phenomenon is still rare.

Huthi ideological objectives are limited and difficult to decipher; this clearly differentiates them from other political movements. Abdul Malik al-Huthi has made no statement of his political objectives and his interventions are always based on abstract religious scripts. But in practice the Huthi movement has actively worked to re-establish *sada* power. The vast majority of their senior appointments since 2015 have been of *sada* throughout all institutions, both military and civilian. Their claims to support the poor and disinherited, although still occasionally part of their rhetoric, have been demonstrated to be as spurious as those of other politicians. When they control any institution, personal gain and alliances take precedence over managerial competence or quality, as employees of all Sana'a institutions have found to their cost when trying to operate according to ethical administrative practices. Revolutionary Committee members dominate various institutions, and this in turn has led to rampant mismanagement. Efficiency and effectiveness have certainly not been the determining decision-making criteria for the new Huthi rulers.

Throughout the areas under their control, they have foisted their norms and beliefs on others, thus demonstrating that their claim of respect for other views is vacuous. Typical of the retrograde culture of fundamentalist Islam, they imposed restrictive rules on women's lifestyles, with respect both to their clothing and to their movements outside the home, all supposedly to follow religious dogma. They did so first in Sa'ada, and then in the other towns they occupied, starting with Amran in 2014. In this respect there is no noticeable difference between one variety of fundamentalists and the others, whether Sunni or Shi'i.

The assassinations during the NDC deprived their movement of their most experienced thinkers and politicians. Since then their surviving leaders have been young and inexperienced men who operate without clear objectives beyond imposing their authority. Instead their cohesion is based on war and a highly active common enemy. Within their alliance with Saleh, few would seriously back young Abdul Malik al-Huthi in any contest in guile skills against Ali Abdullah Saleh, given the latter's four decades-long experience of largely successful political manipulations at the national and international levels. However, the long duration of the war has enabled the Huthis to strengthen their military capacity, even though it is composed mostly of informal militia units. This increased armed strength now enables them to counter-balance Saleh's elite forces and affords them an increasingly loud voice within their alliance. Besides manning checkpoints they have also developed some administrative capability in their home area of Sa'ada. Yet overall, their expansion has relied on a mass of young, inexperienced and uncommitted individuals, motivated more by the pleasures of power and the prospects of financial gain, through 'taxation' and other impositions on the citizenry.

The decade since 2007 has been one when the Huthi movement moved from being a marginal though important problem to one where they cannot be ignored. At the other end of the country, the Southern separatist movement re-emerged in 2007, but its development over the past ten years has been very different; the next chapter will try to explain why and how.

CHAPTER SIX

Southern Separatism in Perspective

Although unification was the most popular political slogan in both the YAR and the PDRY, the reality of a united Yemen under the Saleh regime turned out to be a bitter disappointment and experience for many in the South. People of all political persuasions re-imagined a mythical past to which they hope to return by ending unification. Lack of clarity of vision is manifest by the inability of separatists to unify on any issue beyond mere secession. While some want to return to a state within the former borders, which they occasionally name South Arabia, this is unlikely to happen as internal divisions between much smaller entities are at least as strong as the wish to leave the broader Republic of Yemen (ROY).

Hadramaut, as the largest and wealthiest of the entities, is unlikely to be willing to stay in a state alongside the people from the western mountainous tribes whom they regard as petty warlords. When discussing differences with the North (here understood to mean the area of the former YAR), otherwise reasonable Southern intellectuals are wont to assert that 'our Southern tribes are different, they were civilised by the British for over a century', a laughable statement which reveals a lack of understanding of both tribes and the colonial period when the British ignored the hinterland tribes for most of their period in the region. Another revealing Southern joke in recent years goes as follows: 'Northerner asks: Why do you hate us? Southerner replies: when the British ruled, we hated them, once they left, we loved them. When the socialists ruled, we also hated them, and when they left we loved them; now you are here, we hate you, but we'll love you when you leave.'

Among the many aspects of Yemeni politics and society which are complex, the situation in the South is possibly the most confusing. In part this is due to the region's political fragmentation over the past century. Tribal and other social structural features are discussed in Chapter 7, but other factors are directly political. This chapter attempts to explain actual conditions and the socio-political characteristics of the region which differentiate the South from other parts of Yemen. It also addresses the widespread and varied perceptions of Southerners towards Yemen as a unified state, and the role of the South since 2011. In the few weeks between his escape from house arrest in Sana'a and exile in Saudi Arabia, Hadi named Aden as Yemen's temporary capital. Although 'liberated' by August 2015, the south cannot be said to be under the control of Hadi's internationally recognised government, as a wide range of forces control and administer different parts.

Is the South a Coherent Entity?

The South covers the area which was the People's Democratic Republic of Yemen (PDRY) and earlier Aden and the Protectorates. In the colonial period, in addition to Aden colony, it was composed of twenty-five states and statelets ruled by local potentates, who were variously known as sultans, emirs and shaykhs. They governed entities of different sizes and significance. Some enjoyed basic potential viability in economy, population size and geographic area, such as the Eastern Protectorate's Qu'ayti Sultanate with its capital in Mukalla which ruled over a substantial area, as well as population, throughout the Hadramaut region; it was only challenged by the far smaller Kathiri Sultanate based in Seiyun in the wadi (valley). By contrast, statelets in the Western Protectorate were mostly very small geographically and had tiny populations. Their sources of income were restricted to rain-fed and spate agriculture, as well as customs duties on goods and people travelling through their areas. In addition, after they came under British protection most of their leaders received modest funding as well as weapons from Britain.

Aden itself was composed of a widely mixed population, many of whom had migrated there in the decade after the Second World War when the port needed labour, and the British military base expanded. Between 1946 and 1955 the majority population described as Arabs' rose from 58,000 to

104,000, an increase which clearly shows the attraction of the city and its lively economy to the populations from the Western Protectorate as well as from the Imamate in the North. Immigrants from the latter area moved not just to improve their economic situation, but also to have access to modern education and other facilities and to escape political repression at home. By 1955 a further 10,000 Adeni residents were Somalis (more than twice the number in 1946) while the Indian population rose from 9.000 to 16,000 in that decade. A coherent Adeni identity was thus difficult to identify, due to the wide range of cultures and languages brought from these different places; nor did the short-lived Federation of South Arabia in the 1960s create a common identity for its citizens. Yet many Adenis shared a belief in their urban superiority over the hinterland tribes which they tended to consider backward and uncivilised. This perception was still much in evidence during the PDRY period among those 'old Adenis' who had not fled to more profitable pastures.

Although the socialist regime of the PDRY made considerable efforts to reduce the influence of tribalism and of solidarity based on areas of origin, as discussed in Chapters 3 and 7, the creation of a deeply ingrained national identity would have taken a lot longer than the twenty-three years during which that state existed. One of the regime's nation-building policies had ambiguous results: by trying to ensure a good balance between all areas and avoid regional and tribal domination, the regime ensured that leaders from all areas were included in the government and the leading party institutions. As a result, when disagreements emerged, it was easy for participants to emphasise the tribal/regional aspects of the problems, at the expense of the more complex policy issues. Thus leadership disputes within the ruling Yemeni Socialist Party pitted men from different regional origins against each other, thus allowing many to see politicians as having objectives solely rooted in tribal/locality origins. Such regional perceptions spread to the popular level, which in turn prevented and slowed down the process of nation-building to which the regime was committed.

These factors played a major role in the January 1986 'events' discussed in Chapter 3. Although not initially tribal/communal either in origin or in objectives, when fighting moved out of the Political Bureau meeting and reached the streets, and news spread about the killing of the main leaders of the party, fighting degenerated into killings based on location of origin. At checkpoints and when encountering other armed men, those involved linked origin with loyalty and commitment in the absence of any understanding of the political issues involved. Moreover, the political differences between the two rival Southern groups were largely obtuse and opaque. To most educated observers, the conflict seemed to be simply a fight over positions, rather than based on fundamental differences of policies.

It is worth pointing out that creating a nation out of social groups with other initial loyalties is not an easy or rapid process. It takes much time, political, social and cultural work, and needs long-term commitment at all levels from a regime as well as from all other superstructure social entities, culture in particular. Destruction of such feelings, on the other hand, can be very rapid. While it took generations to create a 'Yugoslav' a few killings and strong propaganda destroyed the concept within weeks in the 1990s, leading to the fragmentation of the state and even the division of families. This remains the case in both former Yugoslavia and in former South Yemen, with lasting resentments among the population, despite a widespread longing for a return to a system which is remembered with nostalgia.

So when Yemeni unification came, only four years after the most murderous of internal struggles within the YSP, Southern society was an easy target for Saleh's 'divide and rule' tactics. He used these to strengthen the revival and re-emergence of a multiplicity of competing social identities throughout the country, thus destroying what shared identification people had developed with the state. This process intensified with the return of many exiles. The positions of the sultans, shaykhs and emirs of the colonial period were not officially restored after unification, but in practice things worked out differently. Some have come on visits and tested their popularity and likelihood of reclaiming their political leadership, for example in al-Mahra and coastal Hadramaut. Others have become far more influential and returned on a permanent basis, settling down and claiming both properties and authority; a prime example is Tareq al-Fadhli whose group of Islamist 'Afghans' played a significant role in the Saleh regime's success in the 1994 war against the short-lived separatist Democratic Republic of Yemen established by al-Beedh in Aden in May 1994. Al-Fadhli remained a significant political force in Abyan Governorate, and was a major player there certainly up to 2011.

In view of these historical divisions and their persistence today, it is difficult to assert that there is a coherent Southern entity. That remains true despite common experiences shared by inhabitants of the former PDRY, including that of the socialist period with its education and health systems, as well as the rule of the centralised PDRY administrative structures. However, given the fact that over 70 percent of the population is under twenty-five years old, and that unification happened in 1990, the vast majority of the population of the Southern governorates have no direct experience of these earlier periods, and their perceptions are based on the imaginary memories promoted by a range of individuals and organisations.

Unification and the 1994 War

The euphoria which greeted Yemeni unification in 1990 was all too short-lived and different aspects have been covered in Chapter 3. Yemeni unity had been the most popular state slogan for the previous two decades throughout Yemen and there are many reasons why unification was so welcome. In brief, they include the following:

- Most Yemenis from one part of the country had relatives in another through common tribal origin, migration or mixed marriages.
- The prospect of freedom of movement within the country as a whole was a major incentive.
- Hopes for better economic conditions: Southerners often believed that economic conditions were better in the YAR; they were soon disillusioned once unification happened.
- The recently discovered oil fields were along their common borders and the realisation that the alternative to sharing them within a single state would have been to fight over them.
- For people with nationalist feelings, the prospect of a stronger Yemeni republic in the Arab world and beyond held a strong appeal.

In the early months, the South experienced positive changes which were perceived as side-effects of unification: the broadening of personal and political freedoms with the multiplication of newspapers and journals, the creation of any number of political parties and the open discussions which were taking place throughout the country in qat sessions and elsewhere. Some negative features also appeared in the earliest days: deterioration of living conditions due to the changes in currency and rapid price rises, the liberalisation of trade, and mainly the ending of a basic basket of subsidised food. With the transfer of many senior politicians and officials to Sana'a immediately after unification, Aden soon lost its political and administrative importance, which in turn led to economic decline. Many deplored two immediate changes: the spread of the Northern qat, and family laws to the whole country. Until the 1994 watershed, the administrative system in the Southern governorates remained largely unchanged from the socialist period, with middle- and low-level administrators staying in place, whether they were politically aligned or independent. The fundamental changes included the re-privatisation of agricultural land and housing, industrial assets, and anything else around. All these contributed to the increasing alienation of the population of the former PDRY from the new regime.

In addition to these early disappointments, worse features started emerging as early as 1991 with a series of actual and attempted assassinations of senior political figures opposed to Saleh, within both the YSP and other parties, and mostly targeted at Southerners.[2] These attacks increased in number and intensity until the 1994 short civil war. The 1993 elections brought a major change, as they ended the YSP's strong position in government and accelerated the transformation of the regime in what was, by then, known as the Southern Governorates. At those elections, although it came second to the GPC with 18.5 percent of votes, the YSP only took 56 seats while Islah with 17 percent of the votes took 62. The fifty/fifty sharing agreement of the unification deal came to an end as Islah with more seats joined the coalition with Saleh's GPC, alongside the YSP. Tension between Saleh and al-Beedh worsened on a daily basis.

Despite the formation of a government with the three main parties, the issues of the distribution of power and the role of the vice presidency were the focus of the struggle while numerous personalities tried to mediate and achieve a peaceful solution. But the two main protagonists, Saleh and al-Beedh, were busy preparing for more drastic strategies, the first for military victory and the second for a political breakaway. Months of mediation, tension and building up of alliances or military forces led to the final break a year later and the short civil war of secession in 1994.[3]

The war itself officially lasted three months, from 27 April to 7 July 1994, though some consider that it started immediately after the signing of the Document of Pledge and Accord on 22 February 1994 in Amman, Jordan. While the military had remained separate since 1990 and both sides had made sure that units were not merged, mysteriously al-Beedh's group had failed to notice the way in which the strongest Southern units were isolated in Amran Governorate, far from the South and with no means of reaching their home base. Meanwhile, some of Saleh's stronger and better equipped units were conveniently installed in Abyan within easy reach of Aden. Moreover, as mentioned earlier, Saleh benefited from having under his control the Southern military units who had been defeated in the 1986 civil war and had then joined the YAR forces. These men were all too familiar with the southern terrain. In addition, Saleh enjoyed the active support of Islamist factions, ranging from those aligned with al-Zindani in the Islah party to returning 'Afghans', some of them under the leadership of Tareq al-Fadhli. Despite the strong organisation and previous history of victories of the Southern forces over Saleh's military, for example in 1979, this time the balance of power was clearly in Saleh's favour.

Al-Beedh declared secession on 21 May 1994 and proclaimed the establishment of the Democratic Republic of Yemen (DRY). His government included leaders from the colonial period, who had remained active separatists since then, in particular Abdul Rahman al-Jifri and Abdullah al-Asnag. Both were close to the Saudi leadership and had been in exile in Saudi Arabia during the PDRY period. The former is still active while the latter died in 2014. Most other DRY ministers were from the YSP, including some who were abroad and were not consulted on their nomination. However, many YSP members and even leaders supported unity and rejected participation in the DRY. The result was a split of the YSP, one of many more, which further weakened the party. Overall, the government formed by al-Beedh included both YSP members and people who had been firm enemies of the YSP in earlier decades, and that merely indicated the political desperation of his move.

Discussions with Saudi Arabia and other Gulf Cooperation Council (GCC) states in previous months had led al-Beedh to believe that the GCC would recognise his Democratic Republic of Yemen, but they fell short of doing so. Saudi support came in the form of arms and other discreet backing, but there was no official recognition, which made the DRY's position all the more difficult internationally. Ultimately only one state recognised the DRY, and it was a collapsing one at that, Somalia. Active diplomatic moves by the Saleh regime at the United Nations, led by then Minister of

Planning* Dr Abdul Karim al-Eryani, successfully prevented the UN from recognising the regime.

Military action focused on Aden which was under siege from June onwards, and was the last place to fall to Saleh's troops on 7 July. The city was then sacked by 'Northern' forces, although many of those involved were Southern jihadis who directed their fury at the beer factory, outlets selling alcohol, women's clothing, Sufi shrines, and other religious signs which did not conform with their extreme Salafi interpretation of Islam. They also ransacked and destroyed civilian institutions, such as schools, health centres, training establishment or indeed anything else. The sacking of Aden left a bitter memory in the South and encouraged the strongly anti-Northern feelings which fuel the separatist movement in the 2000s.

The 1994 war marked the final demise of any remnants of the earlier regime in people's daily lives as the Saleh regime increasingly filled senior administrative and security positions with its supporters, mostly from the Northern governorates or from its allies among the exiles of different phases of the internecine socialist struggles. The new senior appointees actively undermined the administrative structures, intent on destroying southern capacity. Even when southerners were appointed, or stayed in position, they rarely had any meaningful authority within their official remit. The most prominent example was Abdu Rabbu Mansur Hadi who was named vice president by Saleh in 1994 and remained in this position for the following seventeen years, during which time he had neither power nor influence.

Marginalisation of the South

Perceptions of marginalisation and bitterness spread throughout the Southern governorates, particularly after the 1994 war. Only a few groups benefited directly from the new regime: some returnees from exile who participated in, or initiated, businesses with the Sana'ani elite, others who received land and properties, some emigrants who invested in real estate, and the few who managed to integrate into these structures. But the vast majority of professionals, farmers, other rural and urban people, and

---

*   It is worth noting that during much of his long political career, Dr Abdul Karim was
      Minister of Foreign Affairs or Prime Minister. He died in 2015, aged 81, many said 'of a
      broken heart' at the collapse of the country into civil war.

in particular the elites from the socialist period, all considered that they were being marginalised: that jobs were given to Northerners rather than to them, that all regulations and rules were set in Sanaʿa for the benefit of Northerners, and that their living conditions continued to worsen, with no prospect of improvements.

These perceptions were felt particularly acutely in Aden and in the south-western highlands. Hadramaut was less affected, partly because its population had been less committed to the socialist regime, despite the fact that some of the highest ranking PDRY politicians were Hadrami; but most importantly because many Hadramis benefited more from the new regime. This was thanks to their large diaspora based in Saudi Arabia, which promptly started investing in various enterprises in the governorate and consequently created employment for local people. They also financed some infrastructure as well as charitable organisations. The only group which suffered systematically from the new regime was that of the lower-status Hadrami *fellaheen* (cultivating group not entitled to own land) who lost their lands to the previous owners or others.[4] Many of them either returned to their earlier situation as sharecroppers or alternatively found other casual work locally. Again, diaspora connections helped: some of the leading and wealthiest Saudi-Hadrami businessmen are of low-status origins and helped others to obtain visas to Saudi Arabia.

Despite its official status as the economic capital, Aden lost out in the industrial sector and its professionals suffered discrimination, either because jobs moved to Sanaʿa or because they were unable to organise the contacts and networks that they needed in either location. People from the western governorates (Lahej, al-Dhalaʿ, Abyan and Shabwa) had limited income from small holder agriculture, and there were few large agricultural projects. Large numbers of their men were former military who became the core of the Southern separatist movement a decade later. In any case, most recruitment to the security/military forces was limited to men from certain areas surrounding Saleh's own home in Sanhan, who benefited from top quality training and equipment. By contrast, other military personnel were exploited and deprived of their fair share of food and equipment, and their allocations disappeared into the pockets (or foreign bank accounts) of their commanding officers.

While there is no doubt that the situation in the Southern governorates deteriorated and its people lost many of the advantages of the socialist regime, what basically happened is that they were brought to the level of living and working conditions which had prevailed throughout the YAR prior to unification. In other words, what people perceived as deliberate discrimination against them was simply being reduced to the same status as the majority of the population throughout Yemen. With the notable exception of the small groups who benefited directly from the Saleh regime, most Yemenis everywhere in the country received the same treatment. In short, they formed the norm, not the margin.

The issue of privatisation was a major change in policy for Southerners. The Saleh regime was encouraged to privatise factories and other productive assets by the IMF and World Bank, following neo-liberal principles. Some industrial units were returned to their former owners while others were sold off at bargain basement prices without much recourse to transparency or internationally recognised procedures. Homes which had been handed over to their occupants as private property – among the last actions of the PDRY regime – largely remained as they were. Adding to the confusion, each previous change of Southern leadership had been followed by a game of 'musical chairs' in which desirable villas and other buildings were taken by the victors; so determining who the 'real' owners might be would have been extremely complex. In Aden in particular, much housing had been built in the last years of the colonial period for the armed forces and other government personnel, so should these buildings and villas be claimed by the UK government? The mechanisms through which people close to Saleh obtained land for construction and other assets, particularly in and around Aden, confirmed many Adenis in their perceptions of discrimination.

The socialist agricultural land reform had redistributed agricultural land throughout the country during the PDRY years. While some of these lands were returned to their previous owners, much of the land had belonged to former sultans and other rulers who were excluded from Saleh's re-privatisation programme. Council of Ministers Decree 65 of 1991 stated that all agricultural lands were to be returned to their pre-independence owners and that dispossessed farmers would be compensated with five feddans (or acres) of irrigated land ready for cultivation. The text addressed issues such as previously uncultivated lands and improvements to the lands carried out by the beneficiaries. However, in reality the confiscation of the lands from the agrarian reform beneficiaries took place efficiently and systematically, while the compensation aspect barely took place at all. An internationally funded project to prepare state lands for allocation to the newly dispossessed operated with great difficulty. Most of the 'state' lands allocated to it were then claimed by various armed groups who denied state rights over these lands. In a sense they successfully merged the concepts of political control over territory with that of private ownership. Half-hearted support from the authorities in Sanaʿa, combined with effective resistance at the local level, resulted in the achievement of 236 families receiving compensation land, by comparison with the 1,950 targeted by the project and the estimated 24,000 dispossessed as a result of the re-privatisation process.[5] The difficulties and problems of this exercise certainly confirmed the views of many rural Southerners that the centralised unified Yemeni state had little concern for their problems.

The Rise of the Separatist Movement

The Southern separatist movement started officially in late 2006 with the establishment of the Association of Retired Military, Security and Civilian Personnel in Lahej Governorate. It included people from al-Dhalaʿ Governorate, mainly because that part of al-Dhalaʿ had been in Lahej Governorate prior to 1998.[*] After the 1994 war more than 86,000 military and other security sector personnel were dismissed in the Southern governorates, most of whom returned to their rural homes in Lahej and al-Dhalaʿ. This was officially described as retirement, but the people concerned had neither served for decades nor were they old. Their dismissal was an entirely political move by the Saleh regime which considered them a security risk and doubted their loyalty. During the 1994 civil war, the men involved had either remained neutral or been serving in units or locations that supported unity: hence the decision to exclude them was more an attempt to remove and isolate a potential perceived threat, rather than to address a real one. It also saved the formal government cash in over-stressed budgets.

Many of these 'retired' officers considered their dismissal and the implied lack of trust to be insults added to the injury of losing their livelihoods and

---

[*]   In that year a new al-Dhalaʿ Governorate was set up, composed of the northern part of Lahej and the southern and eastern parts of Ibb. Many believed it had been created to dilute the earlier connections and loyalties of people within Lahej.

being sent home to environments low in income-generating potential. Moreover, their pensions were increasingly worthless, because of inflation and high cost of living, and payment was at best irregular.[6] After a decade of frustration and worsening relations with the regime, the movement they formed initially demanded compensation, reinstatement to their previous positions, or adequate salaries. From the beginning they asserted their determination to remain peaceful: 'We call on the people of the south to actively participate in this event ... while holding dear their civil values and civilized manners and peaceful means in changing opinion.'[7] Their decision to be peaceful was both tactical and strategic.[8] There is no doubt that, like all other Yemenis, they had easy access to small weapons, though they did not have the equipment to resist a major assault. However, resorting to arms would basically have meant they were yet another anti-regime rebellion, whereas initially their demands were not directly political. They gave the regime the benefit of the doubt by providing it with the opportunity to correct unjust decisions and restore their civil rights. They maintained their resistance through unarmed demonstrations, despite the fact that the regime responded with violence. By using civil and peaceful means, they also wanted to demonstrate higher moral and cultural values than those of the 'Northern' regime.

The relevance of their economic demands is evident if one considers the living conditions prevailing in that entirely rural area. In addition to rain-fed sorghum and other cereal cultivation, most of these mountains are unsuitable for anything other than rangeland for small ruminants, although there are pockets of qat farms where irrigation is available or where rainfall is particularly high. Yafi' forms an exception to this rule, as it is one of the country's most famous coffee-growing areas and also produces high quality qat. Not only did people have to cope with the dramatic increases of commodity prices due to the Triple F crisis – food, finance and fuel – which affected everyone in Yemen after 2006, but this area also suffered a long series of drought years, which had killed off most of the coffee trees by 2008, thus eliminating the main local source of cash income. Due to its tough agro-ecological conditions, Yafi' has long been a source of emigration. Yafi' in particular has significant migrant communities in Saudi Arabia and beyond, but was also the source of military personnel for Hadrami sultanates in the nineteenth century.

Visiting Yafi' in 2009

Travelling and working in Yafi' in 2009, the sense of hopelessness and despair of the people was striking. The mountains were covered in terraces of dead coffee bushes, as these bushes can survive up to five years of drought, but no more. Men were assembled where different branches of wadis met, near kiosks selling the usual set of basic necessities (cigarettes, tea, sugar, sweets and sugary canned drinks), hanging around and ready to speak to any passing consultant. They usually explained that either they had been dismissed from the armed forces or they had returned from Saudi Arabia and no longer had any sources of income. The rocks were already covered in roughly painted separatist slogans and flags of the former PDRY. Unfinished projects such as dams were all around. The sudden threat of a downpour raised the spirit of a group we met, and we took refuge in a school to hold our meeting. Their disappointment was enormous and impossible to ignore when we came out and found that the rain had lasted less than half an hour and had been insignificant.

Initially, what became known as the Hiraak movement was exclusively concerned with the problems of those who had been employed in the military/security sectors prior to unification and, to a lesser extent, between 1990 and 1994. Hence it was effectively a PDRY-related institution. Rather than respond reasonably to these demands, the regime reacted with violence, as it had done in the far north against the Huthis. Hundreds were killed and wounded in the following years; some fell in genuine armed clashes involving groups which did not subscribe to the peaceful approach, but the overwhelming majority of casualties occurred during street demonstrations when the only violence came from official government forces. There is little doubt that the repressive response of the regime contributed to the transformation of the movement away from the initial objectives of restoring their civil and economic rights, towards a movement with broader political objectives. Second, it strengthened resentment against the Sana'a-based regime and helped the emergence of separatist views among the retirees. Further, the overall brutality of the response increased popular support for the demands of the retirees, and helped the movement spread beyond the ex-military, and become broader in its aims, explicitly demanding Southern secession. By 2010, there were frequent and regular demonstrations throughout the governorates of Lahej and al-Dhala' and in Aden.

A related movement emerged in Hadramaut, led by different former YSP leaders from the area, such as Hassan Ba'um, which called for secession as soon as it started. As Hadramaut produced few military personnel, this movement was more of a civil society initiative from the beginning. Demonstrations there, mainly in Mukalla, met the same level of repression as those in Aden and its neighbouring areas.

The Separatist Movement and the 2011 Revolution

Southern movement demonstrations continued and escalated in the last years of the decade, with increasingly large protests on the various historic anniversaries, such as 7 July (Southern separatist defeat in 1994), 13 January (anniversary of the main internecine 1986 war in the YSP but renamed 'Reconciliation Day'), 14 October (anniversary of the beginning of the liberation struggle against Britain), and 30 November (independence from Britain).[9] Their stated objectives were increasingly separatist. Mostly peaceful, these demonstrations were met with brutal force, including killings. It is therefore interesting that the peaceful methods of the demonstrations, if not their objectives, certainly served as a model for the revolutionary uprisings that emerged on a mass scale in 2011.

During 2011 the Hiraak partly merged with the overall national anti-Saleh regime uprising. Some Southern activists asserted that the main problem was Saleh and that unity might be possible and reasonable once he was gone. Others, however, called for separation. Demonstrations and encampments in the Southern governorates were sometimes split between the two groups, for example in Aden. Elsewhere the separatist trend was the dominant, if not exclusive, element of the movement, as was the case in the part of al-Dhala' Governorate which was formerly in the PDRY. Here anyone supporting unity was effectively isolated and excluded from the political discourse. In Aden and Mukalla, separatists formed the bulk of the crowds in demonstrations, though the overall support for separatism among the population at large was far lower.

While young people dominated street demonstrations and encampments in Southern cities and towns, as elsewhere, their demands were straightforward: a democratic system representing the population, dignity, justice, a national economy, and an end to corruption. Just as in other parts of Yemen, the inability of the movement to produce a new leadership was one reason why the uprisings turned into a struggle between the pre-existing political forces and leaders. In the South, demonstrators supporting unity who held on to their original political, social and economic ambitions, were left out on a limb as they had no national movement to join. The absence of a new strong leadership upholding the values and ambitions of the youth was a fundamental problem of the uprisings, but is also very much a reflection of the absence of new politics worldwide. This vacuum was an opportunity for the older, mostly exiled, leaders of the colonial period and the PDRY to re-emerge in the media and on posters, if not in person. They soon took the helm and redirected the movement towards separatism, diverting it away from general political aims and restricting their demands to separation alone. This was made possible largely thanks to their access to cash to finance activities and thus create a body of supporters.

Another issue which bedevils analysis of the South is that the number of separatist 'organisations' is vast and variable, usually numbering something close to 100. Furthermore, they all have extremely similar names, an additional hint that the movement finds it hard to agree on anything beyond the desire for secession. While there is little doubt that some of them are 'clones' established by Saleh's agents to create confusion and dilute support, there are far too many of them for this to be a sufficient explanation. Although some are willing to accept federation (as a temporary or permanent solution) others want to return to earlier state borders, specifically those of the PDRY. Nor can they even agree on the name for the entity they support. Abdul Rahman al-Jifri and others associated with the colonial period leaders, for example, want to call their proposed state South Arabia, recalling the Federation of South Arabia of the 1960s. Others are willing to use Yemen in the name, either following on al-Beedh's short-lived Democratic Republic of Yemen in 1994, or suggesting an alternative. The main characteristics of all the separatist organisations forming the Hiraak is that they each:

–   Claim to represent everyone while in reality they usually represent no more than a handful of their close relatives and friends.

- Are remarkably stubborn and refuse to compromise with anyone, even those with positions close to theirs.
- Lack long-term political programmes which would address the area's economic, social or financial problems.
- Probably include organisations which are under some influence from the various security institutions of the different governing factions.
- Frequently advertise forthcoming conferences in various locations to reach decisions and a programme, which either fail to happen at all, are boycotted by individuals claiming leadership, or achieve nothing.

These divisions within the movement are largely based on the revival of rivalries from the past half century and should be of serious concern to their potential supporters. As explained in Chapter 3, deep divisions between very small political entities existed throughout the British period and were exacerbated by British policy. The socialist period was unable to eliminate them and its own internecine struggles were hardly models of negotiating skills. Many of the current leaders of the separatist movement stood on opposing sides in 1986 and, despite attempts at reconciliation, they still bear deep grudges connected with the killing of their friends and associates at that time. So this fragmentation can be summarised as combining the factional divisions of the tribal and other social divisions of the colonial period, with those which emerged during the socialist period, topped by those sponsored by the Saleh regime. Anyone with any understanding of this historical background would be unwise to look forward to effective government from any of the individuals currently claiming leadership.

Southern Separatism and the Transition (2012–2015)

During the transition, the Southern issue was partly addressed in the National Dialogue Conference[10] which sat from March 2013 to January 2014. Here again, leaders from the earlier generation came to dominate the discussion. While most irredentists (including al-Beedh, Baʿum and others) refused to participate as they considered that the only dialogue possible was between two equal separate states, many others did participate. Yet their leadership changed three times over the period, due to either political clashes or financial reasons when the Hadi regime failed to provide sufficient supporting funds. Although Southern participants in the NDC formed 56 percent of the total, most had far more reasonable attitudes than the eighty-five Hiraak representatives. They were not part of the separatist group, nor did they have any influence over it, which gives the lie to the claim that the separatist movement is representative of all Southerners. Here again the UN could have done better: by concentrating its efforts on the existing political elite, it failed to identify and involve Southerners who could have been considered more representative of the Hiraak movement or indeed of the South as a whole, and thus they allowed the old guard to continue its fruitless in-fighting.

With the conclusion of the NDC, very important issues remained unsolved. As far as the Southerners were concerned, the main one concerned the number of regions in the proposed federal state. The Regions Committee decided on two regions for the former PDRY area, one in the west and one in the east, the latter including Shabwa, Hadramaut and al-Mahra Governorates, in addition to the islands of Socotra which had become a governorate in 2013. The other governorates would lie in the Aden region, while Aden city itself was to have a special status, similar but not identical to that of the national capital Sana'a. This proposal was supported by many Southern NDC members, particularly in Hadramaut. Yet it was considered completely unacceptable by the majority of separatist factions, who asserted any number of reasons for their opposition. Chief amongst these was that the main economic resources of the area as a whole are oil in Hadramaut and the gas pipeline and port in Shabwa. Most separatist leaders favoured the alternative of a single Southern region, but many inside the South and beyond considered this to be no more than an interim step towards secession. Others elsewhere in Yemen had far stronger objections to this proposed set of regions: the Huthis in particular, as well as Saleh and his allies, who object to federation altogether.

During 2014, Southerners, including some separatists, participated in the Constitution Drafting Committee, where they actively obstructed and prevented progress of the committee's work. The draft constitution was finalised in December 2014 and was to be submitted to the post-NDC authority in January 2015, the event which triggered the civil war, as is discussed in Chapters 1 and 5.

Throughout the three years of the transition, the situation in the South bore many similarities with that elsewhere in Yemen, with a dramatic reduction in the presence of the state and its institutions and a perceptible deterioration in administrative and other services. The most noticeable change was not positive: jihadis in lower Abyan had achieved dominant status in March 2011 and the international sponsors of the transition regime considered their presence a major threat. These foreign states duly encouraged the Hadi regime to address this problem. An offensive a year later returned Abyan's capital and its neighbouring town of Ja'ar to state control by June 2012, although it did little more than disperse the jihadis further into the remote mountain regions of Abyan and Shabwa Governorates. There they have remained active ever since, despite a major military offensive that dispersed them in April and May 2014. Since the war started, they occasionally attack and re-establish a presence in these towns and are entities that need to be taken into consideration.

The War: The Intricate Relationship Between Internal and External Participants

The civil war which engulfed Yemen in 2015 has significantly different characteristics in the Southern governorates from those elsewhere. Aden was the main fighting front between March and the end of July 2015. At first, during March, Saleh's Republican Guards controlled it, and threatened to oust President Hadi from his temporary capital, where he had moved after escaping from Sana'a. In a kind of blitzkrieg, the Republican Guards and the then-Yemeni Air Force came close to a complete takeover of the city. Their offensive forced Hadi to take refuge in Saudi Arabia, despite some fierce resistance from local forces dominated by armed separatists who had different political visions, and included Salafis and jihadis. Ordinary citizens, too, joined in the defence of Aden, as they feared a repeat of the 1994 ransacking and destruction of their city.

Only the intervention of the Saudi-led coalition air strikes, which started on 26 March 2015, prevented this disaster from happening. In July the city was liberated with the help of ground troops from the United Arab Emirates and other coalition partners. Since then, ministers have come and gone, as have the president and prime minister. Hadi's fleeting visits to

Aden have been described by some as the first case in history of a president making an official visit to his own capital.

Despite the presence of a few ministers, Aden (let alone other 'liberated' governorates) is far from being under the control of the Hadi government. Its population experiences daily attacks on security officials and others, and robberies of banks, payrolls and citizens. Since July 2015, Aden has hosted the UAE forces headquarters in Yemen. While they occasionally act as arbitrators in fights between other groups, they have also established their own militia, known as the Security Belt, an unofficial force which has no status in the Yemeni administrative structure. The UAE has equipped and trained it, and pays its members, who are mostly Salafis from Aden itself and neighbouring governorates. The Security Belt is in daily conflict with various Hiraaki groups who support a wide range of ideologies and are therefore often also fighting each other. While Huthi-Saleh forces are clandestine, if present at all, there is open conflict between Islamists, Salafi and others, followers of different leaders, as well as AQAP/Daesh elements. The latter claimed responsibility for atrocities in 2015 and 2016 that killed large numbers of young men.[*]

In December 2015, after the assassination of the previous incumbent, Hadi was pressurised to appoint a well-known separatist as governor of Aden alongside the latter's close friend and ally as security chief. Both were supported by the UAE and have their own militias which consists of at least 10,000 men from the al-Dhala'-Lahej areas. During his tenure as governor, Aydaroos al-Zubeidi placed men from al-Dhala' and Lahej in all administrative positions throughout the Governorate, at the expense of people from the city itself. In mid-2016 Aden's security forces also expelled more than 5,000 'Northerners', including workers and other residents, mostly originally from Taiz and neighbouring areas. They were

---

[*] The following mass killings were all claimed by Daesh: on 22 May 2016 more than forty recruits to the official army in Khormaksar were killed with a body-borne explosive belt. On 29 August 2016, a booby-trapped vehicle exploded killing more than seventy young men in al-Sanafer school in Mansoura. The victims were in the process of joining Salafi-dominated forces to go and fight with the Saudi-led coalition on the northern border. On 11 and 18 December 2016, in two suicide attacks directed against the same military camp of Solaban in al-Areesh in Aden, more than 150 recruits were also killed. In two of these cases at least, the perpetrators were from al-Dhala' and Lahej and the majority of victims from Abyan. In response, the Abyan tribes sent a strong message to Yafi's after the Mansoura killings.

unceremoniously trucked to the former border between the YAR and PDRY, despite protests by Hadi and his government at the time. This xenophobic campaign had popular support and was a manifestation of the sad rise of social tensions in the country. There have been other similar expulsions in 2017. Such activities suggest that the likelihood of economic recovery and the renaissance of Aden as an economic hub seem like distant dreams. Reconstruction efforts are limited and only concern the restoration of basic services, such as electricity and water. Power cuts remain the norm, leading citizens and others to wonder what has happened to the millions spent by the UAE, Qatar and others on the installation of the numerous large and smaller power plants which feature daily in the media. Demonstrations complaining about the absence of these services are almost daily occurrences in 2017, alongside others demanding salaries and pensions.

The Situation in Mid-2017

Underlying the complexity and contradictions of this situation is the rivalry between the Abyan-Shabwa network and the al-Dhala'-Lahej group. While some elements of the former express limited support for Hadi, who originates from the midlands in Abyan, the latter is firmly committed to separatism. Hadi's record of military support for Saleh in the 1994 war also means that many from Abyan and Shabwa consider him a traitor, and this certainly includes separatists from those areas. In May 2017, the conflict between the two groups burst into the open when, following a series of incidents focused on control of Aden airport, Hadi dismissed Zubeidi, thus illustrating the dramatic deterioration of his own relations with the UAE. Within days, while accepting his dismissal, Zubeidi had been given the title 'leader of the Southern Resistance' by numerous separatist groups and established the Southern Transitional Council which he co-chairs with a Salafi former minister of Hadi's government, Hani Bin Breik. Among the semi-comical aspects of the situation, Zubeidi's friend and colleague, the Aden Security chief, remains in position and operates largely from Zubeidi's house. While clearly unfinished at the time of writing, this situation is illustrative of a number of important more long-term political issues:

-   the ambivalent relationship of people in Aden to Hadi and his role

as president, and his lack of popularity in the South and particularly in Aden
- while the Saudis and the Emiratis have clearly had different tactics in the past, this is the first time that their more fundamental long-term strategic divergences have come out into the open
- although Hadi took the risk of dismissing Zubeidi, he did not dismiss Shalal Ali Shaye, the security chief as, between them, Zubeidi and Shalal had successfully reduced insecurity in Aden
- most significantly, this is a symptom of overall instability in Aden, but also of the likely future conflicts between Southern elements, should they declare secession from the rest of the country.

The UAE has sponsored and established security forces beyond Aden: there are Security Belts in all Southern governorates except al-Mahra which act as police forces, while Hadramaut and Shabwa also have 'Elite Forces' equivalent to the army. Their leadership is Salafi, as are many members, and they are all composed of local individuals who have been trained, equipped and are paid by the UAE. It is unlikely that they would follow UAE agendas should these clash with their own personal or collective interests, but what is clear is that any loyalty they may have is more to the UAE than to Hadi's internationally recognised regime. Despite their presence, most of the Southern governorates are under the control of a variety of groups, mostly local and including some community and tribal entities. Al-Dhala' Governorate is the heartland of separatism and is the one area where that trend seems least challenged. Here Zubeidi reigns supreme. Lahej is the site of confrontations between jihadis, separatists and Security Belt units, while the UAE and other forces are fighting the Huthi-Saleh alliance further west. Abyan and Shabwa are contested between local forces of separatists and jihadis. They also have to cope with the presence of AQAP and Daesh in some areas, a subject discussed in greater detail in Chapter 4. Officially, Hadramaut and al-Mahra are aligned with the Hadi government; yet in practice local forces are in charge and there is also a jihadi presence. While details of who is aligned with whom may be different at the time of reading, the basic trend is clear. There are deep divisions, historic and contemporary, political and regional, all of which bode ill for the stability of this part of the country in the future.

Hadramaut is also the only area which could be a viable social, political and economic entity. It has access to financial resources for investment thanks to the past success of many of its migrants to Saudi Arabia and south-east Asia. However, it suffers from divisions between armed groups. Moreover, a number of Hadrami leaders have also made it clear that they are committed neither to Yemeni unity nor to remaining attached to the rest of the South. The likelihood of them declaring independence is high, with or without al-Mahra and Shabwa, as per the region envisaged in a proposed federal state. Hadramaut is likely to get enough international support from its neighbours to survive, though the widely advertised and long-prepared All-Hadramaut Comprehensive Conference held in May 2017 failed because wealthy Hadramis based in Saudi Arabia withdrew their support at the last minute – another event which could well be connected to the tense Saudi-Emirati relationship over the future of Yemen.

Conclusion

The Southern question is clearly complex. While separatism still appears to be a dominant ambition in the first decades of this century, its visibility may well conceal widespread scepticism about its wisdom. Southerners do not need deep knowledge of the history of the PDRY to have serious doubts about the political reliability and honesty of the separatist leaders, let alone their commitment to a specific ideology. Those old enough to remember will be fully aware of last century's divisions and full-scale military conflicts between the many disparate factions which now form the leadership of the movement, conflicts whose philosophical content could be summarised as a struggle over a position. Younger people need only look at the present failure of these groups to form a united leadership. In addition, the glaring lack of concern for the future welfare of the population is manifest in the absence of a political programme addressing future political, economic and social problems. Above all, Southerners, like all other Yemenis, yearn for a reasonable living standard, good access to essential services, and respect for their basic human rights. While the loud separatists are visible in the streets and the media, the silent majority may well not support their views.

Certainly the South has more natural resources and a smaller population than the rest of the country, as will be discussed in Chapter 8. But most of these resources are found in the east of their region, that is, in Hadramaut and the eastern part of Shabwa, through which the gas pipeline runs. Prospects for the western part of the former PDRY are far less positive. It faces the likelihood of endless factional and sub-regional political and military conflicts which in effect seem to prolong the struggles of the Protectorate period and of the in-party factional fights of the socialist period. The very limited economic resources of this sub-region of the South would merely exacerbate these tensions. Aden might remain a focal point for the battles of different factions, while dreams of economic prosperity based on reviving the port of Aden reveal wishful thinking and ignorance of the changes in maritime trade over the past half-century.

As this chapter has pointed out, regional differences and others based on the changes in social structure still play a major role in Yemeni political, social and economic life. The next chapter analyses the changes in Yemen's social structure over the past few decades, complementing the specific area and historical details presented in Chapter 3.

CHAPTER SEVEN

From Tribes to Elites

The Development of Yemen's
Social Structure

Most Yemenis believe that they are marginalised and excluded from the benefits and services which they expect from the state. But the reality is that the truly marginal are the tiny group who benefit from the patronage system and have enriched themselves at the expense of the majority. They include top-level kleptocrats in the military/security establishment, a few wealthy investors, whether from tribal, military or trading backgrounds, leaders of the elite security and military forces, and some former exiles, now complemented by war profiteers. Altogether this privileged group adds up to a microscopic proportion of the total population and are the core of a new type of elite which is transforming Yemen's social structure. The political and economic changes of recent decades have undermined a complex societal pyramid in which people's statuses were defined by occupation and birth. Yet there is some room for optimism, for Yemen is currently incubating elements which will eventually generate a new social structure reflecting the parallel transformation of current and future economic relations.

This chapter examines how tribal and other social roles have been transformed through the emergence of the military-kleptocratic nexus during the three decades of Saleh's regime.[1] It also explores how other social groups either increased or decreased in influence, and in particular how the country failed to develop 'standard' working and middle classes.

Instead, the regime created a system based on patronage which allowed the rise of individuals and families through this nexus, regardless of their position in the pre-revolutionary social structure; the earlier structure had been based on inherited ascribed status and was characterised by lower levels of inequality. Changes affecting women will be addressed separately, though it is essential to emphasise that most of what is said about people in general also applies to women, something which is often neglected.

Given that the vast majority of Yemenis are tribespeople, they must be given priority in any analysis of Yemeni social structures. Tribes are a fundamental element of Yemen's social fabric and they are vastly misunderstood and misrepresented. The term 'tribe' is often used in an anti-historical way as if it represents a static and unchanging group, ignoring the constant changes taking place, both within tribes and in their relations with others. Tribal people are subject to multiple prejudices which stereotype them on the basis of imagined characteristics. Disparaging and indeed insulting assertions about tribes are all too often found in the media, in academia and even among educated people, as when the word *bedu* (literally nomad) is used to disparage both tribespeople and nomads.

American analyst Daniel Corstange presents an excellent summary of these prejudices: 'In the Yemeni context ... tribesmen are often stylized as uneducated, backward, ignorant, uncultured, tradition-bound, irrational, uncivilized and violent. These views are often strongest among city-dwellers, the educated elite, and those who strongly oppose the current governing regime in Yemen, which is associated with tribalism and tribal traditions. Unflattering jokes abound about the ignorance and stupidity of tribesmen, and the epithet "tribal" is not infrequently used as a synonym for "backward".'[2] While tribes attract much attention, other social groups are neglected, including both ends of the spectrum, the *sada* and the *akhdam*; changes in both the nature and evolution of different social entities are given insufficient attention. Inadequate understanding of the country's social structure enables the spreading of widespread misconceptions about Yemen abroad, which could almost be said to be caricatures of reality.

Other than demystifying the tribal question, Yemen's contemporary reality can only be understood in the context of its socio-economic transformations in the past half-century. This chapter addresses these issues

briefly and, given the importance of tribes and their complex nature, I start
with a brief discussion of the concept of the tribe before addressing the
overall hierarchy of ascribed social groups which remain relevant today.

What Is a Tribe? Can It Be Part of a Modern State?

Both in ordinary life and among academics, tribes in the Middle East are
usually assumed to have the following characteristics: they are rural, and
membership is based on kinship relations combined in sets of segmentary
lineages.* Mutual solidarity is the basis for relationships within the tribe
or sub-tribe. Tribal political economy is based on nomadic pastoralism,
sometimes supplemented by oasis agriculture, in which raiding settled
communities and each other is a basic source of income. The assertion
that tribes are rural is clearly limiting, as people do not cease to be part
of their tribes when they move to urban environments. Many authors,[3]
and not only those from the Marxist tradition, see tribes as pre-state
forms of political organisation, while others see them as alternatives and
challengers to the state. Most writers accept that tribes are egalitarian
internally, but hierarchically ranked on the basis of their economy, with
camel herders coming first, followed by sheep and goat herders, and then
settled agricultural tribes.[4] For each of these characteristics, exceptions can
be found, as we will see shortly.

The following definition of tribes as they exist in the Middle East is a
reliable summary: 'Tribe may be used loosely of a localised group in which
kinship is the dominant idiom of organisation, and whose members consider
themselves culturally distinct (in terms of customs, dialect or language, and
origins); tribes are usually politically unified, though not necessarily under
a central leader, both features being commonly attributable to interaction
with states. Such tribes also form parts of larger, usually regional, political

---

* As neatly explained by Swagman, 'tribal structure is segmentary, that is, tribes are
composed of sections, subsections, sub-subsections and so on; the actual number of
levels can vary ... a subsection might include ten or twenty villages spread out over a
twenty or twenty-five square kilometre area ... a *qabila* is made up of a number of sections,
covering hundreds of square kilometres and may number thirty or forty thousand
members' (Charles Swagman, 'Tribe and Politics: an Example from Highland Yemen',
Journal of Anthropological Research, vol. 44, no. 3, 1988, p. 252). While segmentarism is
out of fashion in recent writings, it may still be of some relevance.

structures of tribes of similar kinds; they do not usually relate directly with the state, but only through these intermediate structures.'[5]

Tribes and the State

Academic[6] debate about tribes and their relationship to the state swings wildly between two extremes. Some see tribes as entities which, by definition, oppose and compete with the state, while others see tribalism as a structure complementary to the state, acting as an intermediary between the state and communities. In fact, most contemporary discussions on the subject return to the analysis of the father of sociology, Ibn Khaldun (1332–1406), to either support or challenge it. While in practice over the past century there have often been tensions between centralised state authorities and the tribes within their territories, the hierarchy seems clear, and tribes continue to operate within the various states around them.[7] More recently, social anthropologists have adopted similar interpretations, most prominent among them Maurice Godelier.[8] Much media and political discourse on Yemen systematically asserts that tribes oppose the state, regardless of the evidence. Indeed these sources often make mutually contradictory statements: on the one hand stating that tribes challenge state authority, and on the other, for example, mentioning that the objective of the latest kidnapping of foreign tourists was to get the state to provide a service. This narrative was routine in Yemen in the 1990s. Similarly Saleh, while asserting that Yemen is a 'tribal state', behaved in a way totally contrary to tribal norms. Although he used standard tribal (and indeed European) dynastic models to strengthen his position by marrying into as many tribal and other groups as possible to expand his loyalty base, his respect for tribal values, such as honour and consultation, was rather less noticeable.

There has been widespread cynicism about what have become known as jumlukiyas[9] in the Arab world, that is, the process whereby almost all the leaders of so-called republican states have tried to pass on their leadership positions to their sons. (Most came to power through military coups and later got themselves elected, and re-elected, again and again). In Saleh's case, given his view that Yemen is a tribal state, he might argue that he was following tribal tradition when trying to pass on the presidency to this son. Saleh's own tribe, Sanhan, is a minor branch of the Hashed tribal confederation, and his struggle against the al-Ahmar family can also be interpreted as an attempted takeover of the leadership of the confederation. His whole strategy in building an authoritarian state has been based on manipulating and distorting tribal procedures to strengthen his position at everyone else's expense.

In brief, the central state rulers of Yemen over the past centuries have tended to cooperate with and co-opt tribes living within their territories. Such a tactic is necessary to retain and consolidate their power, and to harness tribal military strength so as to face both external and internal potential threats. Tribes and tribal confederations are constituent elements of broader entities. Responsibilities are distributed between the tribe and the state, and each has a complementary role; they work best together in alliance through negotiations.

Social Structure Before the Revolutions of the 1960s

Yemeni social structure bears similarities to that found in other tribal societies, yet has specificities which ensure its uniqueness. The ascribed or inherited nature of the country's occupation-based categories has led to academic debate comparing Yemeni social structure with the south-east Asian caste system.[10] Likewise, ascribed statuses also exist in many African tribes, which share some common features with the situation in Yemen. For example, the blacksmith group in many African societies has its own status, and North Africa has 'saints' whose role can be interpreted as equivalent to that of Sufi elements in Yemen.[11] Regardless of theory, shifting from one category to the next is possible, though not easy, in both Yemen and regarding the most hierarchical case of castes in India.

The following are the groups in Yemen, though there are regional variations particularly concerning exactly which occupation goes into which lower group. While no statistics are available on the status-based distribution of the population, estimates are that at least 70 percent, possibly up to 80 percent, of the country's population are members of tribes. So what are the other social groups? And what is or was their relationship to the tribes?

The top ranking social group is that of the *sada* (sg. *sayyed*), sometimes and in some places known as Hashemites or *ashraf* (sg. *sharif*). They claim descent from the Prophet and their responsibilities are primarily religious and judicial. Throughout the country, *sada* are also landowners. They often live in villages where they form the totality or the majority of the population, rather than being dispersed in tribal villages. Until the 1962 revolution, the northern part of the country was ruled by Zaydi *sada* Imams. *Sada* also took the leading political positions in Hadramaut, where their dominance was partly based on wealth through trade with south-east Asia and the political and economic power they derived as a result. There are Zaydi and Shafi'i *sada* and while the *sada* from the northern areas found their political role seriously diminished after the revolution, those in Hadramaut retained their social and religious status. Some even held senior political positions in the PDRY though they did lose their properties and their political predominance as a group during the socialist period.

Generally *sada* are perceived as non-tribal, yet the reality is that they are originally tribal given that the Prophet was himself a tribesman, hence all his descendants are equally so. The transformation of *sada* into a separate social category took place over time. Scholar Marieke Brandt describes their descent and activities in the Zaydi areas: 'Zaydi Hādawī doctrine[12] ascribes to the *sadah* a leadership role in both religious and secular affairs, and *sadah* henceforth occupied the position of the imam (the spiritual and secular leader of the Zaydi community) as well as leadership positions in government administration and the military ... Due to their alleged non-Yemeni origin, in genealogical terms the *sadah* are still considered an immigrant community: Whereas almost all South Arabian tribes regard Qahtan (the putative common ancestor of the Southern Arabs) as their progenitor, the *sadah* still trace their descent to the Prophet, an 'adnani Arab of the Banu Hashim clan of the Meccan Quraysh tribe, 'Adnan being the putative common ancestor of the Northern Arabs.'[13] Two important additional points need to be addressed: *sada* are considered non-arms-bearing people in Hadramaut and some other parts of Yemen, whereas they certainly bear arms in most of the Zaydi areas, so this may be due to a distinction between Zaydism and Shafi'ism.

Just below *sada* in status are the *quda* (sg. *qadi*), whose status has originated from their learning and who in the past acted as judges and bureaucrats. They have tribal origins and only became a distinct social group over centuries of practice, and nowadays the status is inherited.

The next group, who form the vast majority of the population, are the tribespeople, the mainstream of Yemeni society. In pre-revolutionary

Yemen they were settled agriculturalists, in most cases smallholder owner-cultivators, though some worked as sharecroppers. Another myth holds that the southern highlands are not tribal, yet tribes are in fact found throughout the country. The difference in definition resides in the level of political consolidation of tribal units, which ranges from small tribes of a few thousand people covering a village or a district to the well-known major confederations, in the northern highlands of the Hashed, Bakil and less cohesive Madhaj, and in the southern area of the Awlaqi. Tribes are the main arms-bearing group and were dominant in society as they were the formal and effective protectors of the rest of the population, that is, those ranking above them and those below.

Below them were the groups considered to be weak (*da'if*). Most notably they depended on the tribes for protection because they were not entitled to bear arms themselves. These were headed by traders and followed by *bani khums*, artisans of all kinds, as well as the less despised among the service providers, such as 'restaurant operators', heralds, barbers and blood letters, and 'henna decorators' among women. Different analysts provide varying lists of activities and hierarchy of statuses for this group: this may reflect either the interpretations given by each analyst, or an actually different ranking of trades and hierarchy between one area and the next.[14]

While slaves[15] (*abeed*) had been servants of wealthier households, they also formed the army and the administrative and bureaucratic class of local rulers, whether in Hadramaut, Sana'a, the Tihama or elsewhere. As enforcers of state rulers' authority they gave orders and were entitled to obedience from all groups above them in the hierarchy; and they could bear arms as soldiers. Thanks to this history, in the era after the abolition of slavery they currently enjoy higher status than the *akhdam*.

The low-status groups who cultivate but are not allowed to own land mostly work as sharecroppers. They have different names in different parts of the country: most of them are dark skinned and of largely unknown origin. In the Lahej and Abyan spate-irrigated cotton plantations developed by the British in the 1940s and 1950s, they are known as *zubud*, (originating from Zabid) as most of them were initially brought from the Tihama plain along the Red Sea. In Wadi Hajr, on coastal Hadramaut, facing the Arabian Sea they are known as *subyan* or *hujur*. In Wadi Hadramaut they are known as *fellaheen*. It is interesting to note that these social groups are mainly found in all the areas where there are permanent water flows (such as Wadis

Masila, Hajr and Zabid). The other main characteristic of these areas is that, by virtue of the presence of permanent slow-flowing water, they are areas where malaria and other water-borne diseases are prevalent.

The lowest social group is that of the *akhdam* (servants) who nowadays prefer to be described as *muhamasheen* (marginalised). Up to now, their main occupations have been cleaning and begging, though they also occasionally work as casual cash labourers. They also are semi-nomadic as many of them spend different times of year in different localities. As they are not socially allowed to own land they often live in temporary settlements and are forced to move when the site of their homes is needed for other purposes. While not 'untouchable' in the south-east Asian sense, their status is very similar, given that they are generally despised and suffer from a range of prejudices which still prevail today.[16]

Slavery and formal ascribed statuses were abolished by both republics and, according to all constitutions since 1962, all Yemeni citizens are equal. But in reality, inherited status remains central: most people know and mention that those around them belong to one or another of these groups and behaviour towards them varies accordingly, even though in recent decades ascribed status categories have both weakened and changed. The main indicator of the persistence of this situation concerns intermarriage which is, indeed, the standard social anthropological method for assessing the strength of ascribed status. Endogamy within groups remains the norm and any infringement of this is considered exceptional and often results in some degree of social exclusion. Overall, 'marrying down' is acceptable for a man, but not for a woman, as status is inherited through the male line. Recent years have seen increasing cases of exogamy when it involved improvements in wealth and status for women and, more exceptionally, for men.

Pre-revolutionary social structure reflected the economic structure in a straightforward manner. Except in the most arid areas, where nomadic herding prevailed, and the coastal areas where fishing was the main activity, the Yemeni economy was based on cultivation. Tribespeople and *sada* owned land, and tribesmen and women cultivated their own land with assistance from their household members; at times of peak activity, family labour was supplemented by exchange of labour and occasionally by hired workers.[17] Holdings were small, but sufficient to provide a limited surplus which farmers used to pay for services from the non-cultivating groups, whether of higher or lower status. The few large landowners were mainly rulers, but some leading tribal families were also part of this group. Tribesmen's governance duties were to provide armed protection to the other groups. There were a few tribal sharecroppers though they were usually the result of family impoverishment resulting from some misfortune or other.

In very rare cases, *sada* did cultivate their own land in some areas in the northern highlands; but usually they had sharecroppers, either tribesmen or others. In Hadramaut and some of the lowlands, where there were fewer agricultural tribesmen, cultivation came to be seen as a low-status occupation and the *fellaheen* cultivated the land for the *sada*.[18] Hadrami tribes were more involved in nomadic and semi-nomadic pastoralism. They complemented the limited resource of the remote pasturelands by grazing their animals on crop residues after the harvest and thus fertilising the soil and improving yields of the crop production economy.

So in the pre-capitalist and pre-revolutionary era, agricultural production was the mainstay of economic life for the majority of the population; and the higher-status groups had access to the services of artisans producing agricultural tools and other objects needed for household use and clothes. The few large landowners had recourse to sharecroppers and agricultural labourers, mostly from low-status groups, but also including impoverished tribespeople. Trade was minimal in the rural areas and exchange of crops for services was standard practice. The currency, the Maria Theresa dollar, a silver bullion coin (locally known as the riyal fransi) was heavy and inconvenient; it was used for the few cash transactions, mostly in the towns and weekly markets. The service-provider lower-status groups resided in villages or small towns near the weekly markets and travelled around as needed.

Sada and *quda* performed their judicial tasks, as called for, at home, at weekly markets or in the *hautas* (or *hijra*) where people brought them their problems and conflicts. Many market towns became *hijra* or protected areas where tribal feuds and military activities were suspended, both to enable markets to proceed peacefully and also to ensure safety for conflicting groups while they sought remedy or mediation from residing judicial authorities. State rulers, central administrators and traders resided and practised their activities in the towns, which rarely qualified for the term city.

In brief, the economy was based on agriculture with households operating on a more or less self-sufficient, not to say subsistence, basis.

Tribal people paid for services in staple grains from the groups which they also protected. Some tribes formed long-term alliances which created the larger confederations, though sub-tribes within them could shift alliances. The majority of tribes remained small. International or even internal trade was insignificant, with a few exceptions, Aden being the main one. From the late nineteenth century onwards, the port displayed strong urban characteristics, based on the needs of the comparatively large administrative sector, whose positions were mostly filled by Indians and Somalis. Hodeida and Mukalla had trading and sea-faring activities such as the import of basic commodities (rice, tea and sugar), and Mokha was an important exporter of coffee in earlier centuries.

With Ottoman occupation in the North after 1872, and later attempts at centralisation of taxation under the Imamate after 1918 on the one hand, and British rule in the South, the situation changed during the twentieth century. The presence of dominant urban-based structures had only a limited impact on rural life, but it was at the root of what came later. Alongside taxation in the North came some mechanisation, particularly of irrigation, in the Protectorates, and increased trade. Meanwhile emigration expanded due to the discovery of its income-generating potential, and second because people now needed cash to acquire the goods arriving through the ports.

Changes in Social Structure Up to Unification (1970–1990)

The decade of the 1960s can be summarised as one of struggle to establish the new republican regime in the North and of anti-colonial struggle in the South. These military-political developments generated major political, social and economic transformations which, once the fighting was over, took off in a big way under the new regimes which controlled the country in the following two decades. Given the very different nature of the two regimes and the consequences of their different development today, I will outline the new socio-political formations for each state in the 1970s and 1980s separately.[19]

The Yemen Arab Republic (YAR)

Life for citizens of the YAR changed dramatically in the 1970s when the previous agricultural economy was undermined by mass migration to Saudi Arabia and other Gulf states after the 1973 oil price rises and the construction boom that then flourished in those countries. Most affected were the central and northern highlands which had previously seen little migration, whereas men from the eastern and southern uplands had been migrating in large numbers via Aden for a few decades; their main destinations had been the UK and the US.

In 1975, 89 percent of the resident population was rural[20] and 74 percent of the total population worked in agriculture,[21] with a further 5 percent engaged in construction. Hundreds of thousands of (mostly young) Yemeni men migrated to Saudi Arabia and other Gulf states to work in unskilled jobs. They would return home for short periods to spend time with their families and to distribute cash and goods to a broad range of relatives. This simultaneously demonstrated their success, improved their status within the community, and shifted the economy away from self-sufficiency. It was also a first step in undermining traditional authority structures within households and villages. As their financial contribution increased in importance, some younger men also started demanding the right to take part in deciding on community level investments through the Local Development Associations[22] discussed further in Chapter 10. Development also became widely understood throughout the country to mean modern health care, formal education, roads, electricity and water supply.

In the relatively well-watered terraced highlands, which had depended on rain-fed cultivation of staple crops (sorghum, maize, wheat), many terraces were allowed to deteriorate for a number of reasons: first, most young men were away and therefore not available for the heavy labour involved, although women were also involved in terrace maintenance. Second, imported cereals, mainly wheat, were much cheaper, so people bought them; and third, remittances from the migrants were far greater than what could be earned from the fields, so there was no perceived need to maintain the terraces. The long-term negative implications of their deterioration only emerged in the last decade when the loss of absorption capacity of the terraced land contributed to water shortages. As a result rain-fed agriculture suddenly regained its earlier importance. When

I worked in al-Baidha and Sana'a Governorates in the 1980s, the cost of locally produced sorghum and wheat was about four times that of imported grains and they were considered luxury items for festivities or for wealthier people.

A commercial economy emerged and weekly markets became permanent. The production of local handicrafts declined, partly due to their high cost; instead they were replaced by imports of cheap and fashionable industrial goods. This gradually changed the status of traders: as trade's financial returns improved, the profession ceased to be considered demeaning: tribesmen, *sada* and *quda* all took it up. Status rankings thus shifted from occupation to wealth. Anthropologist Richard Tutwiler noted in 1987 '[there is a] major cultural redefinition of an entire occupational category as more and more tribesmen seek to enter petty commerce. Since the revolution tribesmen moving from agriculture to commerce have not suffered a loss of social prestige or political status.'[23] Thanks to remittances, by the 1980s the regime had 'replaced a national dependence on grain cultivation and a self-contained system of stratified redistribution of surpluses in kind with an open door policy that avowedly sought integration with the global capitalist economy.'[24] The combined effect of cheap imports, the rise of a commercial bourgeoisie and the appropriation of land by large landlords and officials resulted in the emergence of a new class structure. The resultant exacerbated socio-economic differentiation also led to comparable political changes in the power structure. Tutwiler's analysis of the Mahweet area in the northern highlands is largely valid for many parts of the YAR in the early to mid-1980s when he did his fieldwork.

My own experience in al-Baidha Governorate at that time confirms Tutwiler's analysis; in particular the reliance of ordinary rural households on their migrant men for cash which, once daily needs were covered, was invested in buying a four-wheel drive vehicle and building a new house. Migrants also invested in income-generating enterprises such as drilling wells to irrigate their fields and change their cropping patterns, opening a shop, importing construction equipment or a small generator. At that time, if I met a young or middle-aged man when visiting a home, conversation was based on when they had come back from Saudi Arabia, when they were returning, how they were investing their earnings, what they thought of Saudi Arabia, and the like. The likelihood of them not being on a visit from their locale of migration was negligible. At the time Yemen had a population of 9.274 million and 1.168 million or 13 percent of the total population were international migrants,[25] most of them in Saudi Arabia. Another result of the high incomes for migrants was a significant rise in the cost of labour locally; thus even those who stayed at home could improve their living standards. Most local labour was involved in construction of the investments made by the migrants, which in turn led to further neglect of agriculture.

This commercially based rural economy was gradually modified by the emerging power of the military and security forces, as Saleh, from the early 1980s onwards, tightened his control over the country through three basic mechanisms, which he later refined and expanded. First, he subsidised favoured tribal leaders, particularly after 1986 when his financial means increased through access to income from the export of oil; second, he ensured the presence everywhere of security agents from any one of the many security and military institutions he established; and third, he enrolled local leaders, tribal and other, into the General People's Congress. This process enabled those in political favour to accumulate wealth through appropriation, and created a real division within communities between the emerging kleptocrats (albeit on a small scale), and the rest of the population, who felt oppressed. The result of Saleh's interventions also distorted relations between citizens and tribal leaders.

In brief, by the time of unification in 1990, the country's social structure had been significantly redesigned due to the replacement of occupation as main criterion for the definition of status, by wealth (from migration, trade, concentration of land ownership and corruption). Power at the local level came from support for the Saleh regime and through involvement in the security/military apparatus. The lowest social status group of *muhamasheen* or *akhdam* remained unchanged, however, and it became clear that discrimination against them was based on prejudice[26] rather than any other rationale. Meanwhile the original high status of the *sada* and *quda* was also reduced, partly through the egalitarian ideals promoted through the republican ethos, by contrast with the situation during the Imamate, but mostly because of the overall economic changes discussed above. Taking up trade was a form of compensation.

The People's Democratic Republic of Yemen (PDRY)

Social and economic changes in the PDRY during the 1970s and 1980s were different. Although downplayed by the regime, migration was almost as important in the life of most rural households. The regime was very ambiguous in its attitude toward migration: on the one hand, it badly needed the foreign exchange from remittances and appreciated the direct support migrants gave to their rural communities. But on the other hand, the PDRY was concerned about the loss of both skilled and unskilled labour, the 'brain drain'. A major political concern was the involvement of migrants with anti-regime activities. While most migrants were, as in the YAR, tribesmen from mountain villages with small agricultural holdings and low-status people from all areas, they also included political exiles from different social strata, particularly the rulers of former statelets and the urban 'bourgeois', some of whom were educated and whose loss to the labour force was detrimental.

The previously strong urban economy of Aden collapsed immediately after independence with the departure of the British from their military base and the closure of the Suez Canal after the 1967 Arab-Israeli war. Between them these events left the port idle; indeed, it has never fully recovered. Despite ambiguous policies towards the private sector, Aden gradually developed a few industries which provided goods for the local market and reduced dependence on imports. These new enterprises thus created the elements of a traditional working class in whose interests the pre-1990 socialist regime defined itself. Aden also remained the most important city: as the capital, its administration was economically significant and, until the 1980s, it had the only university in the country. The only other location which could boast the term city was Mukalla, whose population was about 44,000 people in the early 1970s.[27]

In most areas socialist-type cooperatives and state farms transformed the rural economy. The main social impact of these changes was to make all farmers formally equal and remove the distinctions between tribal/ *sada* owners, sharecroppers and lower-status cultivators. The regime's ideological opposition to tribalism and its commitment to socialism meant that deliberate efforts went into undermining the former social structure. Some tribal leaders emigrated, particularly those who had ruled the various statelets of the federation; many *sada* and the wealthier traders and businessmen did likewise. Discrimination based on status was made illegal. Low-status groups were given land and thus improved their social standing to be similar to tribespeople; they also improved their potential future status through education, and in time began achieving professional positions.

Education played a big role in establishing a social stratum of qualified employees as teachers, medical workers and in administration. Among other achievements, this created a large group of educated women who were able to get jobs mostly in the public sector and join in building the country. They were employed as teachers but also found work in other administration and technical professions. The Family Law improved women's status and gave women economic and social opportunities which they had not previously enjoyed. Officially, according to this law, 'husband and wife were jointly responsible for maintaining the household'[28] – something which became a realistic proposition as educated women could now obtain employment.

In summary, by the time of unification, the PDRY's social structure was less tribal, more explicitly egalitarian, and its economy was showing signs of socialist characteristics. In addition, the regime strengthened the state and cooperative sectors in agriculture and industry and fostered a new public sector administrative and professional group. The gap between rich and poor was minimal, partly as a result of policy and partly thanks to the almost complete absence of corruption. The economy was more diversified, with some industries and a larger professional class; although migration played a role, it was not a defining one. By 1990 the social structure of the PDRY did not fit firmly within the Western description of a class society, but it was heading in the direction of an East European one. Changes in the social structure which had been initiated in the final decades of the protectorates strengthened during the socialist regime, despite taking a different direction in each of these two periods. But in both cases, the direction was one in which status was strongly associated with activity, rather than birth.

The New Social Structures: The Kleptocratic Nexus (1990–2010)

The two decades between unification and the full-scale crisis in 2011 saw fundamental transformations of the new state's social and economic structures. Essentially the whole of Yemen moved in the direction that began in the YAR with the Saleh regime's ascendency in the previous decade.

Underlying Trends

Agricultural holdings became smaller due to land concentration and rapid population growth. Agriculture ceased to be the primary economic resource for the majority, replaced by male casual urban labour. As tribespeople became poorer, they sold land, thus worsening their long-term prospects, and the vicious downward spiral continued. Many of these tribesmen experienced acute shame at their deteriorating social status, as they stood on street corners waiting for unskilled work as daily labourers. Rural poverty undermined the status of tribes as institutions and upholders of principles of social behaviour as people compared their deteriorating conditions with those of the few individuals connected with the rewarding patronage system. Water started to run out in some areas. Due to the limited natural resources and the absence of high quality education, a 'standard' capitalist economy based on production could not emerge. In any case, such an economy would have been difficult to establish in the globalised international free trade environment. The working class existed only in the small advanced industrial sector. Militancy was not a characteristic of the workers: either they were involved in small family units or else they were relatively content to receive regular salaries and have stable employment.

Emerging Social Classes

The fundamental transformations in the economic base greatly accelerated the establishment of a new social structure based on access to resources, rather than birth or profession. As a result, the tribal system was undermined: traditional solidarity and egalitarianism declined dramatically as social structures became politicised and based on the relationship between community leaders and the Saleh regime. The main criterion to retain or increase power was the extent to which shaykhs supported the regime: alignment was essential to ensure access to financial subsidies, and state employment opportunities in the military/security sectors, and development projects needed to fulfil their obligations of hospitality and care to their tribespeople. These pathways to survival became all the more indispensable in the face of an overall deteriorating economy.

In the past, a poor but honourable tribal leader's decisions and skills were respected and ensured he remained popular and kept his position. However, by the 1990s, a leader lost support unless he could provide jobs or financial assistance – a task made yet more difficult by rapid population growth and reduced opportunities. Despite this, tribal shaykhs continued to solve conflicts within their communities and thus retained some influence, even when they were unpopular with Saleh, at least as long as they stayed in position. One way or another, tribal leaders' independence was reduced: a shaykh who did not cooperate with the Saleh regime faced critical difficulties which challenged his position.[29] Saleh did not, and indeed could not, select or depose shaykhs directly. Instead he and his agents discreetly and indirectly sponsored intra- and inter-tribal conflicts which would eventually lead to changes and the promotion of one of his supporters. This affected any group which did not explicitly support the regime.

Given that the working class formed only 0.8 percent of the population, including those in family enterprises, it did not emerge as a powerful social force. It was also composed of people of different original social status, tribespeople as well as members of the low-status groups; this was a further constraint on the establishment of class solidarity. The professional middle class might have been expected to emerge through the strengthening of capitalism and higher educational standards. However, it was numerically insignificant as inflation, corruption and rising living costs held it back. People were compelled to depend on tribal connections to cope with daily administrative and other problems. Potential bastions of this professional group, such as teachers and health workers, remained poor. Overall, solidarity based on birth status prevailed over possible groupings based on new shared interests, such as profession. For example, in the health sector the divide between high-status doctors and low-status nursing and other staff prevented the emergence of strong solidarity movements. Trade and professional unions were either under the control of the regime or of a rival political party (usually Islah), and were more concerned with politics than traditional objectives of improved working conditions and salaries. In short, workers and professionals neither expected nor received support from their professional institutions.

These points contribute to explaining the decline of the traditional ascribed social statuses: the new twin markers of status became wealth and access to central power. Though there were obviously exceptions, tribesmen and *sada* were no longer respected for upholding values such as honour and just behaviour. As wealth and the ability to provide material benefits became the main criteria for improved status, so traders became powerful through their ability to make gifts, loans and investments. As a result tribesmen as well as *sada* became involved in trade themselves. The image of trade soon changed from low to high status.[30] The military/security elite was increasingly led by Saleh's relatives and composed mainly of men[31] from his own sub-tribe and neighbouring areas. They were (and largely still are) above the law and used their positions, first to ensure Saleh's political position, and second to increase their personal assets, each according to his rank. Leaders included some of the more efficient and better known kleptocrats.[32] They have accumulated wealth through land, industry and control of, or participation in, the major economic enterprises.[33]

Changes in migration patterns were relevant to these developments. By contrast with the situation in the 1970s and '80s, when Yemenis throughout the country experienced gradually improving living standards and were optimistic for their future and that of their children, the situation was reversed after unification in 1990.[*] At the village and household levels, medium- to long-term international migration[34] was replaced by internal migration. In addition, dependence on casual labour within Yemen increased tensions within households as short-term, low-status work in towns and cities meant more frequent visits home while producing less income. A dramatic change from the rapidly improving living standards in the 1970s and 1980s to bare survival in the 1990s and 2000s accentuated tensions. By its very nature, casual employment militates against the creation of organisations of common interest.

---

[*] Although by the 2000s the number of Yemenis in Saudi Arabia had again risen to about 1.5 million, this represents about half what it had been twenty years earlier if considered as a proportion of the Yemeni population. Moreover, their working conditions were far less rewarding, so the impact of their remittances on the economy did not compare.

How Political Parties Affect Social Structure

Political organisations, in particular Saleh's General People's Congress (GPC) and the Islah, emerged in modern Yemen as 'new' mechanisms of access to status and benefits. The largest is the GPC. It was created in 1982 on Saleh's initiative to bring together as many local personalities as he could, whether tribal leaders, *sada* or others, into an organisation whose primary purpose is to keep him in power. It has branches and representatives throughout the country, including individuals connected with the security services. Its agents monitor changes in local power structures; and the GPC systematically attempts to co-opt anyone who emerges as a potentially influential personality, most of the time successfully. Involvement with the GPC helps supporters access jobs and other advantages. Its national presence goes beyond any regional, tribal or other group allegiances, and thus it had the potential to become a base on which to build a genuine national democratic entity. Indeed, the late Dr Abdul Karim al-Eryani tried to move it in that direction and transform it into a genuine party that could respond to the population's needs. His initiative was defeated by Saleh's determination to retain his position as an all-powerful authoritarian ruler who was not interested in such a democratic organisation.

The second most prominent party is the Islah, the only party which offers a genuinely popular programme, as is discussed in Chapter 4. Many people from under-privileged groups, including the low-status social strata, have joined it. As stated by social historian Mikhail Rodionov (2006) with reference to Hadramaut, 'another way of getting rid of hereditary stigma is to join an Islamic organization or political party, e.g. al-Islah, which stresses the principle of equality of all Muslims before God and People.'[35] Rodionov here refers to the low-status *fellaheen*. However, in my view two additional factors led this group to support Islah: first was the condescending, not to say insulting, treatment they received from the returned *sada*, tribesmen and other newly privileged groups. The second was the fact that they had lost faith in the ability of the YSP to protect their interests after 1994. Their support for the Islah enabled that party to have significant parliamentary representation from Wadi Hadramaut in the last parliament elected in 2003.

The Yemeni Socialist Party (YSP) is now a social democratic party and a member of the Socialist International, alongside the British Labour Party and many others. This transformation represented a significant step; but it is still perceived as the party of the Southerners, even though much of its current leadership and membership are from the former YAR. Its failure to support Southern separatism has lost it much popular support in the South. It split in 1994 as a majority supported unity and did not join al-Beedh's breakaway secessionist group. The YSP, the Baathist and Nasserist parties are the only groupings which can be described as standard political parties and they attract mostly intellectuals and professionals. Their lack of tribal base and inability or unwillingness to provide material benefits also contribute to their weakness. By contrast, al-Haq and the Union of Popular Forces are *sada* parties, so their even smaller membership is based on inherited status loyalty.

Overall, political parties in Yemen do not represent specific class interests. Nor have they become standard institutions or mechanisms for those seeking political progress or change, primarily because election after election demonstrated Saleh's complete control over the political process, sometimes in alliance with Islah. This remained the case regardless of the regime's failure, deliberate or otherwise, to create an economy which allowed the population to improve its living conditions. The GPC's capacity to provide material benefits as well as its systematic manipulation of the electoral process contributed to its success. Access to patronage remained the main reason for anyone joining or supporting either of the two major parties. Tribespeople form the majority of all parties' membership, given that they make up most of the national population. Islah includes many individuals from lower-status groups and was also in a position to provide employment in the al-Ahmar business empire. The following incident helps to understand many Yemenis' attitudes to parties. When in 2014 the Huthis ransacked the home of Sadeq al-Ahmar, the leader of the Hashed tribal confederation and the Islah party, other tribal shaykhs considered this unacceptable. As one of them put it: 'Hashed as a tribe was insulted. We are tribal leaders first before we are heads of political parties. What we saw from Houthi supporters and their militia is scary. They've insulted sheikhs like us in other places.'[36]

Changes in Women's Status and Activities

Of course, everything which has been written above concerns women as well as men, and indeed also children. The current fashion for 'gender mainstreaming' in development often implies that unless women are mentioned separately, it is assumed that the discussion does not cover their circumstances. Clearly this is wrong. However, the changes in social structures have had certain specific impacts on women, which are different from those for men, and I will briefly discuss them now.

Myths and misconceptions about Yemeni women's roles and levels of authority and autonomy abound and are worsened by the widespread prejudices about Muslim women in general. The issue of head and face covering is the most obvious focus for these misconceptions. Women also suffer from generalisations which ignore differences due to time and place. Over the decades of my involvement with Yemen, women have experienced many changes, both individually and collectively. The increased use of 'Islamic' outer clothing is the outcome of two different and conflicting trends: the first is the increasing influence of Islamism which encourages women to follow Islamist dress code, while also making life unpleasant for those who do not. The other is an advantage experienced by many women, who find that wearing such garb enables them to go out to work or study in a more relaxed environment as it reduces harassment in the streets, as well as facilitating these activities for women from conservative families who would object to their presence in the public sphere without the 'protection' of the concealing outfits.

Throughout the half-century covered by this book, rural women have been actively involved in the productive economy. They work in the fields and carry out most routine tasks (weeding, sowing, and harvesting) while men are basically responsible for ploughing and land clearance. But women also participate in male activities when necessary. Studies have demonstrated that women carry out about 90 percent of agricultural work, in terms of time and activities. Although there was much talk of women taking over all agricultural responsibilities as a result of the mass migration of men to GCC states in the 1980s this happened less than had been predicted, as there were always a few men around to lead animals in ploughing.

Livestock husbandry was and remains women's work, with the exception of care for camels (where they are found). That said, notable differences existed between highland and lowland areas. In al-Mahra, for example, as is the case in Dhofar in Oman, women did not milk cows or camels in the past, though this may have changed in recent decades. The only aspect of agriculture that tribal women eschewed was marketing because it takes place in public markets. Of course, this puts women at a disadvantage when selling their livestock, as they are unable to control the price or guarantee that they receive the full income; instead they trust their husbands, brothers or sons to carry out transactions in their best interest. Similarly rural women were always involved in building their own homes, even in the highlands where stone is the main building material. Prior to the overwhelming use of plastics and imported cloth, women's work also included sewing and the manufacture of basketry household goods, although weaving has, until recently, remained mainly a male activity.

In cities women work as administrators, teachers, medical staff, and more recently cashiers in supermarkets and banks. These positions are taken up by educated women of tribal origin, but are also acceptable for many *sada* women. Nursing is still largely considered a low-status occupation which families reject as not being respectable, but this attitude is changing. Poor tribal women also make bread for sale near eating places. Low-status women, meanwhile, often work as street cleaners and beggars. Crucially, seclusion was and, to a large extent, remains an indicator of higher status and wealth, regardless of reality. So, for example, *sada* women are far more restricted in their movements than low-status women; even when very poor, it is extremely rare for them to engage in economic activity outside the home, whether agriculture or trading.

In recent decades international organisations have been particularly active in promoting activities aimed at women. This is based on two main assumptions: first, that Yemeni women are particularly oppressed and disrespected, and second, that their high illiteracy rate (45 percent) bears considerable responsibility for the continuing high fertility rate. Therefore to reduce rapid population growth, development agencies operate on the concept that increasing education for women is essential, and that this will also give women more autonomy once they earn their own incomes. Major investors in support of projects designed to improve women's overall status include, among others, the Netherlands and German governments and the World Bank. The latter targets education and health projects, while the Netherlands supported women's units in various ministries and established

Women's Clothing and Seclusion

In Aden during the socialist period, women usually wore headscarves at school and at work. In the afternoons and evenings, they wore a *shador* (an overall black loose bag-like garment open at the top which was wrapped around their faces) over their *deras*, which are the standard women's wear in the hot climate of the city. These are loose garments made of a veil-type material which are basically transparent. Short of displaying one's underwear to the world, it was clearly necessary to wear a less revealing outer garment in public. Only low-status working women wore these during working hours. This situation changed after unification, particularly after the 1994 civil war, when Islamists became powerful in the city and rapidly put pressure on women to take up the loose black coats and head coverings. They also encouraged the full face covering which totally changed the atmosphere at places like the College of Education of Aden University.

The only two rural areas in the PDRY where I ever witnessed women systematically covering their faces were on coastal Hadramaut, where even secondary school students wore the full niqab, and women working in the fields also covered their faces, as did women in Wadi Hadramaut. In the YAR, women in towns and cities were generally fully covered in the 1980s, wearing the *sitara* (literally 'curtain', a multi-coloured pattern sheet-like garment) or the black *shirshaf* (a two-piece garment, with a long pleated skirt and a cape-like top). Professional women were the exception and their standard 'uniform' at that time was a Western raincoat and headscarf. These were worn throughout the day in offices, the street or anywhere, and were definitely not removed indoors, except at home or when visiting women friends in an exclusively female environment. After unification, the raincoat fashion died out and professional women wore long loose jackets and suits, although some Yemeni professionals took up the long black loose coat known as a *balto* which, in the 2000s, got renamed the *abaya* following Gulf fashions. The name change came with a range of increasingly fancy and decorated cloaks, while schoolgirls wore simple ones according to the uniform colour of their schools.

There is a direct relationship between changes in status and the adoption of face covering. The two groups who do not cover their faces are very low-status women at one end of the social spectrum, and highly educated Westernised professional women at the top end. Because urban environments included many unknown and unrelated people, there was greater need to conceal women's faces. I distinctly remember working in villages around Rada' in al-Baidha in 1982 and giving lifts to women who wanted to come to town for one reason or another: when they got into my car, their faces were visible and they wore multi-coloured clothes and head scarves of the then-current rural fashion. By the time I dropped them off in town, they were fully covered in black, and I would have been unable to identify them in a crowd.

Another relevant factor is visibility to 'strange' men, that is, men not related by close or distant kinship, or even tribe. In highland rural areas throughout the 1970s and 1980s, in both the YAR and PDRY, women wore coloured head scarves but did not wear the balto. This was because in their villages and neighbouring fields where they worked, they were highly unlikely to come across any male strangers. This situation changed considerably with the rapid expansion of motorable tracks and the consequent traffic of passing vehicles which meant that unrelated men travelled through their villages and near their fields. Rural isolation thus decreased rapidly, a phenomenon that coincided anyway with the widespread adoption of more conservative Islamist behaviour. As a result, women and even young girls took up wearing both *baltos* and niqab face coverings whenever they left home, even when fetching water or working in the fields.

Similarly in cities the tendency is for increased covering to indicate higher status, until some achieve high professional levels and take up more European-style clothing. The only women who normally show their faces and are seen in public are the lowest-status women, particularly the *akhdam*. In the last decade or so, they have also taken up wearing full black cloaks and face coverings, to suggest higher status, despite their low-status activities. With increased economic difficulties, more women are forced to take up work in public places (as teachers, medical staff, cashiers in supermarkets, bread sellers). Others are students, and most wear *abayas* and many also wear full face coverings.

Women's Studies Centres in the universities of Sana'a and Aden. The US has also financed many scholarships for women.

There is no doubt that these investments have improved the literacy rate among women and have enabled many to obtain employment after their studies. However, external financiers' focus on women also contributed to a backlash among many officials who opposed these policies on the grounds that they interfered in Yemeni culture. Similarly, support for the *akhdam* gave many other Yemenis the impression (probably mistaken given the level of investment) that they were being given privileged attention at the expense of the majority of the population who were also suffering worsening living conditions.

Conclusion

Yemen's current social composition can be summarised as follows. Against the background of the population doubling every twenty years and extreme water scarcity which contribute significantly to the crisis, this period saw a fundamental change in the social structure of the country. Status based on occupation and birth was partly replaced by status based on wealth, regardless of how it had been acquired. This is particularly relevant given worsening poverty which forces many people to seek assistance from individuals whom they do not respect

Tribes remain the fundamental element of Yemeni society though the importance of tribal norms declined markedly: tribal leaders have either consolidated their positions through their political connections or lost power and position when perceived to be dissident. Many shaykhs also became 'city shaykhs' so their constituents either have to wait for their visits home or travel to Sana'a themselves to seek their support. Although tribes constitute the majority of Yemen's population numerically, fundamental changes in the country's social and economic structure over the past half century have expanded political allegiances beyond their remit. Such changes have also allowed some non-tribal individuals, particularly among those of low-status, to improve their status. The move towards an economy based on trade, administration and the military, has contributed to weakening the power of tribes per se. Most fundamentally, the rise of what has become known as the kleptocratic-tribal-military nexus has not, in fact, been the rise of tribal power as such, but rather of a small clique around Saleh. Not entirely facetiously, it could be suggested that his attempt to pass on the presidency to his son reflected his ambition to be Yemen's most powerful 'super'-shaykh (shaykh mashaykh) and to establish a dynasty on a tribal basis, replacing that of the al-Ahmar family which led the Hashed confederation for the past century. In this context, Saleh's current alliance with the Huthis takes on yet another possible interpretation.

At best, the new social structure has nurtured embryonic working and middle classes based on solidarity through shared professional interests. For the most part, however, the ascribed social groups remain the first basis for solidarity. Finally, the rise in unemployment, and the changed economic circumstances within households and villages mean that the younger generations are increasingly frustrated and disaffected, as they cannot achieve the basic ambitions associated with 'normal' life: marriage, children and the ability to maintain a household.[37] While much of what I have said is very specific to the Yemeni context, Yemen is by no means alone in the world in having hundreds of thousands of young people whose future is bleak. Traditional political parties fail to address these issues. As discussed in Chapter 4, faced with this situation, it is not surprising that some youths succumb to the attraction of extremist organisations which offer them empowerment, as well as simple recipes for solutions. What is more surprising is that these youths still remain a very small minority.

Another significant change has been the empowerment of youth beyond the domestic sphere, as a result of their becoming the main income earners. The war has caused a shift from employment as casual urban labour to participation in armed groups, whether in the national army or militias, all of whom provide salaries, at a time when most staff remain unpaid for months on end. Individuals joining Salafi and other groups are increasing their influence within the war economy. This trend undermines both relations within the tribes and the structures set up by Saleh, who had, by 2010, concentrated real power among his closest associates. Tribes used to bear arms in order to protect their group; under Saleh they lost power to a modern military/security apparatus whose members were defined by close relations with the ruler, and which acted with impunity. It remains to be seen how these various transformations will play out over the coming decades, given the many challenges which Yemeni society faces.

Interestingly in this context, the rise of the Huthi movement presents a fundamental challenge to the social structure that emerged under Saleh. Their belief that *sada* are 'natural' rulers of an Islamic country means that the Huthis have appointed *sada* to senior positions throughout the area, and in all the institutions which they now influence, thus shifting power away from social groups based on wealth and political connections to Saleh towards the former 'ascribed' status where birth determines social and political position.

CHAPTER EIGHT

Resources Scarcity and Their Capture

Matters of Life and Death

The volcanic wadis on the Rada' plain in al-Baidha Governorate are fertile. In the early 1980s, when I worked there, they were covered in beautiful, mostly rain-fed gentle terraces of wheat and other cereals. Local men were buying diesel pumps with the income from their labour in Saudi Arabia and increasingly irrigating their fields, some of them introducing qat and other high-value crops. Pumping ground water for irrigation seemed like the perfect solution to ensure increased wealth. Within two decades wells had dried up and, by the early 2010s, many villages have been completely abandoned, as all the ground water has gone, and unpredictable rainfall is insufficient to provide even domestic water. Mismanagement and misuse of this basic resource has turned lovely villages into abandoned and collapsing buildings.

The basic elements needed to build an economy are adequate natural resources, sufficient skilled labour and capital. Yemen is faced with an even greater challenge than its current war, poverty and geopolitical position: its natural resources are very limited. In particular it is one of the most water-scarce countries of the world, a scarcity that threatens its very existence as a populated area. This chapter examines the constraints imposed by the situation, then looks at the role of oil and gas, whose comparatively recent discovery and exploitation raised hopes of a Yemeni bonanza. Yet mismanagement of the income from hydrocarbon exports has reduced benefits for the population as a whole, but high profits for a few. While new oil or gas reserves might be found, only an entirely different polity would ensure that benefits would accrue to the nation as a whole. An additional cause for concern is climate change, whose damage is already causing crises and tragedies due to lack of preparation.

Water: Absolute Shortage and Unsustainable Policies

Let's start with some basic facts: the shortage of water in Yemen is absolute; current annual use of water at 3.5 billion m³ exceeds renewable resources by 1.4 billion m³. In other words, one third of the water used annually is mined from non-renewable fossil aquifers. Per capita availability of renewable water has dropped to less than 85m³, which is significantly below 10 percent of the internationally recognised scarcity threshold of 1,000m³. As population increases annually by 3 percent, this quantity reduces proportionately, because the basic water resource remains unchanged. Yemen is almost exclusively dependent on ground water. The renewable aquifers depend on annual and more long-term rainfall. Greater use of irrigation pumps in agriculture has contributed not only to the depletion of the shallow renewable aquifers but also to that of the fossil aquifers. As agriculture is estimated to use close to 90 percent of Yemen's water, and 70 percent of the country's population live in rural areas, it is essential to develop sustainable water management policies if Yemenis are to continue living in the country's urban and rural areas.

Until the early years of this century, development policies encouraged irrigated agriculture with subsidies for equipment and fuel, contributing to the exhaustion of both rechargeable shallow aquifers and deep fossil aquifers. By the mid-2000s, well irrigation covered 33 percent of all cropped land. Extraction greatly exceeding recharge had reached critical points in many governorates, including Sana'a, Taiz, Amran and Sa'ada. According to the 2002 Agricultural Census, about 265,000 landholders owned 160,000 deep wells, 124,000 shallow wells with pumps, and a further 94,000 unequipped shallow wells. Only 7,000 of these landholders used modern irrigation methods in 2003. Farmers had to deepen their wells every two years or so if they were to reach the water table. Many wells had already completely dried up and farmers' options are now mostly negative: they can revert to rain-fed agriculture, give up agriculture altogether or sell their land.

Lack of clean drinking water is a notorious health hazard which has a debilitating impact on productivity and wellbeing, let alone life.[1] Not only are many urban areas not served by public water distribution systems, but where they do exist, they are often polluted, as are the tanker loads purchased from private suppliers. In rural areas, the cost of domestic water is prohibitive in terms of cash and labour time for women and children who collect it from wells, irrigation pumps, springs and standpipes; and then have to carry it to their homes, usually up steep hills,. Doing this not only consumes time and is physically exhausting; it also takes precious time that could be spent on education or more productive activities. In addition, although often used for drinking, water collected from surface sources (wells, springs, irrigation pumps) is mostly heavily polluted. The extremely rapid spread of cholera in 2017 in urban and rural areas, has once again confirmed the important role of water in the transmission of disease.

In 2010, the World Bank estimated that Yemen's ground water reserves are likely to be depleted in about three decades.[2] Of course there are regional differences, but overall, those areas with the greatest water shortage are also those with the highest population density. The western highlands and escarpments depend almost exclusively on renewable resources; with the spread of irrigated agriculture and large populations, it is the area already most affected by shortages. These highlands are also the areas from which people have started emigrating in greatest numbers: when wells which supply domestic water dry up, households first purchase water from tanker operators, who travel increasingly long distances to refill their tankers, thus making their water more and more expensive. Once this supply has run out, or people can no longer afford to pay for it, the population tends to move away. Initially, families leave temporarily to stay with relatives in villages or towns where water is still available. They then return home after good rains when the wells have filled. Eventually they move permanently: there are already cases of abandoned villages in highland governorates such as Amran, al-Baidha, al-Dhala' and Sa'ada.[3] The latter, of course, has seen mass war-related emigration since the Huthi wars started.

The major cities of the lowlands are likely to see big influxes of population as a result of such movements from the highlands. For example, many al-Baidha families have close relatives in Hodeida and Aden and are therefore likely to head for those cities. These transfers of population towards the coastal areas cause additional problems: in the short term, saline intrusion into the coastal aquifers used both for human consumption and for agriculture reduces the amount of water available for both, worsens soil deterioration and reduces crop yields. The over-exploitation of the rural aquifers in the hinterland of these cities has, for the past two decades, already exacerbated other problems for people in those areas as well as accelerated the process of exhaustion of the sources. Rural-urban conflict over access to water is another cause of insecurity: there is a well-documented history of such strife in connection with Taiz[4] over the past two decades, so the problem is not new.

Although extreme, the case of Taiz illustrates what may well happen elsewhere. Other cities also need to address their water shortages. Aden used to get its water from the wells of Bir Nasser and Bir Ahmed on the way to Lahej. But travellers passing through the area this century would not even guess that this was once a major source of water, as all that is left are some collapsing steel water tanks. The trees and other greenery have completely disappeared. Today Aden's water comes from much further afield in Lahej Governorate and from the Batees area in Abyan, above Ja'ar in lower Yafi'. People in those areas complain about the worsening salinity of their drinking and irrigation water. Residents of Aden itself used to rely on water flowing directly from the taps. That is no longer the case. Over the past two decades domestic water tanks have become essential household infrastructure, installed in the street near their homes, on balconies, or basically anywhere, and carefully locked.

Domestic water in rural areas comes from shallow wells, springs and irrigation networks. Most families get their water from relatively nearby sources, and it is collected by women and children, though also occasionally by men. The 20-litre jerry cans are then loaded on their donkeys or carried on women's heads to their homes, an exhausting and time-consuming task. Water collection can take many hours daily.

Water Management Policies: Who Benefits?

State water management policies since 1990 have been characterised primarily by their absence or, at best, weakness, in addressing this life and death problem.[9] They started in the early 1990s with an exclusive focus on increasing mechanisms to extract water for irrigation without any consideration for long-term sustainability. On the contrary, subsidies to

Water in Taiz: An Extreme Case, or Foretaste of the Future?

International media focus their attention on the prospect of Sana'a being the first capital city in the world to run out of water, but Taiz is far ahead with respect to suffering a desperate crisis. Taiz is in the southern uplands area of ground-water scarcity. Although its rainfall is relatively high, water is not stored in the ground within the city or its immediate neighbourhood due to its geology and inclination. With its high population density and rapid population growth over the past half-century, its water supply situation has systematically worsened, despite a number of projects designed to solve the problem. By the mid-1990s, the 40 percent or so of households connected to the urban network in Taiz received water once every forty days. Thanks to projects implemented at that time, this gradually increased to once every fifteen days in the early 2000s[5] only to drop back to once every fifty to sixty days in the second decade.[6] The majority of people in Taiz get most or all their domestic water from water tankers and much of it is recycled waste water which has not been adequately purified. It is universally agreed that Taiz water is undrinkable, hence people have to buy drinking water separately. The average price of water in 2013 ranged from US $0.9 /m³ for water from the urban supply to US $4.5/m³ for tanker supplied water and US $23/m³ for purified drinking water.[7] The above figures are indicative as cost varies according to seasonality, availability of publicly supplied water, and rainfall, let alone fuel for pumps and transport. Households were spending an average of YR 4,500 per month on water, representing 5 percent to 15 percent of their income, with the poor spending as much as 20 percent of household income on water. Given that low- and medium-level civil servants earn about YR 25,000 per month, the importance of their spending on water reflects clearly on people's ability to cope and their desperate need for this essential utility.

The Taiz water crisis also illustrates an important aspect of rural-urban relations, that of potential conflict. From the mid-1970s onwards, the search for a water source to supply the city expanded into the neighbouring rural areas and the first area to be exploited was al-Haima in the late 1970s. The limited compensation to farmers for the loss of their main income, agriculture, was appropriated by the local shaykh and, by the end of the 1980s, the farmers had lost their livelihoods as their shallow wells had dried up and their crops died. Their frustration and anger were ignored, largely because the tribal groups in that region are weak and isolated, as they are not members of larger, more powerful tribal confederations, as is the case further north. Their impoverishment forced many to become casual labourers in Taiz and beyond.

The lesson was not lost on their neighbours. Attempts at drilling in Wadi Warazan in 1995 were abandoned thanks to strong resistance by local tribesmen. The area immediately adjacent to al-Haima, Habeer was the next target. Unlike Warazan, it turned out that much of the land in that area was state land as it had been nationalised in the nineteenth century by the Imam because local people had refused to pay their taxes. The track from Habeer to Taiz goes through al-Haima, so the people of Habeer were well aware of what had happened to their neighbours whose water had been taken to supply the city without compensation, and who had become destitute as a result. The people of Habeer resisted these plans, and armed confrontations took place with security forces.

To address the issue, in the mid-1990s, the World Bank and government initiated a project which would include 'compensatory'* development initiatives for the communities whose water would be

---

* The word 'compensation' was taboo as government wanted to avoid at all costs the suggestion that it might have responsibility to compensate populations for any of its interventions.

transferred to Taiz. The project included a participatory and consultative process with the population affected, involving them in the selection of development activities as well as the design of domestic water supply mechanisms for their villages. This was also accompanied by unwelcome control mechanisms over their own use of irrigation water. The operation failed due to a combination of the use of military force against demonstrators opposing the project, as well as a change of management in the World Bank team where staff committed to the participatory community development approach were replaced by others whose sole concern was ensuring supply to Taiz city. The wells were drilled by force in 1997–8, though local action ensured that the amount of water reaching Taiz city was substantially below plans.

By the turn of the century the populations of Habeer and Haima were still demonstrating and tension remained high. Meanwhile in Taiz, the water distribution interval had risen to over fifty days, the quality of the water had dropped even further reaching EC of 5,000 uS/cm (way higher than WHO standards of EC 1,500 uS/cm) and the population was increasingly reliant on low quality water trucked in at high expense from wells mainly to the south-west of Taiz city, in Wadi Dhabab; the cost of that water had risen to over YR 1,000 per m^3.[8]

Taiz city can no longer rely on extracting water from neighbouring areas for domestic consumption. Water trucked in can only satisfy minimal needs. Taiz is also one of Yemen's two main industrial areas. The Hayl Saeed Anaam Ltd conglomerate owns most industries in the area and built a desalination plant near Mokha to supply its factories and provide some water for Taiz city. The government of Yemen negotiated with Saudi Arabia to build a new desalination plant and a pipeline to supply the city's domestic needs. By the time the current war started in 2015, these plans had not moved beyond the planning stage. Sadly, even the conglomerate's desalination plant, the only one in all of Yemen, was destroyed by bombings in November 2016 and most of its factories are at best only partly operational.

import equipment and supply cheap diesel encouraged farmers to expand their irrigation and grow thirsty crops, ranging from qat in the highlands to mangoes and bananas on the coastal plains. However, by the end of the century, the need for conservation had become inescapable and new strategies were devised. Most were elaborated with the active participation of the three main funding agencies working in the sector (the World Bank and the German and Netherlands governments), though their impact was limited by largely ineffectual state decisions. The first of these was the establishment of the National Water Resources Authority in 1995, followed by the passage of the Water Law in 2002, and the creation of the Ministry of Water and the Environment in 2003. The ministry was made toothless within weeks of its establishment when responsibility for irrigation water was returned to the Ministry of Agriculture and Irrigation by presidential decree.

The middle of that decade saw a consultative process involving the administrative and management elites concerned with water and the main financiers; it produced the National Water Sector Strategy and Investment Programme (NWSSIP)[10] in 2005. This initiative was updated three years later, and the final event prior to the 2011 crisis was the Presidential National Conference on Management and Development of Water Resources in Yemen in January 2011. Its Sana'a Declaration on the Yemeni Water Partnership includes worthy aims but largely unrealistic strategies. Events overtook it and it has remained a dead letter ever since.

An effective strategy to address this fundamental challenge to the country's very existence is fairly straightforward. In order for people to be able to continue living in the area, priority has to be given to human needs for drinking and personal hygiene, followed by those of livestock. As 90 percent of Yemen's water is used for agriculture, reducing this demand substantially would ensure that the people's needs could be supplied adequately for generations to come. It would even enable the establishment of more industries should other conditions be favourable. So why has this not happened? Removing water management from the control of the large rural landowners, who are over-exploiting the resource for irrigation of high value and other crops, would require challenging a group of powerful individuals whose support Saleh needed to remain in power. Hence all efforts at water conservation were deliberately undermined to ensure that this group could continue and increase its use of the scarce resource at the expense of the future of all other Yemenis.

While Saleh can be blamed for giving priority to his powerful supporters at the expense of the population as a whole, he is not alone in sharing responsibility. Despite much rhetoric on their part, external financiers prioritised their international neo-liberal agenda which emphasised the development of high-value export crops at the expense of local food security and the living conditions of the majority. Agricultural development investments focused on more efficient irrigation mechanisms; the subsidies on offer were accessible primarily to the rich who thus further profited. The development agencies neglected the crops of the poor, and particularly rain-fed staple crops, as there has been no serious research in this area. This is discussed further in the next chapter.

With respect to domestic water, there is no doubt about the value of the various small town projects linked to the construction of sewerage systems, mostly financed by Germany. By contrast, the General Authority for Rural Water Supply Projects (GARWSP) remained a prime example of a model which should not be followed. Equipped with pumps and other technology provided by the Netherlands, its modus operandi in rural areas led to an extremely high failure rate, because little or no attention was given to the complexities of local level social structures and political power. As a result, well over half its projects failed either immediately on construction or shortly thereafter; let alone those which were never completed, with wells without pumps or pumps without wells.

Given the severity of the nation's overall water shortage, the surprise it that desalination has barely featured in Yemeni plans for water management. The only desalination item in the 2005 NWSSIP is a mere US $500,000 allocated for studies of desalination, solar and wind energy! Other than the above-mentioned project to supply Taiz, there are no plans.[11] This despite the fact that desalination of water for domestic purposes is clearly essential if people are to continue living in Yemen later this century, and is the main solution for water supply to all coastal areas, including the country's main cities of Hodeida and Aden. And while still expensive, costs have dropped considerably and technologies have improved. As for Sana'a, the real problem is the cost of pumping the water two kilometres in altitude over two chains of mountains, rendering desalination an unrealistic option.

The water situation presents an existential threat for Yemen as a populated area. Unless it is given urgent and serious attention, within a generation only parts of the country will be inhabitable. What will happen to the majority of the population in areas without water? To date, state action can be described as short-termist, completely ineffectual and responsible for the worsening of the problem by encouraging mining of non-renewable aquifers for the immediate profit of those in least need at the expense of the survival of the majority. Remedial policies are feasible but demand strong and effective central and local governance to ensure the best possible use of the limited resource. This means transferring use from agriculture to domestic and livestock needs in exploitation of limited aquifers, and restructuring agricultural use to maximise income from rain-fed agriculture while limiting irrigation to be supplementary and exclusively on high-value crops. The years of war have made no fundamental change to this problem.

Other Symptoms of Climate Change

Yemen is located on the edge of the monsoon zone, and its rainy seasons throughout the western highlands (the only areas with regular rainfall) are determined by seasonal downpours. However, climate change has disturbed the earlier predictability of rainfall, and thus accelerated the depletion rate of aquifers. The replenishment to rainfall ratio is going down just when the need and demand for water is increasing as a result of population growth and improved hygiene demands. Whereas the rainy seasons used to be relatively well defined, falling in March-April and July-August, recent decades have seen significant changes with far more unpredictability in both timing and intensity. Given that over 60 percent of Yemen's agriculture is still rain-fed, the unpredictability of rains has a major impact on rural people's livelihoods. More violent and sudden downpours damage crops, wash away top soil, and do not allow sufficient time for water to penetrate the soil and be absorbed in the aquifer. Only 3 percent of the country's surface is suitable for agricultural use, including pasture land. Hence the impact of climate change presents a further problem: with increasing periods of drought, good top soil is also blown away by the wind. With violent storms the banks of wadis are swept away, wadis widen and agricultural land is lost, homes and infrastructure destroyed.

Desertification, too, is a growing problem associated with climate change. This phenomenon particularly affects the areas which lie closest to the existing deserts. It is estimated that 3-5 percent of agricultural land is lost annually in this way.[12] Today's archaeological sites in the deserts (Mareb, Shabwa and al-Jawf) provide evidence that many centuries ago they were irrigated agricultural areas and trading cities. Since then, deserts have continued to expand, and increasing areas of the governorates bordering the Rubʿ al-Khali Desert are first transferred from cultivation to range land and eventually become completely desertified areas. This is particularly noticeable in the governorates of al-Jawf, Mareb, Shabwa, Hadramaut and al-Mahra.

The year 2015 will be remembered in Yemen not only for the start of the war but also as a unique one climatically. In addition to all its other problems, the country suffered not one, but two unprecedented and extremely violent cyclones in November: Chapala and Megh. Chapala brought hurricane-force winds of over 120 km/h, and 610 mm of rain in forty-eight hours, seven times the annual average. The cyclone displaced some 45,000 people, causing massive destruction mostly on the ecologically unique Socotra island and in Hadramaut and Shabwa Governorates. Less than two weeks later, after causing further destruction in Socotra, Megh weakened but went on to hit western parts of the mainland and even reached the highlands in Ibb Governorate. Such events have been exceptional up to now. However, they are likely to become more frequent and indicate that climate change is not a problem for the remote future but is with us today.

In the long run, the expected rise in sea levels is likely to destroy many coastal fishing villages and to threaten coastal cities which have built sea-front housing and other infrastructure. Three of Yemen's major cities (Hodeida, Aden and Mukalla) lie on the coast and their populations are increasing rapidly, especially as they swell with the relocation of villagers from mountainous areas which have run out of water. Mitigating this situation requires considerable planning, as well as investment, which should start immediately to ensure not only improved domestic water, but also a new climate-sensitive infrastructure. Coastal livelihoods, urban and rural, need highly innovative strategies for their sustainability.

Oil and Gas: New Opportunities for Kleptocrats

Who Controls Oil and Gas?

Yemen is not completely lacking in productive income generating natural resources. Oil is extracted by international companies, according to fairly standard agreements which provide the Yemeni state with royalties. Although oil has provided most state income since unification, much of it has been under the direct control of Saleh and has not entered into the national budgets. However, by comparison with the situation elsewhere in the Peninsula, even in Oman, Yemen's oil production and reserves are negligible. At peak production in 2001, output was 441,000 barrels/day, gradually dropping ever since to under 280,000 in 2010, with a further precipitous decline in the following years, to 131,000 b/d in 2013[13] and close to zero in 2016. By comparison Saudi Arabia, with a comparable total population, extracts about 10 million barrels/day.

Oil's contribution to GDP was just under 26 percent in 1990, four years after first exports, and rose to its highest level of 41 percent in 2005, when production was already dropping but international price rises compensated. Price fluctuations have, when high, concealed the fundamental problem of decreasing production after 2005. Even local consumption depends on imports, though production and exports restarted on a small scale in 2017. It is not clear when oil will completely run out, though most estimate this to be within the current decade. So while production could recover to about 180,000 b/d on a temporary basis, reserves are almost exhausted. The discovery of new fields is not entirely impossible, but the thoroughness of exploration to date suggests that this is unlikely. Therefore Yemen's future will have to be built on other raw materials.

Both the regime and the people hoped that oil income would be replaced by that of gas after significant discoveries were made in Mareb Governorate. Proven reserves were 9.15 trillion cubic feet (TCF) of which 1TCF was to be reserved for domestic consumption and the rest made available for export. Gas resources are managed by a single company, Yemen LNG, the largest foreign investment in Yemen. It is jointly owned by French Total (39.62 percent), Hunt oil (17.22 percent), Yemen Gas Company (16.73 percent), SK Corporation of South Korea (9.55 percent), two other Korean companies owning under 12 percent between them, and Yemen's Social

Security and Pension Fund with 5 percent.[14] Yemen LNG exports the gas through the dedicated port of Balhaf, with the first cargo departing on 7 November 2009. Investment in port and pipeline infrastructure amounted to US $4 billion.[15] The company has three long-term sale contracts with GDF-Suez, the Korean company Kogas and Total.

Prior to the crisis, let alone the war, expected income from gas exports was estimated to 'total little more than USD 250-300 million a year in the period 2010-2015 ... not enough to cover the fall in revenues associated with lower oil output.'[16] Moreover, accusations of mismanagement and high levels of corruption have focused on the contract between the Total-led Yemen LNG and the government. In addition to the unfavourable contract with Total, quantities of gas may also have been exported unofficially, and unrecorded, to the benefit of certain individuals. Regardless of the underhand deals in agreeing the original contract, irregularities in its implementation, or the motivation for the post-Saleh transitional regime to challenge the contracts, the simple reality is that in the second decade of the twenty-first century, the Yemeni state is in a weak position to renegotiate. Making matters worse, there is currently little demand for gas on the world market as supply is more than adequate. One measure which would have a positive environmental impact, among other benefits, would be to build more gas-operated power stations. Certainly the need for greater electricity availability is recognised by all Yemenis, who experience either no electricity at all, or frequent and very lengthy power cuts.

The contract with Kogas provides a clear example of price manipulation which ensured profits for the company and those involved in the contract at the expense of the Yemeni nation. 'In 2010, Korea Gas paid a fixed price of $3.2 per 1 million BTUs (British Thermal Units), which meant it paid about $193 per ton for Yemeni gas, compared to an average of $689 per ton the company paid for Qatari gas. An analyst who works closely on corruption within the Yemeni resources sector argues that if the YLNG contracts met international standards, the country would make an additional one-third of its annual budget each year.'[17] The transitional regime managed to renegotiate the selling price to Kogas five years after it came into force as permitted by the original contract and the government 'achieved a significant increase in the amount the firm paid for its gas'.[18] Attempts by government to renegotiate with Total, during the period when the original contract was still in force, were not successful. Since then, of course, the export facility has closed, on 14 April 2015, declaring force majeure because of the war situation.[19] There have been a number of attacks on the pipeline, but it could be restored to operational order reasonably easily as none of these raids have hit vital equipment. This would allow a fairly rapid return to production and exports once the military situation has been solved.

Fuel Smuggling: How and Why Saleh's Associates Are Benefiting from Subsidies

Diesel subsidies have been a major drain on the state's budget, taking 34 percent of total government expenditure in 2008, dropping to 22 percent in 2009, and constituting the largest single item in both years.[20] The main beneficiaries have been a few people who smuggled diesel across the Red Sea where it was sold at world prices for vast profits. As neatly put by Phillips, 'the Yemeni government buys its diesel at international market rates and then subsidizes it for sale on the local market. Large quantities of the subsidized diesel is then smuggled back out of the country to be re-sold at international market rates by regime cronies for personal profits.'[21] In 2009, a smuggler could buy subsidised diesel for US $25/barrel and sell it for US $300/barrel at sea.[22] One indication of the extent of localised smuggling emerged in 2005, when a single coastal district in Taiz Governorate, Mokha, had a monthly allocation of 5.3 million litres of diesel, but the four governorates of Aden, Lahej, Abyan and al-Dhala' had between them only 7 million litres. Just to emphasise the point, note that Mokha district had a total population in 2004 of 63,960, and the governorates listed had over 2.2 million people, giving an inhabitant of Mokha district 83 litres per month of diesel while citizens of these other governorates each got 3 litres per month.

Diesel smuggling from Yemen to the Horn of Africa provoked considerable public concern for decades. The Bretton Woods institutions have tried to influence government policy, arguing that subsidies do not benefit the poor, and that directly targeted poverty alleviation measures are more effective. Moreover, in the Yemeni case, they also argued that cutting diesel subsidies would save precious water by increasing the cost of irrigation and thus reducing water usage for agricultural production. The main problem of these subsidies is the fact that the beneficiaries are a small group of influential smugglers, most of whom are part of the closest circle of Saleh associates. This is one reason the proposed IMF solution has systematically failed. Contrary to the IMF's position, the poor do benefit from fuel subsidies as most of the population depends on diesel for drinking water, for the transport of basic commodities, and indeed for much of the country's electricity, including both major power stations and small-scale village level generators. The problem of 'elite capture' of the subsidised fuel could have been addressed more effectively with alternative policies. Unsurprisingly, policies intended to reduce water use by increasing the price of diesel failed: the ingenious and well-informed Yemeni farmers promptly demanded electric pumps and, when electricity became scarce, they are now great enthusiasts of solar pumping.

Without the petroleum subsidy the poverty rate would have been roughly 2.5 percent higher (3.6 percent in urban areas and 1.5 percent in rural areas). Subsidies represent 1.9 percent of the total household consumption for the poorest decile section of the population, versus 0.9 percent for the wealthiest decile.[23] When taking into account indirect effects, without subsidies, the poverty rate would be 8.2 percent higher (6.6 percent urban, 8.9 percent rural). Thus, prior to the crisis, petroleum subsidies were keeping roughly 1.5 million people from slipping into poverty, and therefore they had a significant poverty reduction impact.[24] The problem is thus not the subsidies themselves, but rather the mismanagement of diesel distribution.

At the instigation of, and mainly under pressure from, the IMF and World Bank, governments have increased diesel prices more than once, though they still remained way below world market prices. On each occasion (1996, 1998, 2005), an initially substantial price rise led to strong and sometimes violent demonstrations in Yemeni cities, in which ordinary people protested against this fanning of inflation and higher prices. Each time they were repressed, blood was shed, and people were killed. A day or two later the president would intervene and announce a reduction which would leave the actual new price higher than it had been prior to the change. The result: people went home (except for those who had been killed), the IMF had achieved some price increase, and it looked as if the government was trying to comply with its demands. The demonstrations also showed the unpopularity of such moves, Saleh looked good as he had helped reduce the impact on his subjects, and the smugglers among his entourage were happy as, despite slightly lower profits, they were still raking it in without much effort.

Since 2011, smuggling of diesel out of Yemen has more or less disappeared due to overall shortages. The Huthis gained much popular support in August 2014 when President Hadi bowed to IMF pressure and increased diesel prices, though he did it suddenly rather than following the procedures recommended by the World Bank. The Huthis brought thousands of people onto the streets protesting the move and this support from civil society helped them take control of Sana'a without firing a shot. A few months later, they 'freed' fuel prices and these rose dramatically to reach unprecedented heights, making the former black market prices look reasonable by comparison. In a flash, public backing for the Huthis atrophied. Since the war started, the old smuggling networks are back in action, focusing on imports rather than exports of fuel, weapons and all manner of goods.

Several analyses have revealed corruption in oil sector contracts, including 'claiming subsidies on non-existent fuel imports, on the basis of falsified import documents ... YECO [Yemen Economic Corporation]* was among the key beneficiaries of this system. Oil-related corruption was also endemic in the military, with officers benefiting directly from fuel allocated to their units and using military transport infrastructure to move it both within Yemen and to foreign markets.'[25] In 2009, it was 'estimated that about a third of the budget of fuel subsidies, around USD 3 billion, that year, went to diesel smuggling networks.'[26] Corruption is discussed further in the next chapter.

---

*   The Yemen Economic Corporation started life as the Yemen Military Economic Corporation, founded in 1975 by the Hamdi regime in the YAR to provide military cadres with access to cheap subsidised basic food and other commodities. Under Saleh it was turned into a major element of the patronage structure and acquired massive assets, including land, real estate and a range of monopolistic import licences. It became the largest economic enterprise in the country and a major mechanism to enrich Saleh and his closest associates, by producing and selling goods to the population at large. In 1993, under the influence of the IMF's privatisation programme, its name was changed to the Yemen Economic Corporation, but its ownership structure remained unchanged and it officially belongs to the Ministry of Defence with a minor shareholding from the Ministry of the Interior.

Other Economic Resources

In addition to the labour force, which should be seen as a key national asset and is discussed in Chapter 9, Yemen has mineral resources which could be exploited, ranging from stones for construction to valuable metals like zinc, gold and silver. No commercial exploitation had started by 2011 when the country's political crisis interrupted any foreign investment plans. Exploitation of these resources may contribute to future development. Although employment in mining is usually tough and low-paid for the majority, it cannot be ignored as Yemen lacks a 'magic bullet' resource which would provide an easy solution to its problems.

Yemen's main potential resources for future development are its wonderful landscapes, coast, architecture and archaeological wealth. All these could provide the basis for the development of an important and lucrative tourism sector. Of course, this potential could also be ruined by resorts, either high class and expensive for the very few or indeed cheap and nasty for the many. Nonetheless, well-managed tourism could create thousands of jobs and encourage deeper knowledge of Yemen's rich culture. The sector was in its infancy in the 1990s when it was prevented from fully emerging by the rise of kidnappings and later that of attacks by jihadi organisations. Tourism is an economic activity which can be highly labour intensive as well as culturally sensitive. It can be the source of cultural exchanges profitable to both visitors and service providers. Its future will depend on the care and protection given to the country's cultural resources during the war as indiscriminate military strikes as well as smuggling of archaeological finds would seriously threaten this option. It will also require wise development policies – in other words, better governance.

The Future

When the war ends, whoever is in control of the country will have to address the fundamental issue of enabling the population to survive and, ideally, to prosper. As is clear from the above, the first issue will be that of water. Any new regime must ensure that water is used sustainably throughout the country, which simply means reducing agricultural use very considerably and transferring water to the domestic sector as a priority, followed by livestock use, and then possibly industrial use. It also entails eliminating the use of ground-water pumping for agriculture, except possibly in Hadramaut where the Umm al-Rudhuma aquifer may be able to provide water for Hadramaut and al-Mahra as well as parts of Shabwa. Irrigation will have to be limited to spate systems accompanied by firm support for any mechanism which can contribute to the replenishment of water tables, ranging from the rehabilitation of terraces, to breakwaters and other structures which slow down flows resulting from violent downpours. This would enable both human and animal populations to live.

Rain-fed agriculture also needs to be further developed, in two ways. First, through introducing improved drought-resistant crop varieties. And second, by developing high-value crops that demand little water. Both these measures would enable rural households to earn adequate incomes. In addition, the potential for desalination has to be harnessed to boost the supply of water to coastal areas – primarily for domestic and industrial purposes. While gas revenues will hopefully make a significant contribution to national income, this will take time and in any case will generate revenue primarily for the state, not directly to the people themselves. It will not provide much employment, so its income should be used to support massive investment in social sectors, primarily education, which is essential to enable the population to participate in new economic activities which are less demanding of the country's limited physical resources.

For its part, climate change is a recognised phenomenon worldwide whose negative local impact is likely to be worse in Yemen than elsewhere. The World Bank has foreseen three main scenarios for Yemen, the most likely being 'hot and dry' and 'warm and wet'. Regardless of which actually materialises, 'Yemen will be getting warmer, most likely at a faster rate than the global average ... there will be more variability of rainfall patterns within years [and] there will probably be an increased frequency of intense rainfall events and therefore possibly an increased risk of floods.'[27] Regardless of the details, there is no doubt that Yemen will have to address grave issues relating to climate change: rising sea levels, water shortage and limited extractive industries resources. All these issues will persist, regardless of the nature of any political settlement, or the ravages of war. The next chapter looks at implemented economic and development policies which have, sadly, prevented Yemen's population from deriving maximum benefit from the country's natural resources.

CHAPTER NINE

The Economy

Neo-Liberal Policies and Worsening Poverty

Yemeni cities over the decades gave a vivid illustration of the worsening gap between the small wealthy elite and the increasing number of destitute people. In the early 1990s, there were a few beggars at traffic lights and most people travelled by bus or in crowded four-wheel drives. By 2010, people could buy more or less anything portable while waiting for the lights to change: not just newspapers, books and cassettes, but household equipment, clothes, cleaning tools and more. Dozens of hawkers walked along the queues of mini-buses, cars and other vehicles including the latest model fancy expensive 'tape à l'oeil' motors driven by the young – sometimes even underage – sons of the super wealthy. By then sellers were not only low-status akhdam *but also impoverished tribes men, women and children, reduced to such demeaning activities by desperation.*

However bad and deteriorating the situation may have been in the first two decades of the Republic of Yemen, there is no doubt that the decade starting in 2011 has seen a dramatic worsening. The country's economic prospects were dealt a sharp and deep blow within months of the establishment of the state in 1990, when Sana'a's reaction to the Iraqi invasion of Kuwait led to Yemen's isolation. External financial support from all sources was reduced to almost nothing and the return of more than 800,000 Yemenis from the GCC states (Saudi Arabia in particular) instantly eliminated the remittances on which their households depended. In addition, the state had to take responsibility for these people, many of whom returned destitute. They had been away for generations, hence had nowhere to return to. Before the economy could recover, political tensions led to the 1994 civil war which caused considerable destruction in Aden and was a further blow to economic prospects, because of both the cost of reconstruction and an increasing lack of confidence among potential foreign investors. The Aden Free Zone, established in early 1991, never really took off, and the city's status as economic capital was little more than a propaganda ploy.

Instead of entering the era of prosperity Yemenis were hoping for, the new state lurched from one crisis to another, culminating in the full-scale war starting in early 2015. Its weak economic base deteriorated due to the rapacious policies of the ruling clique combined with government implementation of Washington Consensus 'development' strategies and very limited external financial support. It finally collapsed with Yemen's transformation into a war economy, marked by continued predation. Poverty rates, which were already officially high, have rocketed. Yemen's limited natural resources and rapid population growth are partly responsible for worsening poverty since unification, and the political situation has intensified an already bad situation. Neo-liberal economic policies promoted by the IMF, and slavishly followed by most bilateral financiers, have combined with regime complacency to increase poverty and cause long-term social and economic damage through neglect of the fundamental issues, as will be demonstrated in this chapter. Figures provided here should be regarded as indicative of situations and trends, rather than as absolute accurate facts.

Pre-Unification: How Different Were the Two Regimes?

Much has been said about the fundamentally different orientations of the PDRY and YAR regimes, yet their actual economies were more similar than widely believed. Most of the population of both states were rural and depended on a combination of remittances and agriculture. Both states had substantial public sectors, and oil discoveries and production only started in the late 1980s, shortly before unification. The private sector developed in both states, even though the respective governments approached it in decidedly different ways: the YAR had a more laissez faire approach and a pro-private ideology, while the socialist PDRY regime's official rhetoric discouraged the private sector, though in practice it encouraged it to operate with greater ease. Manufacturing was weak in both states, and mainly involved food processing using imported raw materials. Again, despite official claims, there were more similarities in agriculture than is claimed: certainly there were more state farms and cooperatives in the PDRY but they also existed in the YAR, while the PDRY still had a significant percentage of small-scale private farms, and most livestock remained privately owned.

Social sectors were stronger in the PDRY where the ruling powers established functioning and close to universally accessible medical care and schools. Post-secondary education also spread to most Southern governorates and the PDRY even boasted a good medical school. Teachers in the PDRY were almost all Yemenis, while in the YAR Egyptian and Sudanese Salafis taught in the remotest parts of the highlands. Girls' education in the YAR was way behind the situation in the PDRY. School attendance at primary and secondary levels was considerably higher in the PDRY and, most importantly, the school syllabi differed, with a more secular orientation and a greater focus on modern science in the PDRY, by contrast with greater emphasis on Islamic studies in the YAR.

Both states had five-year-plans intended to direct their development and, again regardless of ideology, the PDRY also depended considerably on IMF/World Bank support, particularly as it had far less access to bilateral aid. Indeed, while the YAR obtained bilateral aid from both East and West during the Cold War, the PDRY's bilateral aid was almost exclusively from the socialist Eastern Bloc. Both states also suffered a number of natural disasters which set back people's living standards.

Emigration was particularly crucial in supporting the economies in the 1970s and 1980s. While in the YAR this meant a comparatively wealthy population and a poor state with little control over its economy, in the PDRY remittances provided supplementary income to a population which had access to social services and basic salaries. For example, remittances were expected to cover over 47 percent of financing for the YAR's Second Five Year Plan (SFYP).[1] Remittances obviously implied the migration of labour, with negative as well as positive implications. One reason the PDRY regime attempted to restrict emigration throughout the 1980s was the impact it had on the labour force. In the 1980s about 30 percent of the YAR labour force was out of the country and their remittances peaked at over 70 percent of foreign exchange receipts in both YAR and PDRY.[2] In the PDRY in 1988, out of a total of 2.345 million people, 238,150, or 10.15 percent of the total population, were abroad.[3]

The mid-1980s saw a drop in remittances as demand for Yemeni labour in the GCC states reduced greatly as a result of two main factors: first, lower oil prices reduced demand for labour; and second, these states were replacing Arab labour with south-east Asian workers. The latter arrived on restrictive contractual arrangements and were perceived as less of a threat to the existing social order. The drop in remittances was accompanied by reduced assistance grants from these states to Yemen, leading to worsening deficits and international debt.

Unification was the alternative to the outbreak of another war between the two states at a time when both were politically weak: the immediate incentive was the discovery of oil in an area which was contested between the two states and Saudi Arabia. Either the Yemeni states agreed on its exploitation or, more likely than not, they would both lose it to the benefit of Saudi Arabia. Unification of the two economies was less of a problem than that of the political systems, although the act of uniting created an opportunity for regime predators to grab state-owned productive assets, including agricultural and other land in the former PDRY.

The 1990s: Economic Crisis, Development Plans and Structural Adjustment

At unification, Yemen had a total population of 13 million people.[4] The first years of the ROY were economic disasters, with GDP dropping continuously. According to the Ministry of Planning,[5] each year between 1990 and 1995 experienced negative growth, totalling 1.3 percent for the period; but among analysts, Gerd Nonneman, of Exeter University, found that this masked a 7 percent contraction in non-oil GDP.[6] Balance of payments data indicate the gap between exports, mainly of oil, after 1987 and income from aid. Meanwhile food remained the main source of import expenditure, at US $600 million in 1991. Despite oil exports, the balance remained negative throughout these years, with a deficit ranging from US $250 million in 1990, to US $1,700 million in 1994.[7] In the face of a crisis with no obvious solutions, the regime strategy in the early years of unification was to continue both states' previous policy of combining restriction of imports with a desperate search for increased oil reserves, while boosting production to increase income.[8]

Per capita annual external assistance to Yemen in the late 1980s/ early 1990s was significantly below that of other low-income countries: as this period includes both the pre-1990 period when aid flows were significant, and two years after the recovery started in 1995, this can be considered representative of the overall situation: between 1987 and 1996, Yemen received US $23.90 per capita by comparison with comparator countries which received US $49.11.[9] Between 1990 and 1995, the Bretton Woods institutions were largely absent. The rationale for their lack of involvement included the 1990 crisis, and post-unification political instability between 1991 and 1994. By 1995 the regime in Sana'a was actively interested in re-establishing good relations with the international community to restore its access to financial support. By that time it had been partly 'forgiven' its anti-US position in the Iraq-Kuwait issue.

Restoration of Relations with International Financial Institutions

The first sign of reconciliation between Yemen and international funders was the signature of the Economic, Financial and Administration Reform Programme (EFARP) with the IMF in early 1995. This was followed in 1996 by the World Bank's Country Assistance Strategy, which was characterised by a standard neo-liberal structural adjustment package with the following three objectives:

- Stabilisation, structural adjustment and social protection measures
- Sustainable natural and human resource development
- Improved implementation of the World Bank portfolio of projects.[10]

Unsurprisingly, it proposed to improve the economic situation by complementing oil income with 'the development of a vibrant private non-oil sector needed to provide adequate employment opportunities and diversify exports away from oil. Finally, future growth will need to be increasingly financed from domestic savings, supplemented by foreign capital investments.'[11] Rather than poverty or inequality, it considered that 'the most pressing challenge facing the authorities is the reduction of the fiscal imbalance and the resulting inflationary pressures.'[12] Stabilisation was to be achieved through trade reform, privatisation of public enterprises, and reduction in public sector staffing. Sustainable development would be supported by sector work and 'policy dialogue to protect the Government's budgetary allocations to education and health'.[13] Better performance of the portfolio of World Bank loans was to be achieved through the introduction of more effective supervision mechanisms, including the opening of what started as a modest World Bank Resident Mission in Sana'a.

An evaluation carried out in 2001 reinforced the neo-liberal message: it complained of 'the relatively low priority given to removing constraints to private sector development, a priority for Yemen's future'[14] and that it had ignored the issue of the narcotic qat.[15] It also reflected the extent to which the Bank considers itself to be decider, rather than adviser: the Evaluation Division 'thinks that sector work in the last several years has served to move the dialogue and reforms in the right direction'.[16] While the report admitted that the neo-liberal formula was unpopular, it blamed this on an inadequate communication strategy, rather than the nature of the reforms: 'riots erupted in 1998 protesting the removal of subsidies on basic goods, such as fuel and wheat products. Thus, in spite of concurrent IDA[17] assistance to mitigate their impact, the reforms have been extremely unpopular which will make it difficult to introduce further budgetary restraint in the future.'[18]

The Twenty-First Century Neo-Liberal Economic Visions and Poverty Reduction

The first decade of the twenty-first century was characterised by two parallel processes. First was deepening official government conformity with funder-encouraged structural adjustment policies; and second were increasing budgetary problems (due to reduced revenues from oil exports) restricted the regime's ability to maintain its patronage system at the level necessary to retain popular support. Numerous over-optimistic official documents were produced, only to be described as 'over-ambitious' by the following one. They appear to have been based on public relations visions bearing little relationship to real daily life for Yemenis.

A prime example was the Vision 2025 document produced early in the decade.[19] It proposed to raise Yemen to the rank of middle human development countries by its deadline, an ambition which required a minimum 9 percent annual growth rate of GDP. This was to be achieved by industrialisation, oil and gas, fisheries, tourism, export-oriented production, development of an economy based on innovation and scientific research, achieving a mature democracy and reducing illiteracy to less than 10 percent of the population. Even at the turn of the century, the likelihood of tourism taking off or of basing economic development on export of agricultural production were highly unrealistic strategies, given the rise of insecurity and the ridiculous suggestion to basically export water* in the second. Economic growth never exceeded 7 percent. Reading the document, one can well imagine it emerging late in a social meeting where the participants had consumed considerable quantities of high quality qat.

Other strategy documents from that decade include the Poverty Reduction Strategy Paper (PRSP), a requirement by the IMF and World Bank to enable poor states to benefit from a debt relief initiative and continued access to IDA loans. In the case of Yemen, given that the paper was supposed to be directed by the country (rather than, as in reality, by the IMF and WB), national staff used the opportunity to criticise the neo-liberal agenda. These Yemeni officials pointed out that the 1995 EFARP had caused a deterioration in living standards thanks to the decline in purchasing power of the riyal, and a rise in unemployment. With respect to the removal of subsidies on wheat, a basic staple of the Yemeni diet, the PRSP pointed out that 'the subsidies have ... served as a form of safeguard for maintaining real standards of living ... what makes matters worse, is that the withdrawal of the government from undertaking this role comes, in the light of the retraction of real wages and consumption, the rise in unemployment and the deterioration of the quality of public services – all of which serve, in essence, to fundamentally increase the severity of the effects of the EFARP on the limited income of the poor.'[20]

Regardless of government's success in including serious critical analysis, the programmatic elements of the PRSP follow the neo-liberal agenda to the letter. They emphasised economic stability through fiscal policy which prioritised deficit reduction, public expenditure curtailment, and reform

---

*   While not actually exporting water, the export of agricultural produce requiring considerable water for their cultivation is similar, and 'virtual water' is the term now used to discuss such activities. Concept elaborated by Tony Allen of SOAS and King's College, University of London.

of the taxation system to the advantage of the private sector. They further advocated maintaining a floating exchange rate, controlling growth in monetary supply, establishing capital markets, liberalising trade, joining the World Trade Organisation (WTO), creating a conducive environment for private sector investment, and correcting distorted markets.[21] The PRSP and the Second Five Year Plan (SFYP) were prepared jointly and had four axes: economic growth, human resources development, improving infrastructure, and ensuring social protection.[22] The plan was yet another opportunity for unrealistic ambitions: instead of the projected target of 5.6 percent annual growth, it achieved 4.1 percent;[23] customs duties fell by 3.7 percent whereas they had been predicted to rise by the same percentage.[24] Contrary to intentions, public revenues increased at 14 percent per annum while public expenditures grew by 18.9 percent, thus turning a government budget/GDP surplus of 6.1 percent in 2000 into a 2.3 percent deficit in 2005.[25]

The next plan, the Socio-Economic Development Plan for Poverty Reduction 2006-10, became known as the DPPR. It did not signal any significant policy change; and its over-ambitious objectives were watered down in 2009 when a Mid-Term Review (MTR) was carried out as part of the follow-up to the 2006 London Consultative Meeting with external funding agencies. The MTR noted the many negative phenomena in the previous three years, including increasingly frequent terrorist attacks and unrest which had reduced investment and tourism, internal conflict in Sa'ada, the food crisis resulting from world price rises, as well as severe flooding in the east and the ongoing influx of refugees from Africa. The revised policies for the remaining period of the plan had a stronger focus on continued trade liberalisation, including accession to the WTO and the search for private investment. In addition the MTR committed the plan to raising living standards, ensuring that the poor had an adequate share of national wealth, and making sure that poverty declined overall.[26]

The fourth Five Year Socio-Economic Development Plan for Poverty Reduction 2011-2015 was produced just as Yemen's political crisis blew up, and thus it was never implemented. It was even more closely linked to the World Bank's Country Assistance Strategy as their objectives and timing more or less coincided. It minimises constraints and difficulties while focusing on the usual scapegoats: the tribal system was blamed for limiting state authority, institutions were described as weak, corruption was considered rampant, and the conflict between new and old forces was seen as a relevant factor. Contrary to evidence, none of the problems were ever seen as the outcome of Bretton Woods institutions policies. A prime example was the systematic complaint about the weakness of state institutions, which ignored the fact that the World Bank contributed significantly to this through the Project Implementation Units it established for its flagship projects, the most blatant being the creation of a competing parastatal institution, the Social Fund for Development (SFD).

The Role of Foreign Financing

The impact of the IMF and World Bank's agenda goes well beyond their own financing. Most multilateral and bilateral financiers consider their endorsement as sufficient guarantee to co-finance projects with these institutions or alone, provided they are part of programmes the IFIs support. Development funds come to the state through its institutions; therefore a considerable share remains within the government sector (through salaries at all levels) as well as to major importers (for equipment, etc.). As a result, funding primarily benefits the government structure rather than the people at large. Moreover, the amounts disbursed in Yemen were remarkably small. So why were these neo-liberal policies accepted? In no small part it was probably due to the lack of alternative policies from the Yemeni leadership.

The following table shows the amount of development financing to Yemen since unification. Despite being lower than in the 1980s, actual amounts remained significant between 1990 and 1995, especially with respect to gross national income (GNI). In per capita terms, receipts were much less impressive, which clearly justified the description of Yemen as a 'donor orphan'.[27] One notable exception to the general rule was military assistance from the US: between 2006 and 2010 it rose from US $14 million to US $170 million.[28]

Aid Received by Yemen (1990–2014)

Year	Amount (US $ '000)	Net ODA percent GNI	Net ODA/ capita (US $ units)
1990	449,830	8.02	37.6
1991	296,350	5.17	23.6
1992	253,770	4	19.2
1993	313,180	5.9	22.4
1994	171,140	4.2	11.7
1995	171,230	4.2	11.2
2000	311,280	3.5	17.5
2005	296,530	1.9	14.4
2010	666,520	2.3	28.2
2011	476,240	1.6	19.6
2012	709,220	2.1	28.5
2013	1,039,000	2.7	40.7
2014	1,164,000	2.9	44.5

Source: World Bank Data Indicators, January 2017

The Yemen Consultative Group Meeting held in London in November 2006 was the first significant attempt at coordination between the different international financiers. This gathering pledged to increase financing, and promised US$4.7 billion for the following four years, including US$3.4 billion from the GCC states and their regional multilateral agencies. These amounts were earmarked for major infrastructure projects, including a motorway which would cut the country in two from the Saudi border to Aden. By the time the deadline expired, less than 10 percent of the pledged funds had been disbursed,[29] and each side blamed the other for the slow implementation. Over the following years, many financiers used this shortfall as an excuse to reduce commitments and support.

In January 2010, as a response to the 'underpants bomber' incident, the British government set up the Friends of Yemen (FOY). Britain saw FOY as primarily political, whereas for Yemenis it was perceived as a mechanism to increase aid financing. Its membership grew from twenty states to thirty-nine by 2013, when it described its role as 'to support the Government of Yemen's plans to address the broad range of challenges facing Yemen. There is a specific focus on supporting and monitoring progress on political, economic and security reform during the second phase of political transition ...'[30] The FOY held eight meetings until the end of 2014. Since the outbreak of full-scale war it has vanished from any discourse, even when meetings on reconstruction are held.

The main issue which would eventually lead to its fizzling out, other than the political disintegration which overtook it, was a fundamental difference of perspective between the UK and the GCC states. The former saw itself, alongside the US and the Bretton Woods institutions, as taking the lead on political and economic policy issues, while they expected the latter to finance the different investments, a position which could be described as neo-colonial. By contrast, the GCC states, Saudi Arabia in particular, were unwilling to accept this distribution of responsibilities, as they had managed their political and economic relationships with Yemen according to their own priorities for decades. While the West saw the FOY as both a political and financing entity, in Yemen it came to be seen as the financial arm of the international community, and the GCC states and Group of 10 Ambassadors[*] were seen as the political interlocutors.

Bigger and Better Pledges: The Executive Bureau

The difference between Western and GCC visions became particularly blatant in September 2012 when two pledging conferences were held, the first in Riyadh on 4–5 September, under the auspices of Saudi Arabia and pledging US $6.4 billion of development and humanitarian aid for Yemen; and the second on 27 September in New York, on the margins of the UN General Assembly, when additional pledges of US $1.5 billion were made. These pledges were achieved thanks to an agreement known as the Mutual Accountability Framework (MAF), which the Yemeni regime

---

[*] The Group of 10 Ambassadors is the informal group of ambassadors from wealthy and powerful states, including the GCC, who formed a group to monitor developments in Yemen in relation to the FOY and was then extended to the transition process after the uprisings in 2011. Their numbers varied and by 2017 they were the group of eighteen ambassadors.

and the financiers reached at the Riyadh meeting. The MAF required the Yemeni side to guarantee transparency, while the funding side guaranteed financing for the projects included in the Transitional Development Plan. The MAF commitments, as well as the planning and disbursement of the pledges, were to be managed by an Executive Bureau whose exact role, hierarchical position and senior personnel became the focus of a struggle pitting the Ministry of Planning and International Cooperation against the ambassadors representing the leading funding states: the first wanted to retain control to ensure a fair share of the proceeds for its cronies, while the latter were trying to impose an appointee supported by the World Bank.

It took over eighteen months before agreement was reached on the appointment of a director (the third candidate seriously considered) in March 2014. As a result, and given later developments, the Executive Bureau only operated for about a year before the civil war finally brought it to a standstill. By the end of 2014, that is, a full two years after the original pledges were made, only 39 percent of the originally promised funds had been disbursed, while 70 percent had been approved.[31] Implementation performance ranged from zero percent of pledges disbursed (UAE, OFID, IFAD, Turkey) to 100 percent (UN, USA, Japan, Sweden, Australia, South Korea and Spain).[32] Regardless, nothing was to be seen on the ground.

Yemen's Labour Force: Visions and Reality

Rapid population growth is a fundamental problem for a number of reasons. A demographic boom puts pressure on Yemen's limited water resources and the demands of a large population increase strains on social services and infrastructure, particularly education. In recent decades, population growth has outstripped economic growth, thus creating high unemployment, which this century is one of the main causes of worsening social and political tensions. In 2010, nearly 40 percent (of the then 25 million Yemenis), that is, 9.5 million youth, were of school age (5–19) and there were about 230,000 students in higher education. It is forecast that there will be 14 million school age youth in 2030. Population growth will present major additional challenges for the education and the health sectors[33] for the foreseeable future.

Having re-defined and re-organised its classification system worldwide, the ILO (International Labour Organisation) carried out a Labour Force Survey in 2013-4 in Yemen, the first since 1999.[34] With a total population of 24 million in 2014, the working age population (15–64) was 13.4 million, including 8.5 million people outside the labour force, either students, home makers or others, leaving a labour force of 4.85 million. By comparison, the World Bank estimated the country's labour force at 6.5 million in 2010;[35] the discrepancy seems due to the exclusion of 'subsistence' farmers from ILO figures. The working age population is expected to grow at about 3 percent annually, or 700,000 people, between 2010 and 2040.[36] This is a slight improvement on the situation in the first decade of this century when the labour force increased at 4.2 percent per year while the number of jobs increased by 3.7 percent.[37] However, in absolute numbers the difference is less significant.

The state was and remains the main employer: in 2000 there were 432,351 state employees and the number rose to 1.2 million by end 2014, distributed across 1,450 state institutions,[38] in addition to 700,000 military/security personnel. Agriculture is the main private sector economic activity, providing income for over 50 percent of people[39] although it represents only 20 percent of GDP. Low productivity and low income from agriculture have contributed to a shift of primary source of income away from this sector with a drop from 54 percent in 1994 to 25 percent in 2010. Employment in trade, restaurants and hotels rose from 10 percent to 22 percent[40] during the same period: if one adds the 9 percent working in construction, the overall situation is clear. During decades of work in rural development I noticed that the first source of household incomes was no longer agricultural activity but the labour of men in the towns and cities; the implications of these figures for people's daily lives will be discussed in Chapter 10.

By contrast, the largest contributor to GDP, oil, provides very few jobs, and most of them go to highly qualified foreigners: in 2003 the sector employed only 21,000 Yemenis, while at the same time 190,000 job seekers entered the labour market.[41] The ILO found only 14.5 percent workers employed in industry (9 percent of whom were in construction) and 56 percent in services. Employment in education and health increased by 4 percent, in public administration by 2 percent, and in construction by 4 percent, compared to an increase of only 2.5 percent in manufacturing over the two decades prior to 2015.[42]

Unemployment, Education and Low Wages

As mentioned above, official unemployment figures are generally considered wild underestimates: the ILO data suggest that 70 percent of youth are either unemployed or 'not employed, not in education', and many observers consider even this to be an underestimate of youth unemployment. There is broad agreement that Yemen has to develop a highly skilled labour force if it is to reduce unemployment, improve its economic performance and get away from an economy based on agriculture, construction and low-skill services sectors. Immediate action is urgently needed in education: in 2013, only 8 percent of the labour force had any kind of university degree, while 17 percent were illiterate, including substantial numbers of younger workers. A mere 33 percent were either barely literate (29 percent) or had completed primary school (4 percent) while a further 20 percent had a secondary or equivalent certificate.[43]

When, in addition, one considers that the majority of qualifications are not scientific and that, even among the scientific ones, they are rarely in advanced technologies, the prospects of Yemenis joining a modern scientific economy as suggested by Vision 2025 is not about to be achieved in a hurry. Education policy throughout the decades, and certainly since unification, has been a major area of struggle between the Saleh regime and Islamists; although the latter have been unable to take control of the syllabi and the management of the relevant ministries, they have had considerable influence and Islam and Islamic-related subjects take up substantial shares of the timetable. So although in 2013, 1.8 million youth were in full-time education, including 670,000 females, few of these are likely to be able to participate in a modern competitive economy.

A further economic problem is that official salaries remain way below what is needed to maintain an adequate standard of living: in 2000 the average monthly wage in the public sector was YR 22,800, or about US $100.[44] Private sector incomes were overall somewhat higher, but the majority of casual labourers worked only about fifteen to twenty days per month. In 2013, 24 percent of employed people were earning less than YR 20,000 per month, and 42 percent were earning between YR 20,000 and YR 50,000, with a median income of YR 35,000, with the bottom 30 percent of employed taking 8 percent of total earnings.[45]

Child Labour

Child labour is a symptom of poverty. People send their children to work, rather than to school, when they can't afford to finance their direct or indirect schooling costs and their households need the income. Children also work to help their families in agriculture typically during the peak labour demand periods, mostly the harvesting season, while herding small ruminants is also often a child's occupation. Children (mainly girls, but boys are also involved) collect water for household use with their mothers or alone, and it is mostly girls and women who collect firewood, though the transfer to cooking with bottled gas has made the acquisition of fuel a more gender-neutral activity. In addition, although the labour force is defined as the population aged 15–64, at the same time people aged 15–17 are still considered children in international statistics.

According to the PRSP, the labour of children aged 6–14 years old increased by 6 percent per annum between 1994 and 1999, from 240,000 in 1994 to 327,000, 'which reflects the expansion and severity of poverty and the reliance of poor families on child labour. [46] According to the 1999 Labour Force Survey, girls' work contributed 51.4 percent of the total, but 39.5 percent were both working and attending school. Child labour was concentrated in rural areas (95 percent) with 92 percent in agriculture and general services and sales. Most children (91 percent) worked with their families without pay for between 15-34 hours per week, while 8 percent were self-employed working for cash or material wages. In 2010 a further survey of child labour found that 16 percent of the 6.1 million children aged 5–14 were employed, with a lower rate (11 percent) for those aged 5–11 and a higher one (28.5 percent) for those aged 12–14. [47] At the younger age group, employment of girls is higher than that of boys (12 percent to 10 percent) showing the important role of girls in domestic activities, particularly water and fuel collection. While these figures are often used to deplore a problematic situation, it must be noted that they include both normal help in household tasks within families and cash labour, hence the situation is less problematic than might appear from the data.

Industry and Other Sectors

Economic growth in recent decades has been largely in non-productive sectors, with most employment concentrated in small shops, restaurants and other services activities, the notable exception being construction. Industrial development has remained static, and agricultural employment has declined. The industrial sector remained small: in 2012, just over 200,000 people were employed in industry, half of them in small units, and 162,000 in manufacturing.[48] Workers in the large enterprises, although on fairly low pay, appreciated their position as stable employees on guaranteed regular salaries and were largely considered privileged by the majority who depended on casual employment. Competition from cheap imports, including from other Peninsula states, compromised the expansion of manufacturing.

The few large industrial enterprises are controlled by a select group of families, most of whom were originally from the trader social category from Taiz, Aden and Hodeida. They built food processing and other enterprises, which provide significant employment where they operate. In recent decades, owners of long-established large private enterprises had to include among their shareholders Saleh associates. Refusing to do so would lead to serious problems, ranging from unexpected and unexplained demands for large tax payments, to physical attacks on individuals or the enterprise facilities. Newer larger enterprises were initiated and completely under the control of Saleh associates, and Saleh himself made sure that the 'right' people received their share of contracts and that new shareholders or senior staff were appointed on the basis of providing niches for his cronies.

Private enterprises with over twenty-five employees numbered a mere 1,000, or 0.3 percent of the total number. Most manufacturing takes place in small family units: there are nearly 280,000 small enterprises with fewer than four staff, mostly family members. Such businesses represent 92 percent of industrial units.[49] Although detailed data are hard to come by, the majority of these are in traditional sectors (carpentry, mechanics, tailoring) rather than in advanced technology. The industrial sector is still underdeveloped, as is clearly indicated by the fact that 70 percent of the employed labour force work in the informal sector.[50] Constraints on enterprise development have been considerable and affect both large and small entities.[51]

The main constraints to development listed by the 2013 Enterprise Survey were, first and foremost, political instability (86 percent), closely followed by power cuts (79 percent), corruption (over 75 percent) and insecurity (67 percent). Difficulties in accessing finance and problems with the taxation administration were also mentioned as contributing factors.[52] Overall, the Yemeni private sector failed to develop according to structural adjustment theory for a number of reasons: it is dominated by very small family units which have limited opportunities and whose workers have few skills; the business environment remained very restrictive as a result of corruption and control of profits by a small ruling clique; Yemen's basic infrastructure simply does not function well, whether for production (electricity, raw materials, and customs for imported machinery or raw materials) or for transport; and the country suffers from insecurity and lack of enforcement of existing laws.

Rural life is primarily based around agriculture and is discussed in Chapters 8 and 10; working the land still represents about 20 percent of GDP and fisheries 3 percent.[53] Most important to note is that many of those employed in trade and hotels are rural young men; jobs in these occupations have become the first source of income for their rural households, due to the reduction income derived from subsistence agriculture. So while about 33 percent of the population live directly and mainly from agricultural activities, about 54 percent are involved at least part-time in agriculture. Agricultural output increased in the past two decades thanks to qat, which represents 30 percent of agricultural GDP, while vegetables and fruit contribute another 30 percent, livestock 20 percent and cereals a mere 10 percent. Fisheries employ only 1.5 percent of the labour force but accounts for 3 percent of exports, and it is the third most valuable export after oil and gas.[54]

International Migration and Remittances

International labour migration has been an essential element of Yemeni culture and economy for many centuries and remittances have enabled Yemenis to continue living in the country. Although it excludes informal personal transfers, the following table is indicative of the importance of these remittances since unification. The wide range in percentage rates of GDP from migrant earnings is largely due to the variation in income from oil and other exports. However, remittances are significantly higher than aid flows into the country; moreover these funds go directly to households, mostly to poorer and middle income, rather than either the very poor (who thus remain impoverished due to the lack of remittance incomes) and the very rich who simply don't figure in these analyses.

Remittances in Current US$ millions

Year	Amount	Percent of GDP
1975	329	24
1980	1,417	40
1990	1,133	17
1995	1,081	25
2000	1,288	13.4
2005	1,283	7.6
2008	1,411	5.2
2010	1,526	5
2011	1,404	4.3
2012	3,351	9.5
2013	3,342	8.3
2014	3,350	7.7
2015	3,350	8.9

Source: World Bank Indicators, January 2016

Poverty

Like most data, poverty figures have been adjusted to suit the interests and concerns of the agencies involved in poverty alleviation, which were to demonstrate the success of their policies. In Yemen, the negative impact of structural adjustment was to be compensated by the establishment of a number of new projects in the years immediately following the state's adoption of these policies. In addition to those initiatives discussed below, the strategy also included a project targeted at Southern governorate 'farmers dispossessed of land and other poor families'.[55]

In 1996, the Social Welfare Fund (SWF) was established under the Ministry of Social Affairs. A standard cash transfer programme for the poor, it initially reached 50,000 families, rising to 450,000 in 2000[56] at the cost of YR 7.2 billion.[57] By 2006 it reached nearly a million people, including about 14 percent of the extremely poor, but only 8 percent of those who should receive these funds on the basis of their poverty level and other circumstances.[58] By the end of 2011, beneficiary numbers had reached 1.5 million. [59] In addition to the high percentage of non-poor on that payroll, its impact on poverty remained extremely low, mainly because the amount paid per beneficiary is 'at best 4 percent of the poverty line, while the average income deficit of the poor is 27 percent'.[60] The total amount paid to beneficiaries was capped at US $20 per family per month,[61] an insignificant amount which had not changed by the time the SWF ran out of cash and stopped paying anyone anything in 2015.

The Agriculture and Fisheries Production Promotion Fund (AFPPF) was also created in 1996. Entirely locally funded, the state paid it YR 2.5 for each litre of diesel sold. Its funds were to be spent, as its name implies, on agriculture and fisheries investments. The concept was to compensate farmers and fishermen for the increased price of diesel (which is used for small fishing boats and irrigation pumps) by providing these groups with useful productive infrastructure. It was not specifically intended as a poverty-alleviation fund. By the end of 2000, it had financed 11,863 projects benefiting 6.1 million people and costing YR 11.8 billion;[62] projects included dams, storage facilities, agricultural inputs and fishing platforms. It provided interest-free loans and grants in all governorates, with governorate allocations based on population size. External agencies have systematically denigrated this fund by blaming it for financing inappropriate projects, and for being badly targeted and ill-managed. Their real and fundamental objection was their own lack of control over its management and the types of projects it financed, and the fact that it did not follow the standard neo-liberal agenda.

A third entity established in 1996 was the Public Works Project (PWP, now Programme), a direct 'compensatory' mechanism for the negative impact of structural adjustment. It was initially financed by a World Bank loan and has benefited from a succession of financing agreements ever since from a broad range of other financiers. It is managed by a Project

Implementation Unit, with well-paid staff, and community participation is a fundamental element of its implementation procedures. Its strategy is to build labour intensive social infrastructure, ranging from schools and health centres to roads and water supply. The PWP also intends to develop the skills of its contractors and of the participating communities. By end 2010, it had completed 3,631 projects at a cost of US $310 million and created approximately 648,956 person/months of employment.[63] Alongside others, it is a good example of the ability of the Bretton Woods institutions to influence other funding agencies. They are able to leverage considerable funds as their endorsement is considered to be a guarantee of good development policies.

The following year, the Social Fund for Development (SFD) was created as an independent institution under the prime minister's office, with a board of directors from different relevant ministries. Like the PWP, it was initially set up at the instigation of the World Bank and was similar to other Social Funds established in different countries for the same purpose, namely of alleviating the immediate poverty-worsening impact of structural adjustment programmes. It differs from the PWP in a number of ways, in particular in its institutional structure as a parastatal permanent institution. Between its creation in 1997 and the end of 2011, it had completed 12,296 projects worth US $1.21 billion[64] and created about 40 million days of work.[65] The SFD is the favourite institution of all foreign funders who have managed to continue supporting it at a lower level during the war, despite significant deterioration in the quality and transparency of its performance. Funding agencies treat it as an alternative government, regardless of rhetoric to the contrary, thus further undermining state capacity.

What is clear from all these interventions is that the worsening level of poverty resulting from structural adjustment was recognised. Equally clear, from the two major response programmes funded by the World Bank and other international bilateral and multilateral funders, is that the compensatory mechanisms are inadequate and fail to replace the value of previous support to wheat imports and to fuel. For example, in 2010 about 14 million days of work were created by these two entities: that is, about 1.4 days labour per capita for each poor person, assuming a poverty rate of 43 percent and a total population of 23.1 million that year. In effect this means that the compensatory mechanisms are extremely limited by comparison with the level of losses to the poor suffered through the removal of subsidies.

A brief and superficial analysis of the various poverty surveys since unification confirms the conclusion reached by economist Nora Ann Colton that 'it is in the interest of international agencies to give the impression that Yemen is using the funds correctly. The Yemeni government know[s] that in the end the international agencies and governments will release the funds rather than look like a failure in Yemen ...'[66] Advocates of neo-liberal policies needed to demonstrate success: the World Bank's basic problem was that it had underestimated poverty levels in Yemen at the outset. The 1996 poverty assessment found only 19 percent of the population poor, 9 percent unable to meet their food needs and with an annual per capita income of US $142, and 10 percent in the 'upper' poverty group with per capita annual incomes of US $203.[67] While this was considered laughable and unrealistic by all those who worked and lived in Yemen at the time, the World Bank had to use it as a benchmark. Having started with such a low base poverty rate, later assessments could only look bad!

The 2007 World Bank poverty assessment was based on the 2005 Household Budget Survey and its figures indicated significant progress, with a drop in poverty from 40 percent in 1998 to 35 percent in 2005,[68] thus representing a reduction of almost 2 percent per year. Although urban poverty dropped from 32 percent to 21 percent, rural areas showed little progress with a drop from 42 percent to 40 percent. The assessment noted that overall economic improvement was due to oil-driven growth which provided few jobs for the poor; and also that the IMF-encouraged devaluation of the currency (a move that was intended to achieve macroeconomic stability) had instead 'probably contributed the most to transitional adverse effects on the poor'.[69] In addition, the pet project of reduction in 'petroleum price subsidies between 1998 and 2005 may have resulted in a cost of living increase of around 21 percent'[70] and 'social spending, defined to exclude petroleum subsidies, has declined from 8.6 percent of GDP in 2003 to 7 percent in 2006. Health spending is only about 2 percent of GDP. In fact petroleum subsidies alone equal or exceed total social spending.'[71]

Since then there has been no further Household Budget Survey, due to the political crisis. There were no signs of reduced poverty in daily life, with the numbers of beggars in the cities increasing exponentially throughout the period, and more and more rural people living in worse poverty. The 2007-8 Food Fuel and Financial crisis (the so-called Triple F crisis) had a very negative impact on living standards. Recent surveys by the World Food Programme and the International Food Policy Research Institute demonstrated an 8 percent increase in poverty between 2005 and 2010, from 35 percent to 43 percent. In 2010 the World Bank estimated that 48 percent of the rural and 30 percent of the urban population were poor.[72]

The most recent period has seen further deterioration, beginning with the uprisings of 2011 and followed by the lack of social and economic development investments during the political transition period. By the end of 2012 the World Food Programme estimated poverty to have risen to 54.5 percent,[73] and, by mid-2016, even the World Bank stated a poverty incidence of 62 percent.[74] By mid-2017, 21 million of Yemen's 27.5 million people were in need of humanitarian assistance and 7 million of them on the verge of starvation. The crisis was described as the 'worst humanitarian crisis in the world' by UN Secretary General António Gutteres. The only people who are probably NOT poor in this second half of the decade are military/security leaders, arms traders and the new group of profiteers from the war economy, and in particular the old and new cliques of smugglers of food and fuel.

Corruption

Corruption was intrinsic to the Saleh regime which even staffed its anti-corruption institutions with people known to be corrupt. It was one of the reasons Yemen was excluded from US Millennium Challenge funding in 2005, and the same year saw its World Bank funding reduced by 34 percent. Corruption is visible in a wide range of mechanisms and activities, ranging from the daily graft faced by anyone needing to process anything through a government institution, to the vast amounts paid to senior regime officials. In between are a myriad of other instances: the registration of non-eligible voters in elections, procurement corruption, including that on the import and distribution of counterfeit medication which can kill patients, and the absence of oversight of budget expenditure by Parliament and other institutions.

Under pressure from the international community, the regime created institutions designed to introduce and implement acceptable procedures, such as the National Anti-Corruption Authority (NACA), the Higher

Tender Board (HTB) and the Central Organisation for Control and Audit (COCA). While not all the staff and leadership of these organisations were corrupt,[75] many were. Good candidates have refused appointments in these organisations knowing that their real role would be to serve as a cover-up. Moreover, some of these organisations have overlapping responsibilities ensuring rivalry between them. As Saleh appointees, senior officials had no incentive to uncover malfeasance, unless they wanted to end their own profiteering from corrupt practices.

Daily routine petty corruption simply involves handing over cash, dubbed 'qat money', to get papers dealt with or to get officials to carry out the tasks that are supposed to be part of their official duties. So, to obtain the endless signatures needed to process a simple payment, each person on the list needs to be paid a few hundred riyals, whether to approve the renewal of a vehicle licence, be paid for a few days' work, or even to get reasonable grades on an important paper at school or university. This is 'justified' by the low salaries insufficient to maintain a basic reasonable standard of living. These payments are a serious drain on household budgets.

Construction has massive potential for corruption at all stages and all levels, from the bidding process for contracts to actual construction. In the early-1980s I was working in a foreign-funded rural development project in al-Baidha Governorate, which had built four substantial houses for the staff. The director pointed out that a fifth unofficial house had been built about two kilometres away at the same time, on the same model, and through the same project funding as the personal property of the Yemeni director. Similarly, in the mid-1990s a friend who was managing a foreign-funded rural development project in the far north of the country submitted estimates for the construction of extension centres to the ministry for clearance and approval. His estimates were rejected and later replaced by others costing two or three times as much for similar architectural plans. Such examples abound.

Although extremely widespread, cases of high-level corruption are rarely demonstrated and confirmed. In the oil sector, one of the few documented cases concerns the French company Schlumberger which was investigated by the US Department of Justice in 2010. Its local agent, Tawfiq Saleh Abdullah Saleh (a nephew of the president) and his company Zonic, was paid a bonus of US $500,000 and a further US $1.38 million between 2002 and 2007 for a data bank on petroleum exploration. The main agent for the import of equipment was Dhakwan Petroleum and Mineral Services, which belonged to Ali Mohsen al-Ahmar (vice president of the internationally recognised government since 2016). Dhakwan received US $280,000 between 2004 and 2007 'for making sure the paper work went through'. When Schlumberger tried to put an end to this arrangement, the company was unable to import equipment, thus confirming the widespread view that it was impossible to operate without using this company as an agent.[76] Another notorious example of corruption in the oil sector was the sale of the government share in exploration block 53, where US $27 million were undeclared and disappeared into the pockets of corrupt government officials.[77]

A pervasive form of corruption is the phenomenon of 'ghost workers' which are found in every sector of state employment. For example, in the mid-2000s it was estimated that up to a third of military personnel were ghost workers, some merely absent, others fictitious.[78] In the Ministry of Education 40 percent of staff were estimated to be ghost employees.[79] Corruption in the military goes well beyond ghost soldiers. 'Commanding officers reportedly will receive money for [the soldiers'] salaries, weapons, ammunition, food and blankets, and pro-rated numbers of vehicles, fuel and tires, among other items. The tangible items then get sold on the black market with the profits accruing to the officers. Cash transfers for salaries and the like can be more simply pocketed ... Annual military expenditures are enormously high by percentage, having reached $1 billion, out of a total government expenditure of about $6 billion.'[80] At the turn of the century, I used to eat in a restaurant in Shabwa owned by an officer and staffed by serving soldiers.

Another aspect of corruption is in capital outflows: the UNDP found that Yemen had outflows of US $12 billion between 1990 and 2008, which was 2.7 times the amount of aid received during that period, about US $4.5 billion.[81] This implied that Yemen's shadow economy was worth on average 275 percent, that is, almost three times the country's GDP during the same period.[82]

Corruption is a very sensitive subject and local Yemeni media have been discouraged from investigating it, particularly the large-scale cases involving senior officials. Journalists who write about corruption are likely to be attacked physically in the streets, usually by 'unknown aggressors', and sometimes they even disappeared or were killed. In late December

2016, Mohammed al-Absi, an investigative journalist who had covered numerous corruption cases, including some related to Yemen LNG, the largest investment in Yemen, was found dead just as he was about to reveal his findings on oil-related corruption among senior Huthis. His family and the Journalists' Union arranged a post-mortem which demonstrated he had been poisoned.[83]

The Situation in 2010, the Road to Collapse and Future Prospects

Macro-economic indicators for the first two decades of the ROY were not particularly impressive but the oncoming crisis could be clearly foreseen by looking at the details. With annual population growth standing at over 3 percent, only strong economic performance based on equitable distribution could have improved most citizens' living standards. This did not happen: average growth of 5.6 percent per annum during the first decade dropped to 4.5 percent in the second and was mainly due to oil exports.[84] Throughout the period, the oil sector was responsible for about one-third of growth while the rest came from services, including oil sector services.[85] Productive sectors, industry in particular, lagged behind. The data strongly suggest failure of the neo-liberal agenda, as productive sectors dropped from 23 percent to 20 percent of GDP for agriculture and fisheries, and from 19 to 15 percent for manufacturing, while government services increased from 16 percent to 20 percent, and transport and commerce grew from 11 percent to 14 percent.[86] State revenues have covered recurrent expenditures, mainly salaries (35.5 percent) and subsidies to oil products (24.5 percent) between 1996 and 2014. Capital expenditure made up only 14 percent of the total, leaving high fiscal deficits averaging close to 6 percent of GDP between 2008 and 2014.[87] These figures obviously only include what actually made it into the state budget while unknown amounts went directly into the regime's patronage system and the personal coffers of the top leadership.

The political crisis, which started with the popular uprisings in 2011, was largely brought about by the economic situation. As we have seen, not only have the younger generation of adults grown in numbers enormously since the beginning of the century, but their economic prospects have continued to deteriorate. Some 80 percent of youth are left in limbo after completing school or university. Obtaining employment, in the state and private sector, had become almost impossible and determined more by personal contacts, known as *wasta* – that is, through nepotism, rather than competence or open competition. With the cancellation of conscription in 2001 and, in addition, the requirement that recruits had to have secondary school education, the earlier fail-safe of military employment was no longer available to provide jobs for young men with limited education.

In 2011, the economy shrank by 12.7 percent with slight growth in 2012 (2.4 percent) and 2013 (4.8 percent) and then dropping to negative growth of -0.2 percent growth in 2014. The decline became even more precipitous in 2015, with GDP declining by 28 percent,[88] and 10 percent in 2016. There is no doubt that 2017 is unlikely to show any improvement.

Regardless of its political future, Yemen is not entirely lacking in economic potential though it faces clear limitations, in terms of both resources and political behaviour. The objective long-term challenges are first and foremost the acute water shortage which demands serious and strong political action for the country's expected 50 million people to live there a generation from now. The second fundamental challenge is to develop a highly skilled labour force able to earn a living in modern economic sectors with low water requirements. A third challenge is to reform a culture of corruption locally, and dependence on neo-liberal agendas externally. And the fourth, immediate one, is surely to bring an end to the current war, without which no economic progress is possible.

To respond to these challenges, the country has a number of potential assets: first, its limited gas and oil resources; second, its remarkable tourist potential based on both its scenery and cultural heritage; third, its geographically strategic position on the Bab al-Mandab strait combined with Aden port; and fourth its young population. The development of all these resources requires a stable political regime based on effective law enforcement, with good development policies. These are essential for Yemen to attract vitally needed investment from its expatriate community. Central to future economic development will be intelligent stewardship of the rural-urban nexus, the subject of the final chapter.

CHAPTER TEN

The Rural-Urban Nexus

In Yemen, the labour market is no abstract concept. In the cities, groups of men congregate at intersections or roundabouts waiting to be hired for a day's work. They carry paint brushes, building, electrical and plumbing tools, wheelbarrows and a multitude of other tools or none. When demand is high, no one is found in these places by mid-morning. When demand is low, they are still waiting late in the evening. These casual workers are mostly rural men who stay in the city for months on end to earn enough to enable their families at home to buy the basic necessities of life. They go home during land preparation, harvesting and other times of high demand for agricultural labour. In the cities they live in the cheapest and most basic facilities, hoping to earn as much as possible. On average in the last two decades, they find work for fifteen days per month. Their lifestyles and livelihoods are a microcosm of the intimate relationship between rural areas and cities, economically, politically and culturally.

Yemen, like so many Southern countries, has experienced massive urban expansion in recent decades. However, given the high rate of population growth and the nature of its economy, this increase has not been linked to an equivalent decrease in its rural population. National census findings in 1994 showed that 77 percent of the population remained rural despite the fact that about half a million returnees from the GCC states after the 1990 crisis stayed in urban areas, around Hodeida in particular. Some twenty years later 70 percent of a much larger population still live in rural areas.

Rural-urban movements in Yemen are, on the whole, less definitive than in many other countries, for a number of reasons. First, urban employment options are mostly limited to unskilled casual daily paid jobs, and there are few long-term stable jobs for educated and skilled youth. Second is culture: Yemeni men want to return regularly to their villages where their roots are and which are perceived as more pleasant and where they also participate in agricultural activities. And third, men migrate without their nuclear household members who remain in the villages; families only come to the cities when necessary for medical or other purposes. This approach maximises cash transfers to the village and reduces urban living costs, while retaining the features of village culture. Constant interaction between rural and urban areas has ensured a more cohesive overall society without a vast social, economic and psychological gap between the two. The almost universal ownership and coverage of mobile phones have significantly reduced isolation and the social/psychological gap between urban and rural lifestyles.

Yemeni Cities

Urban development demonstrates the chaotic outcomes of unregulated expansion. The limited, inadequate and low quality of social and physical infrastructure also illustrate the effect of neo-liberal policies and the corruption that they have allowed.[*] A characteristic of urban life has been the increasingly visible and worsening gap between the microscopic group of super-wealthy and the vast majority of the poor: the rich build fortress-villas, while the poor build slums and semi-slums which lack the most basic services. For their part, the very poor spend their days begging or selling all manner of imported goods or wait to be hired for a day's work. Sana'a, for example, expanded vastly with the emergence of luxury housing in the southwest of the city, around the Hadda area, and unplanned and 'illegal' constructions in the north and west, where people overnight constructed basic houses on empty terrains. They did so in the (usually correct) hope that these would be legalised at a later date, and connected to electricity networks, if not water.

The inadequacy of urban services gets far more attention than their total absence in rural areas, thanks to the simple fact that urban riots and

---

[*]   Contracts and the construction and reconstruction of some of the Sana'a sewerage system in the early 2000s is one example, with roads being dug up again and again due to the low quality of the work.

discontent are more visible: electricity availability has remained erratic throughout Yemen. Put simply, not enough electricity is generated to ensure a constant stable supply to urban citizens and businesses. The duration of daily cuts varies according to the construction of new power plants, the condition of the network and mainly the seasonality of demand. Unsurprisingly, cuts are longest and most frequent in the summer, when demand is at its highest, and the effect is felt the hardest in the hottest cities, Hodeida in particular. Of course, matters are even worse in rural areas, where few enjoy any access whatsoever to the so-called national grid.

Due to the country's history, Yemen has a number of significant urban sites. Besides always serving as markets and religious centres, many Yemeni towns and cities have also played political roles at different times. Their character was also affected by their relationship to their hinterland as well as, particularly in the case of coastal ones, their links to other cultures through migration and transport links. Recently Yemen experienced the emergence of a dominant capital, Sana'a, where growth outstripped that of other cities, thus making it the undisputed hub for administration and politics. Prior to unification in 1990, the country had two capitals, Sana'a and Aden. As the main port of the Northern state, Hodeida played a decisive role in the region for centuries. Mokha remained the main port for the Taiz region, despite its decline once coffee exports reduced. Going back into history, other cities were capitals at different times. In the South, Mukalla on coastal Hadramaut and Seiyun in its wadi were the two major political centres during the British colonial period. Meanwhile, other statelet capitals barely achieved the status of towns, let alone cities. For example, as late as 1994 the population of al Hauta in Lahej was 19,421, Zinjibar 15,778, Mahweet 9,668, al-Ghayda 7,829, and Mareb 3,571.[1]

Sana'a

Sana'a was the official capital of the northern state throughout the last century, although Imam Ahmed stayed in Taiz as he rightly thought he was not welcome there after having ordered his troops to ransack it after the failed 1948 uprising. When he became Imam in September 1962, Badr immediately moved to Sana'a from where he was ousted a mere ten days later. The Republican regime settled in the city which grew rapidly, though it remained fairly small till the 1980s, with a population of 135,625 in 1975, increasing to 277,818 in 1981[2]. By the 1994 census its population had increased to 972,011, a massive change that reflected a growth rate of almost 9 percent per annum.[3] Three main factors help explain this sudden spurt: unification, the arrival of the Adeni political/administrative groups in 1990, soon followed by the forced departure of workers from the GCC states. By the time of the 2004 census, the population had again almost doubled in barely a decade to 1.75 million people. It was estimated at well over two million in 2015.

Traffic in Sana'a

In 1980, when the main Abdul Moghni Street was a crowded thoroughfare with vehicles rushing along and making road crossing a hazardous venture for pedestrians, I was told that a mere three years earlier people used to cross it without looking, as there were only a dozen or so vehicles in the whole city. As Sana'a continued to expand with great speed, an absence of four years between 1982 and 1986 meant that I found myself in an unrecognisable city which seemed to have doubled in size. Since then, it is only through regular and frequent visits that I kept up with expansion from the inner ring road, nowadays seen as part of the 'old centre', to the many new layers of rings. The city had expanded from the east at the foot of the mountain, Jabal Nuqum, to climbing on the western escarpments along the Hodeida Road. The capital had also expanded northwards, to bring the airport within the city itself; and southwards, way beyond the Nahdein hills and Hadda village. As recently as the early 1980s we used to picnic in the orchards and fields of Hadda at weekends. Such idylls have all now vanished and been replaced by villas housing the elites.

Sana'a expansion is due to its political role: new inhabitants include not only Southern politicians and administrators after unification, but also an influx of tribal and other community leaders who needed to be near the centre of power to ensure access to jobs and benefits for their community members. Some of the latter have become 'urban shaykhs' while others only visit when necessary. The main military/security institutions had both their headquarters and main barracks in Sana'a, thus bringing thousands more temporary residents. Other long-term immigrants have included waves of exiles from the South, as political upheavals there led to their departure. The first two types of expansion led to an increase in temporary employment in construction and provision of daily services. Yemenis are natural builders, as is demonstrated by the vast range and variety of highly sophisticated and beautiful housing throughout the country, constructed in different styles and using different raw materials.

So the construction boom has provided thousands of jobs for builders with traditional skills, as well as for others involved in decoration and furnishing. The first to meet this need were members of the artisan social group already living there; gradually the construction labour pool expanded to absorb casual migrant labourers from rural areas. Temporary labour migration to the cities has advantages as well as drawbacks. For the workers, it allows them to sustain their rural culture and keep close links with their families; extended households in turn gain access to a broader range of sources of income, which reduces their dependence on unpredictable and erratic rains. For employers, short-term migration provides a pool of casual workers, paid on a daily basis, whose welfare is not their concern. Sana'a has no significant industrial sector: its Chinese-built spinning and weaving factory closed long ago, and there are mostly small workshops and construction companies.

The political migratory waves from the South started in 1967 with the rise of the socialist regime: the bourgeoisie and former ruling groups emigrated, primarily to Saudi Arabia and the YAR. Those who came to the YAR were distributed between Taiz, Hodeida and Sana'a where they transferred their existing businesses or created new ones, mainly industrial in the former two and commercial in the latter. This wave was followed by others in response to political upheavals in Aden: in 1978 the supporters of Salmeen migrated north, followed in 1986 by those of Ali Nasser. On each occasion some were integrated into the General People's Congress and given positions: the deputy president of the Consultative Council (*Majlis al-Shura*) was for decades a Hadrami supporter of Salmeen. Other Southerners joined the military. A prime example was Abdu Rabbu Mansur Hadi, the current president of the internationally recognised government, who was a senior military officer supporting Ali Nasser in the 1986 failed coup in Aden and moved north with his units. None of these Southern groups mixed socially with Northerners or with each other, despite sharing cultural features which differentiated them from the original highlander communities of Sana'a.

Until the beginning of the century, the rule preventing the construction of modern skyscrapers and guiding the general appearance of buildings was largely enforced. Most buildings, outside the old city of six- to seven-floor plaster-decorated high rises, were villa-type constructions with gardens and walls, which compulsorily had *qamariya* (decorative stained glass and plaster half-moon windows located above the main windows) and retained certain 'traditional' features, thereby giving the rooftop landscape of the city a cohesive appearance. The old city within what remained of the walls (reconstructed in the 1980s in a new style) was subject to a range of 'improvements' largely financed by international support for the city's cultural heritage. Donors intended to develop the city as a major tourist attraction. The first decade of this century saw the end of what little regulation had existed, with the construction of buildings of over ten floors, lacking *qamariya*. Different styles and types of stone and cement abounded, which rapidly contributed to the uglification of the city, and the emergence of apartment blocks which also forced a change in lifestyle towards smaller nuclear units. It is unlikely that the destruction brought about by the war will lead to more culturally sensitive reconstruction once the conflict ends; nor in all likelihood will any future restoration of Sana'a's architecture bring aesthetic cohesion to the city, though this would certainly be rare good news if it were.

The city's rapid expansion has merely aggravated an existing problem. Sana'a is widely predicted to be the first national capital to run out of water, although the expected date for this disaster has been extended whenever the deadline seemed close. The city is located in the water-scarce Sana'a basin, where this precious resource is over-exploited for high-value crops (qat, fruit and vegetables). Not that it is a question of an instant transformation from water yesterday to none today. The process is a gradual one and is taking place with supply diminishing over time. In 2007, the last time serious work was carried out on the issue, ground-water levels were found to be dropping at a rate of 6 metres per annum in the aquifers supplying the city; and an average of five wells were being closed down annually.[4] Already at the beginning of the twenty-first century, even in upmarket areas, people buying land allocated for housing were informed that their areas would not be connected to the urban network.

Despite this the city continued to grow, but the percentage of homes covered by the water distribution network dropped to 41 percent in 2007[5] from 61 percent in 1984.[6] Over the first decade of this century, frequency of service reduced from three times a week to once or twice at best. Most households purchase, at far higher cost, tanker loads that are stored in ground level, underground and roof reservoirs. For those who are connected to the network, how much water they need to buy depends on both their storage capacity and their levels of consumption, which in each instance is affected by their income levels. Others have to buy all their water from the private sector.

Despite WHO recommendations and simple basic awareness of the health hazards of unhygienic disposal of used waters, there has never been a systematic link between the provision of water and the construction of sewerage networks. Sanitation coverage systematically lags way behind water supply, reaching only 33 percent in 2007. The predictable health consequences of this neglect became evident in the 2017 cholera outbreak.

Aden

During the British period, Aden was a city-state colony, a major international port, the headquarters of Britain's East of Suez operations, and the administrative headquarters of the very few British officials involved in administration of the Protectorates, all of which contributed to the city's growth and expansion. Aden's population grew from 1,300 when the British arrived in 1839, to 19,000 in 1850, including 5,000 'Arabs', 3,000 Somalis, 1,200 Jews and 7,600 Indians (of whom there had been a mere 35 in 1839) and close to 800 Europeans. As Aden expanded, thousands of Yemenis from the hinterland and the nearby areas of the Imamate came to work as labourers in the port, the base, and the refinery during and after its completion in 1954. By 1955 'Arabs' formed 75 percent of Aden's population[7] of 138,441.[8]

The first population census in the PDRY in 1973 enumerated 239,000 people in Aden,[9] increasing to 294,430 in the 1986 census[10] and 402,232 in 1994.[11] This 5 percent annual growth rate was much lower than that of Sana'a, reflecting the migration of most administrators and politicians to Sana'a immediately after unification. The figure also speaks of the city's economic stagnation during the first years of unification. In 2004 the population of Aden had only reached 590,000, an increase of 24 percent over a decade. In the absence of a census in 2014 Aden's population is estimated to be about 600,000 in 2017.

It is clear from the above that today's Adenis originally came from many different places in Yemen and beyond. Until the 1950s and 1960s when the labour movement brought together most Yemenis, whether from the protectorates or Imamate, Aden's population was characterised by a lack of social cohesion. People from the Imamate mainly came from the Taiz, Ibb and al-Baidha rural areas, while those from the Protectorates mostly travelled from al-Dhala', Yafi' and other statelets closest to Aden itself. Later on, Aden's population experienced both inward and outward migration: in the years following independence many merchants and former political leaders emigrated with their assets to avoid nationalisation. Their departure was compensated by the arrival of rural people seeking employment in administration and industry or joining the higher education facilities.

Aden mostly stagnated during the socialist period (1967–90): only a few state-financed housing estates were built, initially constructed of stone and cement (in Crater, Mansoura). In later years pre-fabricated constructions appeared in Remy City in Mansoura, and more blocks of flats in the Shaykh Othman district. But the basic fabric and appearance of the city up to 1995 would have been immediately recognisable to any visitor who had known Aden in the 1960s, after the construction of the mile of blocks of flats along Ma'alla main road. In the 2000s, Aden experienced a massive construction boom when investments poured in, mostly from successful Yemeni migrants to Saudi Arabia, Europe and USA. For the most part the new money was ploughed into the neighbourhoods of Mansoura and Shaykh Othman and beyond; and the city expanded too: before long Dar Saad, for instance, had been transformed from a village into just another suburb.

Overall, the city's development has always been determined by its geography and the separation of the different sectors by mountains and patches of desert. In the heart of the city, Crater, Tawahi, Ma'alla, Little Aden (Bureiqa) and, to a lesser extent, Khormaksar, retained the architectural character of the colonial years throughout the socialist period. But this was abruptly ended after 2000 with high-rise constructions and the introduction of Sana'ani characteristics to most buildings, such as *qamariya*, which have become pervasive throughout the country. These 'exotic' features have seriously distorted the local architectural characteristics of most Southern areas, introducing a bogus sense of uniformity and damaging the country's cultural heritage.

Aden's two major economic assets are its port and the refinery. Built between 1952 and 1954, the refinery survived the socialist period to retain its importance in the country's economy, even though the fuel it refines is imported by sea, given Aden's distance from the country's oil fields. The port, which is still regarded by many Adenis as a potential miracle solution to the nation's problems, is unlikely to achieve such a status due to changes in shipping patterns and the size of ships. Competition from other major modern ports in the region represents another impediment to Aden's potential rebirth. Such ports include Jabal Ali in Dubai, Salalah in Oman, Djibouti on the other side of the Red Sea, Berbera in Somaliland, as well as Hodeida and Mukalla in Yemen itself. Many small industries of the socialist years have been closed or privatised and Hodeida and Taiz have displaced Aden as a major industrial area for Yemen.

While often explained as a result of the insecurity brought about by the activities of AQAP, the failure of the Aden Free Zone to take off is due to other factors. Established in 1991, it stumbled through the decades, because of lack of support from the regime and the difficulties encountered by potential investors faced with the legitimate and illegitimate demands of officials. A fundamental issue was the administrative separation of the zone from Aden port, which complicated mutual access and therefore cancelled out the main asset of free zones, namely, ease of procedures. In 2005, the management of Aden port was removed from the Free Zone and handed over to the Ministry of Transport. In 2008 Yemen signed a controversial contract with Dubai Ports World (DPW) to manage the container terminal, which appeared to benefit only the contractor and concerned Yemeni officials: DPW failed to deepen and expand the container port facilities so container traffic, rather than doubling as per the contract, dropped from 500,000 twenty-foot-equivalent units in 2008 to 140,000 in 2011. Hadi's transitional government terminated the contract in September 2012 at the cost of US $35 million[12] to the Yemeni state. This was welcomed in Aden where people had perceived the agreement as highly corrupt. There is little doubt, however, that Aden and its free zone could do a lot better and that mismanagement (to be polite) has prevented Aden from taking off as the economic capital of the ROY.

Since unification, and particularly after the 1994 civil war which defeated the separatist movement, Adenis consider that they have suffered discrimination and oppression from Northerners; they complain of Northern 'occupation' of the South and this perception became more vocal since 2007 with the rise of the separatist movement. The days when everyone dreamt of Yemeni unity are long gone, at least among militants, and in particular the younger generation who have no experience of the pre-unification period. Although some Northerners are indeed responsible for much depredation and illegitimate acquisition of land, buildings and goods, as well as of controlling the most senior political positions, most so-called Adenis tend to forget that they are themselves descendants of second- or third-generation Northerners, as can be seen in the population data for Aden over the past century. Moreover, they refuse to acknowledge the fact that most Northerners have suffered equally from the Sana'a regime. Continuous instability and uncertainty about the city's political future, as well as its citizens' treatment of workers from other parts of Yemen, have lessened investors' enthusiasm. Regardless of the outcome of the current civil war, internal social and political tensions in Aden raise doubts about its potential economic development.

Taiz

Taiz was the city where Imam Ahmed resided and where foreign embassies were located during his reign. It thus developed a more 'cosmopolitan' atmosphere than Sana'a, though its residents at the time might not have recognised that description. Its growth rate has been impressive: in 1975 it had 79,720 people, rising to 322 ,063 in 1994[13] and about 500,000 in the last decade;[14] its growth rate of 7 percent between 1975 and 1986 remained high in the following period. Subject to intense warfare since mid-2015, its population had shrunk considerably by 2017, though is likely to recover fast once fighting stops. Taiz is a model of the water crisis, as discussed in Chapter 8.

Taiz's fame rests on its claim to be the most cultured city in Yemen and, indeed, it was officially named 'culture capital of Yemen' in January 2013. In a region of very high population density and limited agriculture, it initiated private schools and its people gave much attention to education. Merchant families turned to industry and made their fortunes there. The leading example is the Hayl Saeed Anaam group, whose factories are in Taiz and who have also established a charitable organisation working in a range of activities. Nowadays Taizis are found throughout the country; many work as teachers, in the civil service and other sectors which need educated staff.

Because of its more socially liberal culture and its higher educational levels, many Taizi women are teachers in remote villages, and they include Islahi militants who have contributed to spreading its ideology among women. Taizi influence in the military was dealt a major blow shortly after Saleh first came to power in 1978, when a group of Taizi Nasserists in the army led a failed coup against the new ruler. The military security establishment was then purged of Taizis, which in turn forced them to move to other sectors.

The region's high population density and insufficient local employment opportunities are responsible for the large-scale internal migration of Taizis. Their better education, more liberal culture, claim to 'modernity' by contrast with tradition and 'tribalism', and their presence throughout Yemen have also led to widespread anti-Taizi prejudice by people from other governorates who perceive them as 'hogging' the few available jobs. The same factors are also responsible for many Taizis perceiving themselves, along with many urban Southerners, as being less tribal and more 'modern' than people from the Zaydi highlands. This identity is partly reflected in their clothing, as urban Taizi men are the only group in Yemen who routinely wear Western clothing outside of working hours. Their self-perception and, in many cases, their ability to speak English and act as interpreters and escorts, is valued by foreigners who find them easier to deal with than other less 'Westernised' Yemenis who remain more faithful to family and tribal connections.

Taiz's reputation for liberalism is only partly justified, as the Muslim Brother faction of the Islah party was born there and has many supporters in this region which also provides members for jihadi groups. Taizis have a self-perception similar to that of many Southerners, yet this has not prevented separatists in Aden from treating them as Northerners and expelling them in waves since 2015. Another characteristic of Taizis is frequent denial of tribal connections. Such claims are ideological constructs with little relationship to reality: other than the traditional social strata of merchants, artisans and *sada*, most of Taiz's population have their origin in villages which, alongside others elsewhere in Shafi'i Yemen, are members of tribes, even if they lack allegiance to large tribal confederations.

Hodeida

Located in the Tihama plain along the Red Sea, Hodeida has the most difficult climate as summer temperatures are extremely high and humidity intense. It has also, up to now, not suffered any major water shortages thanks to a broader aquifer hinterland, though much of its water is increasingly saline due to over-extraction. Like others, it suffers from particularly severe power cuts due to its climate. Hodeida is a port, like Aden, and an industrial city, like Taiz, so it shares the societal features associated with these activities, hence they won't be discussed further. Its growth has also been impressive, starting with a population of 72,895 in 1975, rising to 302,682 in 2004,[15] and estimated at 600,000 in 2010.[16] Another distinguishing characteristic is that it has hardly anything left of its 'old city'. But Hodeida's main differentiating feature has been that many Yemenis returning during the crisis of 1990 have settled there, thus creating large slums in that city. Most of them have remained poor and are only involved in casual labour.

As Yemen's main port with access to the densely populated highlands, it receives most of the food imported in the country. In 2017, it achieved international notoriety as food imports were reduced to a fraction of what was needed. The prime causes of this setback were the blockade, and the destruction of its infrastructure by the Saudi-led coalition fighting the Huthi-Saleh alliance that controlled the coast and the highlands. The city was also under threat of direct attack by land forces in mid-2017, when drafting of this book was being completed.

Mukalla

On the Arabian Sea, 500 kilometres north-east of Aden, Mukalla is the capital of Hadramaut Governorate. Its population of 51,000 in 1978[17] rose to 91,974 in 1994, and numbered more than 400,000 by 2010,[18] with an annual growth rate of around 5 percent.[19] Unlike other cities in Yemen, Mukalla has adequate ground water and its water distribution network has been modernised, which allows for better coverage. Its post-unification building boom began immediately. An indication of the scope of this boom: in Mukalla district a total of 3,354 plots of state land were distributed to individuals for housing or businesses between 1982 and 1989; between 1990 and 1995 the figure was 56,209 (even though the figure for 1995 only covers the first three months).[20]

Mukalla has benefited from Hadramaut's historical links to Saudi Arabia and south-east Asia. Unlike the situation in Aden, the boom has mostly benefited Hadrami investors residing in Saudi Arabia and the UAE,[21] many of whom having achieved the nationality of their adopted lands. Some migrants to Saudi Arabia, in the early decades of the twentieth century, became successful and famous and, in one case at least, notorious. Some of these families have chosen to support their relatives in Hadramaut, not only by sponsoring individuals to become legal immigrants in Saudi Arabia, but also by investing in the land of their ancestors. Although most of these families come from the interior, Mukalla's port and easy accessibility attracted much investment as these seemed more profitable economic options than the wadi. Investors have improved infrastructure, including roads and electricity; they invested in tourist infrastructure, like hotels and beach playgrounds, as well as fisheries and fish processing.

While some consider that the involvement of the private sector in infrastructure indicates the state's failure to carry out its responsibilities, supporters of the neo-liberal approach would, on the contrary, consider this a major success of transferring public goods and facilities into private hands. In recognition of the economic rise of Hadramaut, in 2005 Saleh chose to celebrate the fifteenth anniversary of Yemeni unification in Mukalla. He invited expatriate businessmen to participate including many from Saudi Arabia. Among other achievements, they were invited to admire the dual carriageway road west of the city which they had financed, and appreciate the quality of urban planning, as it is located a mere fifty metres south from the state-financed one which had been widened a few years earlier!

Rural Life

Yemen has a multiplicity of landscapes, ranging from the coastal plains of the Red and Arabian Seas, to abrupt mountains reaching over 3,000 metres above sea level. These peaks have steep slopes and receive monsoon rains, thus providing for a very fertile terrain, from which came Yemen's description from Roman times onwards as 'Arabia Felix' (literally, Happy Arabia). Finally, from the highest mountains east of the Red and north of the Arabian Seas, there are increasingly arid gentle slopes leading towards the desert of the Rubʿ al-Khali or Empty Quarter, most of which lies in Saudi Arabia. The southern plateau is broken by the famous and beautiful Wadi Hadramaut valley, with its history of mud-brick skyscrapers (in Shibam). Elsewhere, particularly in the historic Tarim district, there are mud-brick palaces financed by emigrants who became wealthy in south-east Asia and built these impressive structures which bear the architectural influence of their adopted lands, while Seiyun and its own mud brick palace was the capital of the Kathiri Sultanate; in the colonial period, Shibam was known as New York, Seiyun as Paris and Tarim as Rome, giving a flavour of the different architectures of the three towns.

About 70 percent of Yemen's people still live in rural areas and more than 55 percent depend directly on agriculture and livestock husbandry, while a further 1.5 percent rely on coastal fisheries for their livelihood. In the past, the fertile rain-fed monsoon western highland areas were barely able to sustain a much smaller population. In the period between the oil income boom in the GCC states and the 1990 crisis, the incomes of ordinary rural people were vastly increased by the remittances and the funds brought back by their unskilled men working in Saudi Arabia and other GCC states. Foreign-earned money thus compensated for the reduced per capita income from family farms, whose size had diminished generation by generation. This situation has obviously worsened in the two decades since unification as emigration possibilities have been seriously restricted, while population growth has continued apace. The current war has brought extreme destitution as prices of basic imported produce have risen dramatically, income from urban casual employment has almost vanished and everything has become vastly more expensive.

The Golden Age of the 1980s: Migration and Rural Investments

In this 'boom' period, village living standards improved as migrant workers brought and sent back funds which were invested in the following, in order of priority: a new home, usually built of stone and according to the fashion of the period, larger with one or two floors only, rather than the tower houses of previous periods, reflecting a perception of increased security and reduced community-level warfare. This investment and its associated furnishings and equipment were complemented by the acquisition of a four-wheel drive vehicle, as motorable tracks were built to reach the remotest locations. These generated additional income through their use as collective transport to nearby markets, hospitals and other facilities. Generators were bought and used for the owner's home and electricity sold to neighbours who paid on a monthly basis according to the number of lamps and other items connected. Generators operated from sunset till about 11 pm or midnight, and were used to run at least one refrigerator in a village shop (stocked with the usual supply of unhealthy but high-status cold fizzy drinks) as well as televisions in people's homes.

Productive investments started with drilling wells and equipping them with diesel pumps to irrigate their fields, with the outcomes discussed in Chapter 8. Other agricultural investments included farm equipment, such as tractors. Those with more substantial savings bought drilling rigs and rented out their services. Very little investment went into agricultural processing facilities; however, much more was invested in micro-enterprises associated with construction (such as carpentry, iron work, plumbing, electrical connections) and in the maintenance and repair of vehicles and other newly introduced technology. Some villages installed community-level water distribution schemes, while many improved their wells or springs to facilitate water collection.

The 1980s were a 'golden age', not just with relative peace throughout the country, but also with regular improvements in living conditions. In the YAR, thanks to migration to the GCC, remittances were used for individual households and 'privately supplied' community services; and in the PDRY a combination of remittances and state-provided economic and social investments benefited the local economy. Everywhere ordinary people experienced higher living standards, as shown by the increasingly easy availability of imported commodities, ranging from television sets which gave access to the outside world, to the imported baby foods and soft drinks which damaged everyone's health! For the majority of ordinary citizens, and the poor in particular, things have basically been going downhill ever since; poverty has worsened, the growth of a professional 'middle class' has halted: in Yemen, as in so many other places, this group has divided between the majority getting poorer and a small minority becoming successful and enriching themselves.

Local Institutions: From Local Development Associations to Decentralisation

From the 1950s onwards, migrants from the Hujjiriya south of Taiz and other areas headed abroad in search of income-generating activities, education and what is today described as 'development'. Men from different parts of Yemen got together to set up informal meeting groups; initially these were meant to be mutual assistance institutions to help new arrivals find work, to pay for education, and assist each other with cash for medical or other emergencies. They soon expanded to finance investments in their home area. Such organisations were set up among Yemeni migrants in Europe, and the US as well as in Aden, and later on in the oil-exporting states of the Middle East. In the 1960s, in the YAR, the organisations they set up at home became known as Local Development Associations (LDAs).

Socially and economically, the LDAs were the main development actors in the early years of the YAR. The movement expanded exponentially with the increase in the number of migrants and the higher incomes earned after the oil price rises in the Peninsula during the 1970s. Their contribution to development was vital when the state had a limited budget. The LDAs financed schools, medical centres, community generators, and road/track construction to link their villages with the main markets and towns, thus enabling them to use the newly imported motor vehicles. Sometimes they even paid the running costs of medical facilities and schools.

Politically LDAs were very diverse. Some LDAs were led by young men from ordinary tribal or even low-status households, thus gradually affording them increasing political influence within their communities, and enabling them to challenge the leading shaykhly families. In other communities, associations were led by the shaykhly families themselves and thus did not challenge existing hierarchical structures. So they could be instruments of fundamental social change, or of consolidation of existing power structures, depending on the specific dynamics prevailing in a community.

The independence of these associations and their achievements were soon seen as both threats and opportunities by the regime. In the mid-1970s, YAR President Ibrahim al-Hamdi was the first to mobilise and control them by bringing them together under the umbrella of the Confederation of Yemeni Development Associations (CYDA). Although this institutionalisation reduced the LDAs' independence, most participants welcomed the new

The al-Sinah Development Organisation

A particularly impressive example of an LDA was found in al-Sinah, in Taiz Governorate. Taiz and Ibb are the areas with the strongest community-based organisations, partly because they are also the areas of highest population density and emigration. Al-Sinah is a hilltop community situated between Taiz and Turbah. This organisation started in 1970 when its migrants in Hodeida, Taiz city and Sana'a held weekly social meetings during which they collected whatever funds they could afford towards the development of their home area. Initial contributions paid for the construction of a health centre in the village, which was completed in 1972. The emigrants then funded the purchase of medicines, and the salaries and training for some of the staff.

The group then financed the building of schools, first in the main village and later in the larger hamlets; and also paid the salaries of community-based teachers. In the mid-1980s, they financed and installed a 250 KVA generator and transformers that supplied electricity to forty-seven hamlets of the local administrative unit, the `uzla`. They also built a very sophisticated water supply project, including drilling deep wells in the valley on land plots they had bought and equipped with pumps to bring the water up to a network in the villages. Individual houses were only connected to the system if the households had built a sanitation system. Roads to the area were built over time. Over a period of twenty years, this organisation operated democratically with annual meetings, but remained informal due to its multipurpose status which prevented it from registering either under the Cooperative or the NGO laws. It presented a model which could have been followed by others. The al-Sinah project's success was largely due to the fact that the income of migrants was very high and enabled investment in economic ventures and in community activities, as well as the commitment of its members and leadership.

By the mid-1990s, however, problems arose due to the reduced income from migration and the need for replacement of some major equipment. At that time, international development organisations got involved and, instead of supporting the association with the finance it needed to replace the pumps, they attempted to interfere in its organisational mechanisms, thus contributing to tensions and difficulties in acquiring necessary funds. Politicisation also weakened and eventually destroyed the organisation, which demonstrates one negative role that external development institutions can play.

confederation as it was linked to increased funding and technical support. Besides this, the CYDA was seen as establishing the basis for a national level development agency, as well as indicating that the state was actually accepting responsibility for the provision of services.

Their transformation into local government institutions took place through two complementary tendencies: increased financial support from central government, and reduced ability to finance investments through remittances income. By funding the LDAs, the state both emphasised its role in development, and limited the autonomy and power of communities. By the 1980s communities were suffering from reduced migration income and were willing to hand over to the state financial responsibility for development investments. Saleh continued the process of extending control over these associations, as he regarded their independence as a threat. Within a few years he ensured that they were increasingly dependent on state financing while restricting their autonomy through regulations. Eventually he transformed them into the elected local councils whose members were mostly shaykhs and other supporters of the GPC. Moreover their finances fell under the control of Sana'a's bureaucratic administrative structures.

So by 1990, local associations had completely ceased to exist or function. Now they remain little more than a memory among older people. For the first decade after unification, local representatives of the state and central government were appointed from Sana'a or governorate headquarters. Down to the level of district directors, staff usually came from elsewhere, whereas at the sub-district level they tended to be local leaders who supported the ruling party. In a parallel move, and contrary to this process of centralised authority, new community-based organisations (CBOs) have been created in very large numbers, mostly in the hope of accessing development funds from external financiers. Throughout the 1990s, discussion focused on the mechanisms that would be introduced for decentralisation, and the extent of power that would be devolved to the governorate and district levels. This debate was intimately linked to the process of unification, as a strong movement demanded more autonomy at the governorate level, including access to financial resources and allocations.

The implementation of structural adjustment led to the creation of poverty-alleviation compensatory institutions such as the Social Fund for Development (SFD) and the Public Works Programme, discussed in chapter 9, both of which prided themselves on being participatory. Instead of empowering communities, they have become mechanisms to shift financing for social infrastructures from the state to the people, thus reverting to the LDA model with a notable difference. Rather than being initiated, financed and run by the communities which would empower the beneficiaries, the new model finds communities requesting and 'begging' from foreign-funded institutions, and then being given a limited role which ensures their subordination. The dramatic reduction in remittances and the fact that these are now barely sufficient to keep households in basic necessities, has played a major role in this change. But the regime's determination to demonstrate its control was also relevant, though it attempted to do so 'on the cheap' – that is, without carrying out the responsibilities people expect of the state.

The war which started in 2015 has led to a resurgence of interest in local - and community-level development to compensate for the disintegration of central and local state entities. The concept of broad-based community-level institutions being incubators for a more democratic future is gaining ground. Both Yemeni and international actors are increasingly subscribing to this view. Detailed analysis of the LDA model would provide elements highly relevant to the contemporary situation, even beyond the war. One important feature is that the LDAs operated according to a wide range of development approaches and outcomes, thereby demonstrating the need for flexibility. History has shown that standard universally applied formulas lead to failure, even within the confines of a single country, despite their being favoured by centralised organisations, whether national states, international financiers, multilateral, bilateral or even non-government institutions. Local dynamics are a basic factor of success, which is all-too-rarely taken into consideration.

Rural Life in the Early Twenty-First Century

Living conditions in rural areas depend on physical as well as social infrastructure. The state has built roads throughout the country and the network of asphalted or paved roads has increased remarkably. The need to provide access to remote locations for its military/security forces has certainly contributed to these investments. The only other sector which has demonstrated impressive improvements has been telecommunications:

here the prime investors have been private mobile phone networks. People in the remotest areas can now keep in close touch with relatives in the cities, as well as with world events and changes within Yemen. In short, this process has eliminated rural isolation. The extent to which modern telecommunications have changed the lives of people is often neglected; the younger generations who have not known isolation take it for granted, but this access to the world beyond those within easy physical contact has contributed to social earthquakes in Yemeni life in recent decades, as indeed is the case in many other countries.

While these positive developments are important, people's expectations in other sectors have been disappointed: for example, water and electricity services have failed to materialise. Water has been discussed in greater detail in Chapter 8: Yemen's topography, as well as its water resources, make the construction of a national distribution network inappropriate. All sources, whether improved clean springs, wells and community-level rural networks, lag far behind need, and only about 25 percent of rural people had access to safe water in 2004.[22] By 2010, prior to the political crisis and certainly before the destruction which started in 2015, only 20 percent of the rural population had access to electricity (by comparison with 85 percent of urban inhabitants).[23] Possibly the only positive aspect of the current war is that thousands of both rural and urban households have installed solar electricity. Even if of inferior quality, at least people have light, can operate their televisions and are able to charge their phones, thus ensuring that they remain connected to the world. However, only a few have systems powerful enough to operate refrigerators or fans in the hottest areas.

Another basic household necessity is domestic fuel. Changes in lifestyle and worsening desertification – a symptom of climate change – have encouraged a gradual shift away from collected wood, crop residues and livestock dung, which were all used for cooking, alongside purchased charcoal. Bottled gas canisters are increasingly used, but their cost and the long distances that have to be covered to obtain supplies mean that many households still use locally gathered wood for at least some of their cooking. These are additional burdens for rural women who are primarily responsible for fuel collection.

So it is clear that life is tough for rural people, even though they are surrounded by beautiful landscapes which Yemenis do appreciate. In addition to the daily tasks of water and often fuel collection, the distances to markets to obtain basic necessities and reach medical facilities and schools, people also have to earn a living away from their villages. Climate change, population growth and the shrinking size of holdings have all contributed to the difficulties of rural life.

Land Holdings, Agriculture and New Income Sources

Over generations, family holdings have diminished through both inheritance and sales, as impoverished families sold land, leading to the concentration of holdings. Only one detailed agricultural census has been carried out in Yemen, in 2002, and therefore there are limited comparative data. However, on the basis of overall development trends and anecdotal information, the trend has been toward a reduction in the size of smaller holdings and the increase of larger ones. Of the close to five million households in 2002, 3.3 million lived in rural areas, and just under two million had some land. The distribution of land ownership was as follows:

Distribution of Landholdings

Holding size	Percent of land	Percent of owners
< 0.5ha	8	58
0.5-1 ha	8	15
1-5 ha	28	20
> 5 ha	56	7

Source: 2002 Agricultural Census

Most households in Yemen's countryside have less than half a hectare of agricultural land, so with 60 percent of cultivated land being rain-fed, it is no surprise that a typical rural family of seven members cannot sustain itself from its agriculture alone. Shortage of pasture land in the cultivated areas also means that most families' few small ruminants or cattle are insufficient to raise their income above poverty level. In Yemen's better watered agro-ecological zones, such as the western escarpments, population density is much higher, thus resulting in far smaller average holding sizes of under one hectare (in Ibb, Taiz, Mahweet, al-Dhala' and Raymah). Despite benefiting from a modernised spate irrigation scheme, Lahej has an average holding of 0.58 hectares and its population is very poor, mainly because most of the farmers who work the irrigated lands are sharecroppers. Landholdings are also mostly distributed in many plots, with a national average of 3.6 plots per holding. The following table on governorate level landholdings explains the high levels of poverty found in some of the more productive and watered areas. Trends have only worsened in the past decade, especially since the beginning of the war in 2015.

Most smallholdings are still worked by family members, though they only require a few days at planting time, and a few more at harvesting time for men. Women, meanwhile, are active in weeding throughout the season, which also produces fodder for livestock. Extended households are still largely the norm in rural Yemen. Land, like other property, is officially held by the head of the household, who is usually the senior male member of the family. Younger men of these households are not the main decision-makers even though many of them are in their forties and have their own nuclear families. They may participate in seasonal agricultural tasks, but invariably they have to migrate to cities to find the casual work without whose income many households would simply not survive. The shift to urban income is increasing tension between generations. Younger men are challenging the authority of their fathers – an aspect of changing behaviour which is reflected at the political as well as household level.

Young men, whether recently married or still single, generally have a higher level of education than their elders. However, even secondary school graduates and those who have higher education find it difficult to find jobs, and they form a large class of un- and under-employed people whose frustration with their living conditions is rising. In the first decade of unification, many of them tried to join the security forces, but this became more difficult after 2001 when only secondary school graduates could join. The war situation has, by contrast, meant that joining armed groups is the one source of employment and reliable income for young men everywhere in Yemen. Salaries are higher than elsewhere and in most cases they are actually paid, which is not the case in other sectors. The vast majority of recruits join for financial rather than ideological reasons, and participate in whichever group their friends and neighbours join. This enables them to support their families who, in most cases, have been reduced to abject poverty.

Comparative Landholding Sizes to Rural Households in 2002

Gover-norate	No. Rural House-holds	Total number of landhold-ers	percent land-holders to Rural Hhs	percent land-holders with < 1ha	percent of ag land held by holders of < 1 ha	percent ag land held by holders of > 5 ha
Ibb	253,183	175 508	69	94	65	8
Abyan	43,040	28 112	65	49	8	65
al-Baidha	53,933	34 366	64	51	12	46
Taiz	286,077	153 661	54	93	40	34
al-Jawf	51,008	28 298	55	30	4	72
Hajja	177,134	97 126	55	74	14	62
Hodeida	236,549	86 449	41	33	4	27
Hadramaut	65,022	39 683	61	74	14	61
Dhamar	162,763	110 641	68	79	23	46
Shabwa	44,244	22 310	50	46	8	63
Sa'ada	71,455	48 531	68	75	26	34
Sana'a	113,948	87 851	77	57	14	43
Lahej	95,699	54 910	57	88	37	33
Mareb	24,141	14 279	59	26	1	91
Mahweet	64,464	44 168	68	85	46	14
Al-Mahra	8,125	3 426	42	69	25	27
Amran	87,359	68 572	78	55	13	48
al-Dhala'	51,562	36 245	70	91	58	12
Raymah	55,744	35 567	64	92	61	8
Yemen	1,950,117	1 180 105	60	73	15	56

Source: 2002 Agricultural Census for Agricultural Data and 2004 Population Census

Irrigation and the types of crops cultivated are further relevant factors determining poverty. Farmers cultivating high-value, mostly irrigated, crops are clearly better off than those whose cropping pattern involves only rain-fed staples, such as sorghum, maize and millet, as well as a little wheat and legumes. Of the 1.2 million hectares cultivated in 2002, 685,000 (57 percent) grew staple grains, 14 percent coffee, qat and other trees, 10 percent animal fodder, 6 percent vegetables, and a further 6 percent fruits, and only 4 percent cash crops (sesame, tobacco and cotton). While qat and coffee allow a smallholder to obtain reasonable returns from small areas, the same cannot be said for other crops, and even most qat growers have such small areas of the crop that this is insufficient to sustain their households.

After land, water availability is the main factor determining yields and the type of crops which can be cultivated. The majority of agricultural land is rain-fed, though its relative importance varies from 95 percent in Raymah, 87 percent in Mahweet and 80 percent in Hajja. All three of these governorates have high rainfall and rough terrain unsuited to spate irrigation. By contrast, other areas have few wells and springs, amounting to a mere 1 percent rain-fed fields in Mareb and al-Jawf where rainfall is very low and well irrigation dominates. Spate irrigation covers 11 percent of the cultivated area nationally, including traditional spate systems that are repaired on an annual basis, and modern ones, such as those found in the Tihama, and wadis Tuban and Bana in the south. Changes in rainfall patterns have increased the tendency to irrigate high-value crops, qat in particular, with tanker loads of purchased water; this is clearly an unsustainable strategy due to its cost and the exhaustion of the aquifers.

Raising livestock contributes significantly to the livelihoods of rural households, most of whom have a few small ruminants and ideally cattle. Throughout the highlands, cattle ownership is usually restricted to one cow as its husbandry is very time-consuming. Due to malnutrition, most cows are force-fed manually, a task usually undertaken by older women who sit and chat spending their afternoons feeding the animals in the shade of their houses. Despite these efforts, the average Yemeni cow only produces about 3 kilograms of milk per day, which is barely sufficient for household needs. Some of this is transformed into ghee and buttermilk, the latter being a basic highland rural breakfast meal when served with spices and bread. The very low milk productivity of cows explains why home cheese production has not taken off as an income-generating activity, as there is simply too little milk to make this a viable operation. Just to produce enough ghee for household needs takes a few days.

While the majority of farms are mixed, 16 percent of rural households are headed by landless livestock owners. They include semi-nomadic large herders in the vast rangelands of the arid regions, where livestock is as important as crop cultivation (Hadramaut, al-Jawf, Shabwa, Mareb and al-Mahra). Others live where poor people without access to land are concentrated, either because the cultivable land to population ratio is low (Taiz, Hajja and Lahej) or because most land is held by large owners (Abyan, Hodeida). In the latter case, livestock owners also work other people's land, either through tenancy or sharecropping arrangements, or as casual workers paid in cash.

The economy of the rural coastal areas is based on artisanal fisheries supplemented by livestock husbandry. Artisanal fishermen include both boat owners and those working in them. There are about 65,000 fishermen members of cooperatives, who probably form the majority of fishermen, certainly of boat owners. In addition, about 150,000 men work on the boats as labourers, many of them coming from the same extended households as the owners.

It is clear from the above that the vast majority of rural households need to complement their income from non-agricultural activities, such as the casual labour of their young men in the neighbouring towns and in Yemen's major cities further afield. To a lesser extent, international migration still plays a role: prior to the beginning of the current war, there were again about 1.5 million Yemenis in Saudi Arabia. However, Riyadh's 'Saudi-isation' policy, which aimed at increasing the employment of Saudi citizens, has had a serious negative impact on employing Yemenis. Sectors which are now 'reserved' for Saudi Arabian citizens include many of the small-scale enterprises which had previously employed most Yemenis.

This chapter has hopefully demonstrated the very close and intricate relationship between rural and urban life in Yemen, as well as given readers a flavour of life for most Yemenis. In the process, it has traced the links between daily life and the overall political, economic and social changes of recent decades.

CONCLUSION

Whither Yemen?

This book has presented the many complex historical, political, economic and social problems whose synergy led to the war in Yemen. In brief, by 2011, breaking point had been reached. People's living standards continued to deteriorate; the patronage and nepotism-based autocratic rule had run out of steam (and cash); and rapid population growth combined with mismanagement of limited natural resources, water in particular, threatened the country's very survival. The GCC Agreement had intended to achieve an acceptable compromise between the popular demands of the 2011 uprisings and the power of the rival elite groups. However, the 2012–2014 transitional regime failed to provide the good governance and equitable social and economic policies required to fundamentally transform the country. Such a 'new Yemen' would have challenged autocratic regimes in the region, one of the reasons why the international community was content to watch as rival elite Yemeni politicians sank into a further struggle for power and marginalised the groups emerging from the popular uprisings. The construction of a new polity was supplanted by an increasingly acute power struggle between different factions of the pre-existing elites. Rather than provide an alternative, the GCC Agreement only postponed regime collapse.

The internationalisation of this crisis in 2015 with the military intervention of the Saudi-led coalition failed to restore to power the transitional government, and turned a political and humanitarian crisis into a catastrophe. If the current crisis is dealt with in a piecemeal way, only short-term, superficial solutions can be found. Reaching a sustainable peace will only be possible if all the problems are addressed in synergy and the population is given the opportunity to, at least partially, see their hopes realised.

As we have seen, Yemeni society has been fundamentally transformed in recent decades as tribal norms and ideology have weakened and been replaced by the early stages of a rapacious process of capital accumulation, which favours only a few. Unlike eighteenth- and nineteenth-century Europe, mass industrial production has not been a feature of this change due to the transfer of most industrial production towards south-east Asia and the fundamental transformations of the capitalist system worldwide, which has stifled the economic emergence of so many 'developing' countries.

During the first decade of the twenty-first century, the Yemeni beneficiaries of this financial accumulation split into rival factions in a struggle over political power and the distribution of diminishing resources. The resulting conflicting elements are now leading the many rival militias in the war. War gains from the smuggling of fuel, weapons, food and all other commodities have become a substitute for earlier sources of income from oil exports and patronage. The war has provided an opportunity for the rise of new profiteers. Enrichment of this group is one of the reasons for the leaders' unwillingness to reach a peace agreement, despite the universal popular demand for an end to the war. The foot soldiers on all sides are themselves primarily motivated by the need for cash to maintain their families, given the complete collapse of what little conventional economy existed prior to the crisis.

How Internationalisation of the War Has Worsened Future Prospects

The war has taken a quantum leap towards the abyss with its internationalisation. Although external participants have legitimate concerns in Yemen, most of their involvement is based on treating the country as a proxy for totally different battles. Saudi Arabia, Yemen's closest neighbour and long-time financier, has a real interest in the country's stability, as do other GCC states. However, these have all been trumped by the deceptive claim that the struggle in Yemen is really one against Iranian expansionism, and hence over domination of the Muslim world as a whole. The proxy element is exacerbated by rivalries between Saudi Arabia, the

UAE and Qatar: in Yemen they are played out around the role of Islah, Southern separatism and Saleh's family, yet again ignoring the country's suffering population. Peace-makers like Oman and the weakened United Nations don't stand much of a chance in the face of combined Yemeni and international interests in the continuation of the war. By contrast with the political and military leadership, the priority for all ordinary Yemenis is to see a rapid end to this war, regardless of its outcome. But in 2017, the UN wasn't even able to arrange a ceasefire for Ramadan, thus demonstrating both its lack of influence and the callousness of decision-makers in this war.

As for the US, UK and other Western states, Yemen is simplistically reduced to a site to counter terrorism. The fate of its people ranks way below the priority of retaining and improving relations with the GCC states, who are seen as potential important sources of investment and trade at a time of economic and financial difficulties at home. Western priorities seem to be the expansion of already extravagant arms sales to even more fantastic figures of billions of dollars; weapons that are unnecessary, expensive, technologically inappropriate to respond to any real threat to these regimes, but which offer opportunities for further enrichment of the few on all sides. These states also hope for increased direct Gulf investment in all economic sectors at home. With only minor exaggeration, this can be interpreted as a reversal of the nineteenth-century situation when debt forced countries like Egypt to submit to Western domination.

Internal Political Implications: The Rise of Extremism and Fragmentation of the Country

Unfortunately, despite the urgency of ending the war, there are no immediate visible prospects for a solution as of mid-2017. The leaders of both major warring factions (on the one side the Huthi-Saleh alliance and on the other the Saudi-led coalition and the internationally recognised government forces) prioritise their personal financial gains and continue to behave with complete and utter contempt for the welfare of the now 27 million Yemenis. As stated by the UN Secretary General, 21 million of them are experiencing emergency conditions including about 7 million whose extreme stress means they are liable to die of starvation in an unprecedented famine.

The persistence of the war is allowing the emergence of tendencies likely to have a long-term negative impact on the country's future. It has encouraged the expansion of fundamentalist extremism which currently takes several forms: the Sunni jihadism of the AQAP and Daesh varieties, rivalling other Salafi movement on one side, and feeding the rise of Zaydi fundamentalism under the Huthi banner on the other. These groups' influence on daily life in the areas they dominate is noticeable in their restrictions on civil liberties, mainly of women, but also of men who challenge their stated ideology and attempt to uphold universal human values. In this way fundamentalist social norms are spread and enforced. Although the majority of young men fighting under any of these banners do so due to poverty, a few are drawn to the ideology of the movements. They may genuinely have adopted these beliefs and thus will uphold them once the main war is over, particularly in the absence of socio-economic development. Moreover, the perception that power comes from being on the right side of a weapon can have a long-term nefarious influence on many youth. Some are discovering and enjoying the advantages of simple banditry in the absence of effective and operational state security forces, and may well continue operating as gangs for some time to come.

The fragmentation of Yemen is already a reality. Throughout the country, divisions which existed in past decades have worsened to the point of conflict since 2015. Fragmentation takes different forms with different levels of intensity in the former YAR: many people from the Tihama along the west coast have been treated as second-class citizens for generations, and now demand to have their specific interests taken into consideration. Further east, lasting historic connections link the people of Mareb with communities in the similarly semi-arid regions of al-Baidha and Shabwa: the people from these areas feel excluded from the benefits captured by the ruling clique in Sana'a, particularly the loss of their main resources, oil and gas, to the centralised regime. The frustration of the people of the far north has concretised in the Huthi movement, now allied with its old enemy Saleh and in control of two-thirds of the population, if only one-third of the land.

Thanks to their high population density, Dhamar, Taiz and Ibb exported their people throughout the country in skilled and unskilled jobs since well before the unification of the two states in 1990. In the South, with the worsening economic situation, these people, mostly single men but also settled families, are being hounded out and there have even been cases of people being murdered in the past decade. In the long term, this form of 'ethnic' conflict is far deeper and more worrying than the formal sectarianism currently promoted by various factional leaders. In addition to the widespread hostility to Northerners, people of the former PDRY are now divided into a multitude of micro-groups. Some semblance of order has been created by the UAE-sponsored and managed security forces, but this is no substitute for administration which, where it exists at all, is by local forces with a broad range of allegiances.

The fundamental divisions in the South are between Hadramaut, which appears to be a relatively cohesive entity and whose leaders have ambitions for autonomy, if not independence, and the rest of the area where fragmentation is deep. East of Hadramaut, people in al-Mahra Governorate are torn between wanting to join Hadramaut and hopes of becoming part of Oman, while the more unrealistic among them dream of an independent al-Mahra. With a population barely reaching 100,000, al-Mahra's influence on Yemeni politics is limited, its strategic geographic position being its only negotiable asset. Further west, the abundance of separatist factions demonstrates their inability to agree on any social or economic policies and their political programme is limited to a single word: secession. This lack of perspective and foresight further proves that the struggle for power between old enemies has taken primacy over any concept of good governance and social and economic development. An example which is merely indicative of the complexity and intractability of the situation is the struggle in Aden in 2017 between UAE-sponsored Salafi factions, Hadi's Presidential Guard, and Southern separatists, culminating in the dismissal of Aden's governor and the latter's establishment of a Southern Transitional Council in May 2017. Readers may be aware of further convulsions in this saga.

So it is very unlikely that Yemen will, at the end of the war, resemble the Republic of Yemen which existed since 1990, the two states of the 1980s, or even the six-region federal state proposed in the 2015 draft constitution. It is more likely that an internationally backed peace agreement will, at best, put an end to the external military intervention, while within Yemen itself, fighting will continue at greater and lesser intensity between numerous small entities over access to the country's very limited natural resources. This could lead to fighting between small groups in the south-west, reminiscent of the rival emirates of the Protectorates period, a Shafi'i-Zaydi split in the northern parts which lack major economic resources and support; while the resource- rich areas might become one or more separate fiefdoms.

Reconstruction: Infrastructure and the Economy

In addition to social disintegration, the war has destroyed much of Yemen's physical infrastructure including some very expensive engineering structures built over decades with limited financial assistance from the international community and through community efforts; it has been destroyed by air strikes as well as ground military action. The cost of rebuilding Yemen will be huge: since 2015, a number of pledging and planning conferences for reconstruction have taken place under the auspices of the GCC states and the international financial institutions; there will be more. They pledge vast amounts which are unlikely to materialise, given the previous history of such meetings in Yemen and elsewhere.

Equally, if not more importantly, what does materialise is likely to take the form of multi-million dollar contracts for infrastructure whose main beneficiaries will be international institutions and contractors, rather than Yemeni companies, let alone the Yemeni people. The gap between pledges and reality is demonstrated by any examination of the actual funds provided after earlier pledging conferences. The farce of the multiplicity of projects to restore electricity to Aden since its liberation in mid-2015 is probably the model for what is to come: expensive contracts for a few (Yemeni and other) companies, much publicity, some low-quality construction and equipment, and continued power cuts for the citizens.

In addition, these pledges mostly ignore the equally important sector of human development. All financing and most development organisations prefer large expensive construction contracts (which also facilitate corruption) to smaller ones focusing on improving people's technical capacity; these cost far less and demand more time and work, but achieve significantly greater long-term real human development impact. Much has been said in the book about agriculture and less about other economic activities. Agriculture has a future but it needs a new approach. Other economic activities can only emerge once serious changes have been made to the education system. This needs an interval of about fifteen years between initiation at the primary level and the emergence of newly educated cadres from tertiary education. The urgency of this action cannot be overemphasised: the longer the delays at the beginning, the least likely to achieve a new economy in time to compensate for exhaustion of the limited aquifers. The 'miracle' solution of micro-finance proposed by the development community in the past decades has had minimal impact; the experience of other countries demonstrates that its potential is far below its ambitious claims. Other development initiatives have suffered from corruption, while the absence of an effective judiciary system has deterred private sector investors.

Reaching a Peace Agreement?

In the context of vast war profiteering, neither the Yemeni factional leaders nor their international supporters have yet shown any willingness to give priority to a peaceful environment for the Yemeni people. Unfortunately they cannot be ignored: both local leaders and the international participants will have a determining role in the outcome. The balance of power between the Huthi-Saleh faction on the one side and the internationally recognised government on the other remains largely static in the third year of the war. The former exercise real control over the central and northern highlands and most of the Red Sea coast, though they lost its southern end in early 2017. By contrast the so-called liberated areas have fallen under the control of a wide range of small entities whose legitimacy varies. President Hadi's government controls very little of Yemen's territories; it cannot even pay the salaries of its civil servants and security staff.

The war in Yemen started shortly after King Salman succeeded his late brother, Abdullah, in January 2015 in Saudi Arabia. Then Deputy Crown Prince Mohammed bin Salman looked forward to a rapid victory in Yemen to consolidate his position in the succession hierarchy of the Kingdom. He also hoped to use the Yemeni crisis to win Saudi Arabia's muted confrontation with Iran which has been badly dented in Iraq and Syria. The consequent propaganda effort attributed to Iran far greater involvement in support of the Huthis than it actually has, something which Iranian extremists facilitated considerably through equally propagandist counter-assertions. Treating Yemen as a proxy for Iran also misled the Saudi-led coalition into attributing to Iranian support a far greater role than it actually has, thus failing to realise the actual military strength of the Huthi-Saleh alliance. The coalition partners were initially fooled by the belief that technological superiority would ensure a rapid and easy victory without even needing to commit their own ground forces. More than two years later, in the face of military stalemate and the high financial, human and public relations cost of the war, Saudi leaders must be reviewing their position and seeking an exit strategy which gives at least the impression of victory. Named Crown Prince in June 2017, Mohammed bin Salman has an even greater responsibility to bring this war to an end.

In addition to the disastrous humanitarian situation, the political and financial cost of the war calls for a rapid resolution, a peace agreement which, at the very least, gives each party enough to consider itself victor. There is no doubt that the Huthi-Saleh alliance is formed of two distinct parties, each of which will have to be given some concessions. On the other side, regardless of UAE efforts to suppress it in the South, Islah remains the largest political institution active in some of the 'liberated' areas, and it has considerable military capacity, both used and potential. Islah cannot be ignored or reduced to a pawn in the GCC internal debate about extremism. Given UAE hostility, the ostracism of Qatar which emerged in mid-2017 may have an impact on Islah's future within the coalition, though it is the main fighting element in the Mareb area. Elsewhere, however divided, the Southern separatists must be taken into consideration. It also remains to be seen whether the Emirati leadership can bring back under control the extremist Salafi elements which it has unleashed in its obsessive hostility to the Muslim Brotherhood element of the Islah, Salafi elements which are far more dangerous in the long run to Yemenis and others.

Up until mid-2017 efforts to reach a peace agreement excluded most of these groups, let alone civil society, youth, women and representatives of the majority of the population, tribal or otherwise. The Yemeni people want peace and most of them, by now, want it regardless of who wins. However, if any agreement is to be effective and long-lasting, it must be far more inclusive than the list of current participants in the UN-sponsored negotiation attempts.

In the Long Term

When peace returns, whatever new regime emerges must focus on the long-term issues faced by the people and, first and foremost, the water crisis. Unless appropriate measures are taken, within a generation or less, the most densely populated parts of the country will become uninhabitable. Like most other problems in Yemen, this one can be solved: a regime committed to the welfare of the population can manage use of water, giving priority to domestic and animal consumption; with 90 percent of water used in agriculture, reducing this substantially would be enough to enable an even larger population to live in the particularly beautiful highland water-scarce areas. While this means putting an end to uncontrolled irrigation, the development of high-value rain-fed crops, alongside eco-tourism and other economic activities based on high technology would combine to provide replacement rural economic activities and thus make life in rural Yemen pleasant. Many Yemenis dreamt of such a change a generation ago, in the heyday of the 1980s.

While the water crisis is largely due to over-exploitation and rapid population growth, other climate change factors must also be addressed for the long-term survival of Yemenis in Yemen. The most prominent of these relates to rising sea levels which will affect not only all fisher communities but also three of Yemen's major cities: Hodeida, Aden and Mukalla. Effective mitigation measures are essential to enable their populations to live, particularly as their size is likely to increase considerably from an influx of highlanders driven out of their homes by the lack of water. The hinterlands of these cities are also among the country's main agricultural areas and better management of their ground water is essential for the country to continue producing even a small share of its food.

Long-term economic policies will depend on the emergence of a highly educated population able to exploit the possibilities of the twenty-first century. This obviously means massive investment in education which would enable rural as well as urban people throughout the country to set up and run enterprises, thereby providing them with a reasonable income. Policies promoting equal economic opportunities and an end to nepotism and cronyism would also be elements of a new well-governed Yemen. Such a regime would reduce inequality and operate according to the laws, thus re-establishing people's confidence in politics.

With respect to the external states involved, particularly Yemen's immediate neighbours, it is also likely that their current short-termist approach could, within decades, have a negative boomerang effect on their own countries. Exclusion of Yemen from the GCC increases frustration among the thousands of Yemenis who could otherwise be both earning a good living there and thus maintaining their families at home, while contributing constructively to GCC societies. In addition, in the long run, political mismanagement and exhaustion of water in Yemen may lead millions to force their way past any barriers and become desperate climate and political refugees in Saudi Arabia, Oman and the UAE. A wiser set of policies integrating Yemen into the GCC could result in prosperity for all in a mutually beneficial relationship. Beyond Yemen's immediate neighbours, Europe and the West in general have neglected the crisis as, to date, it has neither brought thousands of refugees across the Mediterranean nor have any of the perpetrators of terrorist incidents in Europe been of Yemeni origin, nor indeed has maritime security in the Red Sea been impacted. Should Yemen and its people continue to be ignored and the war intensify and persist, none of these negative outcomes can be precluded. Finally, returning to an earlier theme, hope: that the distressing outcomes just mentioned do not materialise and instead that the positive ones come to pass and make Yemen a country where its new generations flourish.

Notes

Preface

1. United Nations Security Council, 12 July 2017. Briefing of the Special Envoy of the UN Secretary-General for Yemen to the open session of the UN Security Council
2. Ibid.
3. Lizzie Dearden, 'Yemen War: More Than Half of British People Unaware of Ongoing Conflict Seeing UK Weapons Deployed by Saudis', *The Independent*, 18 March 2017.

Chapter One: How the 2011 Uprising and the Transition Led to War

1. United Nations, Office for the Coordination of Humanitarian Affairs (UNOCHA), Under-Secretary-General for Humanitarian Affairs and Emergency Relief Coordinator, Stephen O'Brien, 'Statement to the Security Council on Yemen,' New York, 12 July 2017.
2. UNOCHA, *Humanitarian Bulletin Yemen*, no 25, 16 July 2017, p. 2.
3. UNOCHA, Statement to the Security Council on Missions to Yemen, South Sudan, Somalia and Kenya and an update on the Oslo conference on Nigeria and the Lake Chad Region, 10 March 2017, p. 1.
4. Z. Abdelkarim, E. Hodachok and D. Monaco, *Yemen's Transition: Electoral Challenges and Opportunities for Reform*, Centre on Democracy, Development and the Rule of Law, International Foundation for Electoral Systems, Working Paper 139, 2013, p. 7.
5. His previous electoral successes had been made under earlier constitutional changes.
6. K. Abdullah and M. Ghobari, 'Thousands in Yemen March for New Government', *Sprucegrove Examiner*, 27 January 2011.
7. I have discussed in greater detail the significance of the 'Change' squares in Yemen in Chapter 6 of A. Roberts, M. J Willis, R. McCarthy and T. Garton Ash, eds., *Civil Resistance in the Arab Spring: Triumphs and Disasters*, Oxford University Press, 2016.
8. Human Rights Watch, *Unpunished Massacre: Yemen's Failed Response to the 'Friday of Dignity' Killings*, New York: HRW, February 2013. Others give higher

figures for the number of dead.

9.   Translation is found in annex 1 of Helen Lackner, *Yemen's Peaceful Transition from Autocracy: Could It Have Succeeded?*, International Institute for Democracy and Electoral Assistance, Stockholm, 2016, pp. 70–71.

10.   *Al Arabiya News* (English-language web service of Al Arabiya News Channel), 22 May 2011.

11.   United Nations Security Council Resolution 2014, 21 October 2011.

12.   Much of the following section is based on my detailed analysis of the transition process and its outcomes in Helen Lackner, *Yemen's Peaceful Transition from Autocracy*.

13.   Official UN translation can be found in Helen Lackner, *Yemen's Peaceful Transition from Autocracy*, annex B, pp. 72–80.

14.   Ibid., p. 72.

15.   UNSC Res. 2051, 12 June 2012.

16.   UNSC Res. 2140, 26 February 2014, paras 11 ff.

17.   *Gulf News*, 11 February 2014.

18.   He was later appointed ambassador to the US where he was in mid-2017.

19.   Officially named the National Authority for Monitoring the Implementation of the NDC Outcomes.

20.   Data from Stockholm International Peace Research Institute (SIPRI) website.

21.   *Stratfor Worldview*, 'The UAE joins an Exclusive Club', 8 December 2016.

22.   BBC News, 'Somaliland Agrees to UAE Military Base in Berbera', 13 February 2017.

23.   Middle East Eye, 'Hundreds More Sudanese Troops Arrive in Yemen', 9 November 2015.

24.   Middle East Eye, 'Senegal Pledges 2,100 Soldiers for Saudi-Led Coalition in Yemen', 5 May 2015.

25.   Katherine Lackey, 'Reports: US Forces Evacuating Yemen Air Base', *Air Force Times*, 21 March 2015.

26.   Oriana Pawlyk, '2 Years Into Yemen War, US Ramps Up Refueling of Saudi Jets', *Military*, 15 February 2017.

27.   Data from the Bureau of Investigative Journalism, using their minimum death toll and only confirmed drone strikes.

28.   Maggie Michael, 'In Yemen's Secret Prisons, UAE Tortures and US Interrogates', *AP*, 22 June 2017.

29.   SIPRI website.

30.   Decision as quoted by *The Independent* on 10 July 2017.

31.   Andrew Mitchell, BYS Annual lecture in the *BYS Journal* 2017 [forthcoming]

32.   See the relevant reports from Amnesty International, Human Rights Watch and Médecins Sans Frontières.

33.   BBC News, 'Yemen Conflict: UN Criticises Saudi Civilian Bombings', 10 May 2016.

34.   *Gulf States Newsletter*, 1025, 3 November 2016, p. 3.

35.   For a detailed analysis of the CBY saga, see Peter Salisbury, *Bickering while Yemen*

Burns: Poverty, War, and Political Indifference, Arab Gulf States Institute in Washington, June 2017.

36. C. Savage and E. Schmitt, 'Trump Administration Is Said to Be Working to Loosen Counterterrorism Rules', *New York Times,* 12 March 2017.

37. World Food Programme, *Yemen: Comprehensive Food Security Survey,* 2014, p. 7. This compared with 22 percent in 2003 and 44 percent in 2008.

38. UNOCHA, *Revised 2016 Yemen Humanitarian Response Plan,* p. 1.

39. UNOCHA, *Humanitarian Bulletin Yemen,* issue 19, 31 December 2016, p. 1.

Chapter Two: Yemen and the World

1. Carla Stea, 'Manipulation of the UN Security Council in support of the US-NATO Military Agenda, Coercion, Intimidation & Bribery Used to Extort Approval from Reluctant Members', *Global Research,* 10 January 2012.

2. Talk at Chatham House, London, 7 September 2016, viewed on the Chatham House website.

3. Askar Halwan al-Enazy, 'The International Boundary Treaty Concluded Between the Kingdom of Saudi Arabia and The Yemeni Republic on 12 June, 2000', *American Journal of International Law,* vol 96 no 1, January 2002, pp 161–173.

4. For a discussion of Saudi Arabia's use of religion as a primary element in its own state construction and as a consolidation mechanism for its internal structures through promotion of Wahhabism as a rival to nationalism in the Arab world, see Adham Saouli, *The Arab State: Dilemmas of Late Formation,* Routledge, 2012, pp. 95–100.

5. See Joshua Rogers, 'The Making of the Tribal Republic: North Yemen's Tribes and Central Authority during the Civil War 1962–1970', *British-Yemeni Society Journal,* vol 24, 2016 pp. 12–18.

6. Saudi-PDRY relations are discussed in detail in Fred Halliday, *Revolution and Foreign Policy': The Case of South Yemen, 1967–1987,* Cambridge, 1990, pp. 154–164, in particular, and various chapters of both Noel Brehony, *Yemen Divided: The Story of a Failed State in South Arabia,* I.B. Tauris, 2010, and Helen Lackner, *PDR Yemen: Outpost of Socialist Development in Arabia,* Ithaca Press, London, 1985.

7. Stephen Pelletiere, *Yemen and Stability in the Persian Gulf: Confronting the Threat from Within,* Strategic Studies Institute, US Army War College, PA, 1996, p. 22.

8. Paul Dresch, *A History of Modern Yemen,* Cambridge University Press, 2000, pp. 196.

9. Embassy Sana'a. 'Yemen's Big Brother: What Has Saudi Arabia Done for Yemen Lately?' Wikileaks Cable: 08SANAA1053_a. Dated 18 June 2008, para 4.

10. Ibid., para 19.

11. G. Hill and G. Nonneman, *Yemen, Saudi Arabia and the Gulf States: Elite Politics, Street Protests and Regional Diplomacy,* Chatham House, Middle East and North Africa Programme, 2011, p. 9.

12. See Ash Rossiter, 'The Yemeni-Saudi Border: from Boundary to Frontline', in H. Lackner and D. Varisco, eds, *Yemen and the Gulf States: The Making of a Crisis*, Gerlach, 2017.

13. Embassy Sana'a. 'Yemen's Big Brother: What Has Saudi Arabia Done for Yemen Lately?' Wikileaks Cable, para. 8.

14. 'Yemen Denies Saudi Air Strike Targeted its Soil', *Al Arabiya*, 5 November 2009.

15. See Ash Rossiter, 'The Yemeni-Saudi Border', in Lackner and Varisco, eds, *Yemen and the Gulf States*.

16. This and other aspects of Saudi Arabia's views on unification in Jean Gueyras 'Ombre Saudienne sur le nouveau Yemen', *Le Monde*, 29 June 1990.

17. Details of the relationship between Yemen and Oman are discussed in Ahmed Baabood, 'Omani-Yemeni Relations: Past, Present and Future', in H. Lackner and D. Varisco, eds, *Yemen and the Gulf States*.

18. BBC monitoring, 25 November 2009.

19. John Xenakis, 'Iran Brags That Sana'a Is the Fourth Arab Capital They Control', *The National*, 27 September 2014.

20. *Al Bayan*, 23 April 2015, issue 2359804 albayan.ae/one-world/arabs/2015-04-23-1.2359804.

21. Stephen Pelletiere, *Yemen and Stability in the Persian Gulf: Confronting The Threat From Within*, Strategic Studies Institute, US Army War college, PA, 1996, pp. 27–8.

22. Edmund Hull, *High-Value Target: Countering al-Qaeda in Yemen*, Potomac Books, Washington DC, 2011, p. 9.

23. Ibid., pp. 115–6. Regarding the World Bank cuts, see 'World bank Cuts Support by a Third Citing Slow Progress', IRIN, 26 December 2005.

24. Sarah Phillips, *Yemen and the Politics of Permanent Crisis*, Routledge, 2011, p. 42.

25. Jeremy M. Sharp, *Yemen: Background and US Relations*, Congressional Research Service, 2010, p. 27.

26. Bureau of Investigative Journalism website.

27. Bureau of Investigative Journalism website.

28. Patrick Cockburn, 'Threats to Yemen Prove America Hasn't Learned the Lesson of History', *The Independent*, 31 December 2009.

29. Embassy Sana'a. 'General Petraeus' Meeting with Saleh on Security Assistance, AQAP Strikes.' Wikileaks Cable: 10SANAA4_a. Dated 1 June 2010.

30. Jeremy M. Sharp, *Yemen: Background and US Relations*, p. 29.

31. Nabeel A. Khoury, 'Yemen: In Search of a Coherent US Policy', *Middle East Policy Council*, Summer 2014, Volume XXI, Number 2, p. 7. At the time Brennan was President Obama's chief counterterrorism adviser.

32. G. Hill and G. Nonneman, *Yemen, Saudi Arabia and the Gulf States*, p. 4.

33. Andrej Kreutz, *Russia and the Middle East: Friend or Foe*, Praeger Security Interests, London, 2007, p. 144.

Chapter Three: The Two Yemeni Republics and Unification

1. Edgar O'Ballance, *The War in the Yemen*, Faber, London, 1971, and Duff Hart-Davis, *The War that Never Was: The True Story of the Men Who Fought Britain's Most Secret Battle*, Century, London, 2011. These books, among others, discuss the British involvement and details of the civil war.

2. For further discussion of this largely forgotten period in the history of the YAR, see Fred Halliday, *Arabia Without Sultans*, Penguin, London, 1974, pp. 118–126.

3. Fred Halliday, *Arabia Without Sultans*, pp. 146–7.

4. According to a joke which circulated throughout Yemen for the first year or two of his tenure.

5. See Richard Tutwiler, *Tribe, Tribute and Trade: Social Class Formation in Highland Yemen*, PhD Thesis, University of New York at Binghamton, 1987.

6. Paul Dresch, *A History of Modern Yemen*, Cambridge University Press, 2000, p. 123.

7. Halliday, *Arabia Without Sultans*, p. 250.

8. Drech, *A History of Modern Yemen*, p. 118.

9. People's Democratic Republic of Yemen, Central Statistical Organization, *Statistical Yearbook 1988*, Aden, 1989, p. 47.

10. More details on this period can be found in Helen Lackner, *PDR Yemen: Outpost of Socialist Development in Arabia* and Noel Brehony, *Yemen Divided: The Story of a Failed State in South Arabia*.

11. Other hopes of the period are listed in Robert Burrowes, 'The Republic of Yemen: the Politics of Unification and Civil War, 1989–1995', in Michael C Hudson, ed., *Middle East Dilemma: The Politics and Economics of Arab Integration*, IB Tauris, 1995, pp. 200–1.

12. R. Leveau, F. Mermier, U. Steinbach, eds, *Le Yémen contemporain*, Karthala, Paris, 1999, p. 112.

Chapter Four: Islamism: Reality and Myth

1. See N. Brehony and S. Sarhan, eds, *Rebuilding Yemen: Political, Economic and Social Challenges*, Gerlach, Berlin, 2015, p. 2, footnote 4.

2. François Burgat, *Face to Face with Political Islam*, IB Tauris, London, 2003, and his other books provide details of his analysis, including significant passages on Yemen.

3. Laurent Bonnefoy, *Salafism in Yemen: Transnationalism and Religious Identity*, Hurst, London, 2011, pp. 57–8.

4. Laurent Bonnefoy, 'Violence in Contemporary Yemen: State, Society and Salafis' *The Muslim World*, volume 101, April 2011, p. 338.

5. International Crisis Group, *The Huthis: From Saada to Sanaa*, 2014, p. 3, footnote 12.

6.	For more detailed analysis of the Islah Party, see Sarah Phillips, *Yemen's Democracy Experiment in Regional Perspective: Patronage and Pluralized Authoritarianism*, Palgrave Macmillan, 2008, Chapter 6, pp. 137–166.

7.	From al-Bab website, *Political Programme of Islah Party*.

8.	Sarah Phillips, *Yemen's Democracy Experiment in Regional Perspective*, p. 150.

9.	The rise of Islah in the former PDRY is discussed further in Chapters 6 and 7.

10.	In 2004 the Ministry of Awqaf only supervised 6,000 of them. Phillips, *Yemen's Democracy Experiment in Regional Perspective*, p. 145.

11.	See Gregory Johnsen, *The Last Refuge, Yemen, al-Qaeda and America's War in Arabia*, Norton, New York, 2012, pp. 40–47.

12.	A fairly comprehensive list of claimed al-Qa'ida and AQAP actions can be found in W. Andrew Terrill, *The Struggle for Yemen and the Challenge of al-Qaeda on the Arabian Peninsula*, US Army War College, Strategic Studies Institute, 2013. However, he does not address the relationship between the Saleh regime and the insurgents.

13.	This particular incident is well documented, see Johnsen, 2012, p. 194, Hull, 2011, pp. 116–7.

14.	Discussed by Hull but also soberly by Sarah Phillips, *Yemen and the Politics of Permanent Crisis*, Routledge, London, 2011, p. 43.

15.	Johnsen, *The Last Refugee*, p. 212–3.

16.	Ibid., p. 222.

17.	Ibid., p. 225.

18.	Attack on 12 May 2003 in Riyadh (Johnsen, p. 196), 8 November 2013 in Riyadh, 24 February 2006 in Abqaiq.

19.	Crown Prince January 2015–June 2017.

20.	Sarah Phillips, 'Questioning Failure, Stability, and Risk in Yemen', in Mehran Kamrava, ed., *Fragile Politics: Weak States in the Greater Middle East*, Hurst, London, 2016, p. 76.

21.	Hull, *High Value Target*, p. 9, with reference to FBI investigations of the *Cole* incident.

22.	Sarah Phillips, *Yemen and the Politics of Permanent Crisis*, Routledge, London, 2011, p. 139.

23.	For more detail, see Victoria Clark, *Yemen: Dancing on the Heads of Snakes*, Yale University Press, 2010, pp. 160–165; also Johnsen.

24.	Olga Khazan, 'Imams, Saunas, and Art Therapy: A Brief History of Jihadi Rehab Programmes', *The Atlantic*, 13 May 2013; Katherine Seifert, 'Can Jihadis Be Rehabilitated?', *Middle East Quarterly*, Spring 2010.

25.	Details of the ups and downs of the early stages of this relationship are described by the then US Ambassador to Yemen, Edmund Hull in *High Value Target*.

26.	Among many reports, see Hull, pp. 60–1.

27.	Johnsen, *The Last Refugee*, p. 123.

28.	Ibid., p. 205.

29.	Details of Saleh's relations with jihadis are found in M. Jerrett, M. al-Haddar, *Al Qaeda in the Arabian Peninsula: From Global Insurgent to State Enforcer*, Hate

Speech International, 2017.

30. Johnsen, *The Last Refugee*, p. 253.

31. Ibid., pp. 260–1.

32. Ibid., p. 264.

33. All data on US strikes from the Bureau of Investigative Journalism.

34. The connection between the allegiance of low-status people to fundamentalist Islamism, whether quietist or militant is discussed in greater detail in Chapter 7.

35. J. Watling and N. Shabibi, 'How the War on Terror Failed Yemen? The West Decided to Make Fighting al-Qaeda its Top Priority – and Only Ended Up Making Things Worse', *Foreign Policy*, 18 May 2016.

36. Nadwa Dawsari, 'The Enemy of my Enemy is al-Qaeda', *Mena Source*, Atlantic Council, 9 February 2015.

37. *Al-Arabiya*, 'Yemen Recruits Tribesmen to Hunt al-Qaeda', Al-Arabiya, 25 October 2010; and Brian Whitaker, 'Yemen Strikes Tribal Alliance Against al-Qaeda', *Al-Bab*, 26 October 2010.

Chapter Five: The Huthi Movement: From Nowhere to Centre Stage

1. A recent study focusing on Nigeria shows one example of Wahhabi proselytising: see James Dorsey, *Creating Frankenstein: Saudi Arabia's Ultra-Conservative Footprint in Africa*, annotated remarks at Terrorism in Africa seminar, Singapore, 18 January 2017.

2. Marieke Brandt, *Tribes and Politics in Yemen, A History of the Houthi Conflict*, Hurst, London, 2017, p. 144. Note that the references are derived from the proofs and the final page numbers may be slightly different.

3. Ibid., p. 37.

4. *Yemen Times*, 6 December 2010.

5. *Al Quds al-Arabi*, 3 December 2010.

6. International Crisis Group (ICG), *Yemen: Defusing the Saada Time Bomb*, 27 May 2009, p. 8.

7. 'A New Political Party: The Birth of The Ummah Party', *Al-Masdar*, 5 January 2012.

8. Brandt, *Tribes and Politics in Yemen*, p. 37.

9. Ibid., p. 154.

10. Ibid., p. 199.

11. ICG, p. 22.

12. Embassy Riyadh, 'Saudi Arabia: Renewed Assurances on Satellite Imagery', Wikileaks Cable: 10RIYADH159_a. Dated 7 February 2010. See also Stephen Day, *Regionalism and rebellion in Yemen: A Troubled National Union*, Cambridge University Press, Cambridge, 2012, p. 218.

13. Brandt, *Tribes and Politics in Yemen*, p. 351.

14. Patrick Cockburn, 'Threats to Yemen Prove America Hasn't Learned the Lesson

of History', *The Independent*, 31 December 2009.

15. Embassy Sana'a, 'Sa'ada War: Despite Claims of Ceasefire, Civilians Suffer, No End to the Fighting in Sight,' Wikileaks Cable: 09SANAA1599_a. Dated 26 August 2009.

16. Embassy Sana'a. 'Yemen's Counterterrorism Unit Stretched Thin by War Against Houthis,' Wikileaks Cable: 09SANAA2230_a. Dated 17 December 2009. It is worth noting, though, that one of the missions of this unit was to search for a group of Western medical staff who had been kidnapped in May that year, some of whom were found murdered. The children were eventually released and their parents were 'declared deceased' by the German embassy many years later. To date no one knows the true identity of the kidnappers, with little evidence to support any of the theories which range from the Huthis (least likely) to AQAP and Ali Mohsen (most likely).

17. Christopher Boucek, *Yemen on the Brink, War in Saada: From Local Insurrection to National Challenge*, Carnegie Endowment for International Peace, pp. 10–11.

18. Brandt, *Tribes and Politics in Yemen*, p. 84.

19. Ibid., p. 76.

20. Boucek, *Yemen on the Brink*, p. 10.

21. With one minister of state Hassan Sharafeddin, formally from the al-Haq Zaydi party.

22. *Yemen Times*, 20 September 2012, issue 1609.

23. Brandt, *Tribes and Politics in Yemen*, pp. 339–340.

24. Ibid., p. 339.

25. Leaked to Al Jazeera TV on 21 January 2015 though it took place the previous October.

26. On Monday 19 January 2015, the only day when there was armed resistance to the coup.

27. Quoted by various sources, including Al Jazeera and Iran's *Financial Tribune*.

28. The total absence of women on these institutions, and their minimal presence in governments, whether Huthi-Saleh or Hadi, reflects the seriousness with which all these leaders take the decision of the NDC that there should be 30 percent women in all leading institutions.

29. Decree 36 of 2017 on 27 April 2017. The SPC president ordered the prime minister to cancel the appointment on 30 April by Presidential Letter 762.

Chapter Six: Southern Separatism in Perspective

1. R. J. Gavin, *Aden Under British Rule 1839–1967*, Hurst, London, 1975, p. 445.

2. Franck Mermier, 'Le Mouvement Sudiste', in Laurent Bonnefoy et al, eds, *Yemen: le tournant révolutionnaire*, Kathala, Paris, 2011, Chapter 2, p. 43; Bernard Rougier, 'Yemen 1990–1994: la logique du pacte politique mise en échec', in Rémy Leveau et al, eds, *Le Yémen Contemporain*, Paris, 1999, p. 112.

3. For a more detailed account of the debates of the period, see Noel Brehony ed.,

Yemen Divided: The Story of a Failed State in South Arabia, I.B. Tauris, London, 2010, pp. 191–198.

4. See Helen Lackner, 'Hadramaut: Social Structure, Agriculture and Migration', in Noel Brehony, ed., *Hadramaut and Its Diaspora: Yemeni Politics, Identity and Migration,* I.B. Tauris, London, 2017, pp. 67–84.

5. More details on this issue in Helen Lackner, 'Land Tenure, Social Structure and the State in the Southern Governorates in the Mid-1990s', in K. Mahdi, A. Wuerth and H. Lackner, eds, *Yemen into the Twenty-First Century: Continuity and Change,* Ithaca Press, London, 2007, pp. 197–220. Also see World Bank, *Southern Governorates Agricultural Privatization Report,* 2006, Implementation Completion Report, 36380-YE, p. 7.

6. Mermier, 'Le Mouvement sudiste', p. 51.

7. Nasir Nuba in November 2008, quoted in Human Rights Watch, *In the Name of Unity: The Yemeni Government's Brutal Response to Southern Movement Protests,* New York 2009, p. 17.

8. The peaceful movement is discussed further in Chapter 6 of Adam Roberts et al, *Civil Resistance in the Arab Spring: Triumphs and Disasters,* Oxford University Press, 2016.

9. See Mermier in 'Le Mouvement sudiste' for summary of events.

10. The NDC and its problems are discussed in Chapter 1. Also see Helen Lackner, *Yemen's 'Peaceful' Transition from Autocracy: Could it Have Succeeded?,* Stockholm, 2016.

Chapter Seven: From Tribes to Elites

1. Much of the detailed research for this chapter was undertaken at Durham University where I held the 2016 Sir William Luce Fellowship. This chapter draws on the paper published there, as 'Understanding the Yemeni Crisis: The Transformation of Tribal Roles in Recent Decades', Durham Middle East Paper, Luce Fellowship Paper n. 17, 2016.

2. Daniel Corstange, 'Tribes and the Rule of Law in Yemen', paper for the Annual Conference of Middle East Studies Association, 2008, p. 9.

3. Sheila Carapico, *The Political Economy of Self-Help Development Cooperatives in the Yemen Arab Republic,* PhD Thesis, University of New York at Binghamton, 1984, p. 79; P. S. Khoury and J. Kostiner, *Tribes and State Formation in the Middle East,* University of California Press, Berkeley, 1990.

4. Among others, see Faleh A. Jabar, 'Sheikhs and Ideologues: Deconstruction and Reconstruction of Tribes under Patrimonial Totalitarianism in Iraq, 1968–1998' in F. A. Jabar and H. Dawod, eds, *Tribes and Power: Nationalism and Ethnicity in the Middle East,* Saqi Books, London, 2003.

5. Richard Tapper, quoted in Khoury and Kostiner, *Tribes and State Formation in the Middle East,* p.5.

6. See the many important contributions in Khoury and Kostiner; Giacomo

Luciani, *The Arab State*, University of California Press, Los Angeles, 1990; F. A. Jabar and H. Dawod, *Tribes and Power*; Hosham Dawod, *Tribus et Pouvoirs en Terre d'Islam*, Armand Colin, Paris, 2004; Shelagh Weir, *A Tribal Order: Politics and Law in the Mountains of Yemen*, British Museum Press, London, 2007.

7. Interpretation confirmed by Weir, *A Tribal Order*, p. 105.

8. Maurice Godelier 'A propos des concepts de tribu, ethnie et état, formes et fonctions du pouvoir politique' in Hosham Dawod, *Tribus et pouvoirs en terre d'Islam*, p. 296.

9. A combination of the terms *jumhuriya* (republic) and *mamlakiya* (monarchy).

10. See Abdalla Bujra, *The Politics of Stratification, A Study of Political Change in A South Arabian Town*, Oxford University Press, 1971, pp. 190–1; Joseph Chelhod, *L'Arabie du sud: Histoire et civilisation*, tome iii, Culture et institutions du Yemen, Paris, 1985, pp. 15–6, 33.

11. Ernest Gellner, *Saints of the Atlas*, Weidenfeld and Nicholson, London, 1969. This is the best known book on this subject.

12. The legal teachings and judgments of Yahya b. al-Husayn are the basis for the so-called Zaydi Hadawi school of law. The main emphasis of Zaydi Hadawi teaching is its insistence on righteous rule through the sadah; for details see chapter 4, 'The Sunnization of Upper Yemen', in Marieke Brandt, *Tribes and Politics in Yemen*.

13. Brandt, *Tribes and Politics in Yemen*, p. 21.

14. Stevenson provides a useful table with the ranking given by a number of different authors, see Thomas Stevenson, *Social Change in a Yemeni Highlands Town*, University of Utah Press, Salt Lake City, 1985, p 94.

15. For a brief discussion of the status of slaves and *akhdam*, see Jeffrey Meissner, *Tribes at the Core: Legitimacy, Structure and Power in Zaydi Yemen*, PhD thesis, Columbia University, 1987, pp. 165–170.

16. Dolores Walters devoted her PhD to analysing the comparative levels of low-status groups and attempting to identify the origins of these phenomena, See Dolores Walters, *Perceptions of Social Inequality in the Yemen Arab Republic*, PhD Thesis, 1987, New York University.

17. See Weir, *A Tribal Order*, pp. 33–35.

18. See Helen Lackner chapter 4, 'Rural Life and Land Tenure in Wadi Hadhramaut: Links with Outmigration' in Noel Brehony, ed., *Hadramaut and Its Diaspora*; also Walter Dostal, 'Squire and Peasant in Tarim: A Study of "Rent Capitalism" in Southern 'Arabia', in Walter Dostal, ed., *On Social Evolution: Vienna Contributions to Ethnology and Anthropology*, Vienna, 1984, pp. 232–3.

19. For more background on the country, see Helen Lackner, ed., *Why Yemen Matters*, Saqi Books, London, 2014, and N. Brehony and S. al-Sarhan, eds, *Rebuilding Yemen: Political, Economic and Social Challenges*, Gerlach, Berlin, 2015.

20. Yemen Arab Republic, Central Planning Organisation, *Statistical Yearbook 1986*, 1987, p. 49.

21. Ibid., p 59.

22. See S. Carapico and R. Tutwiler, *Yemeni Agriculture and Economic Change: Case Studies of Two Highland Regions*, American Institute for Yemeni Studies, Sana'a,

1981.

23. Richard Tutwiler, *Tribe, Tribune and Trade: Social Class Formation in Highland Yemen*, PhD Thesis, State University of New York, 1987, p. 407.

24. Ibid., p. 556.

25. *Yemen Arab Republic*, Central Planning Organisation, *Statistical Yearbook 1986*, 1987, p. 31. This gave a lower percentage of outmigrants than earlier censuses, with 12.6 percent whereas in 1981 the percentage was 16 percent and in 1975 19 percent, though some of this difference is likely to be due to different methodologies, let alone some inaccuracies.

26. Walters *Perceptions of Social Inequality in the Yemen Arab Republic*.

27. United Nations Economic Commission for Western Asia, *The Population Situation in the ECWA Region, Democratic Yemen*, Beirut, 1980, p. 10.

28. People's Democratic Republic of Yemen, Law no 1 of 1974, *The Family Law*, articles 17, 20, 22.

29. See, among others, J.E Peterson, 'Tribes and Politics in Yemen', Arabian Peninsula Background, 2008, Note APBN 007, p. 10.

30. An interesting example of changed living conditions and status in Sana'a and Taiz is given in S. Carapico and C. Myntti, 'A Tale of Two Families: Change in North Yemen, 1977-89', in Sheila Carapico, ed. *Arabia Incognita: Dispatches from Yemen and the Gulf*, Just World Books, Charlottesville, 2016, pp. 65–72.

31. While one or two women from Saleh's immediate family played a major role, this was largely kept in the background, and they operated through their husbands or brothers. The regime discouraged women from participating in active public life.

32. The importance of this group is explained in G. Hill et al., *Yemen, Corruption, Capital Flight and Global Drivers of Conflict*, Chatham House, London, 2013.

33. See among others, J. E Peterson, 'Tribes and Politics in Yemen', pp. 10–11.

34. See Hélène Thiollet, 'The Changing Dynamics of Migration in Yemen', in Lackner, ed., *Why Yemen Matters*, p. 273.

35. Mikhail Rodionov, 'Social Re-stratification in Modern Hadramawt', in *Quaderni di Studi Arabi*, nuova Series, Vol 1, 2006, p. 184.

36. Statement by Abdul Wahed Numrana, a shaykh from the Murad, one of the five major tribes of Mareb and the leader of the GPC, in Nadwa Dawsari, 'The Enemy of My Enemy is al-Qaeda', *Mena Source*, Atlantic Council, 9 February 2015.

37. For examples of this problem, see USAID, Education Development Centre Inc., *Yemen Cross-Sectoral Youth Assessment*, Final Report, 2008, p. 33.

Chapter Eight: Resources Scarcity and Their Capture

1.   See Abbas El-Zein et al, 'Health and Ecological Sustainability in the Arab World: A Matter of Survival' in *The Lancet*, vol. 383, 1 February 2014, pp. 458–476.

2.   World Bank, *Assessing the Impacts of Climate Change and Variability on the Water and Agricultural Sectors and the Policy Implications*, Yemen, report no 54196-YE, 2010, p. 21.

3.   See Lackner, ed., *Why Yemen Matters*, p. 177.

4.   Marcus Moench, *Yemen: Local Water Management in Rural Areas: A Case Study*, World Bank, 1999, and Helen Lackner, *Decentralized Management Sudy*, World Bank, Sana'a, 1997.

5.   C. Ward and N. al-Aulaqi, *Yemen: Issues in Decentralized Water Management*, A WaDImena Research Study, Republic of Yemen, 2008, p. 18.

6.   Personal interviews by the author at different times.

7.   J. Firebrace, A. Saleh Saif, S. Abbas Maqtari, R. Franceys, C. Coles, C. Handley, *Reducing Conflict through the Provision of Affordable Water and Increased Employment in Taiz*, James Firebrace Associates, Woodbridge, 2014, Chapter 1, p. 37.

8.   Ibid., Chapter 2, p. 33.

9.   These are discussed in some detail in Helen Lackner, 'Water Scarcity: Why Doesn't It Get the Attention It Deserves?' in Helen Lackner, ed., *Why Yemen Matters*, pp. 161–182.

10. Republic of Yemen, Ministry of Water and Environment, *National Water Sector Strategy and Investment Program, 2005–2009*, Sana'a, 2005. Its update in 2008 is the latest official policy statement.

11. See James Firebrace, 'Yemen Urban Water: Extreme Challenges, Practical Solutions and Lessons for the Future. The Case of Taiz', Chapter 6 of S. al-Sarhan and N. Brehony, eds, Y*emen to 2020: Political, Economic and Social Challenges*, Gerlach, Berlin, 2015.

12. World Bank, *Climate Investment Funds: Strategic Program for Climate Resilience for Yemen*, Meeting of the PPCR sub-committee, 17 April 17 2012, p. 42, paragraph 79.

13. United States Energy Information Administration (USEIA), Yemen Crude Oil Production by Year, retrieved from Index Mundi website.

14. USEIA, *Yemen Brief*, updated 25 September 2014.

15. Ginny Hill et al, *Yemen*, p. 25.

16. Peter Salisbury, *Yemen's Economy: Oil, Imports and Elites*, Chatham House, London 2011, p. 6.

17. Sarah Phillips, 'Questioning Failure, Stability, and Risk in Yemen', in Mehran Kamrava, ed., *Fragile Politics*, pp. 72–3.

18. Peter Salisbury 'Corruption in Yemen: Maintaining the Status Quo? in Brehony and Sarhan, *Rebuilding Yemen*, pp.71–2.

19. Yemen LNG website, http://www.yemenlng.com/ws/en/Articles/ShowArt.aspx?cmd=showone&at=news&artid=000

20. B. Clemens, W. Engelke, and O. Ecker, 'Petroleum Subsidies in Yemen: Leveraging Reform for Development', Policy Research Working Paper no. 5577, World Bank, Washington, 2011, p.5.

21. Phillips, 'Questioning Failure, Stability and Risk in Yemen', p. 73.

22. Embassy Sana'a, 'Contraband and Confusion in the Gulf of Aden', Wikileaks Cable: 09SANAA1604_a. Dated 29 August 2009.

23. World Bank, *Yemen Poverty Assessment*, 2007, p. 16.

24. Ibid., p. 17.

25. Ginny Hill et al, *Yemen*, p. 21.

26. Salisbury, 'Corruption in Yemen', p. 66, quoting earlier work by Sarah Phillips.

27. World Bank, 2010, p. 20.

Chapter Nine: The Economy

1. Ahmed al-Kasir, 'The Impact of Emigration on Social Structure in the Yemen Arab Republic', in B.R. Pridham, ed., *Economy, Society and Culture in Contemporary Yemen*, Routledge, London, 1985, p. 122.

2. World Bank, Operations Evaluation Department, *Yemen Country Assistance Evaluation*, Report no 21787, Washington DC, 2001, p. 1.

3. People's Democratic Republic of Yemen, Central Statistical Organization, *Statistical Yearbook 1988*, 1989, p. 47.

4. Republic of Yemen, CSO *Statistical Yearbook 1990*, p. 4.

5. Quoted in Gerd Nonneman, 'Key issues in the Yemeni Economy', in E.G.H Joffé, M.H. Hachemi and E.W. Watkins, *Yemen Today: Crisis and Solutions*, Caravel Press, London, 1997, p. 97.

6. Ibid., p. 97.

7. Ibid., p. 98.

8. Charles Schmitz, 'Politics and Economy in Yemen: Lessons from the Past', in Mahdi et al, *Yemen into the Twenty-First Century*, p. 35.

9. World Bank, 2001, p. 5.

10. Ibid., p. 11.

11. World Bank, *Country Assistance Strategy for the Republic of Yemen*, report no 15286-Yem, 1996, p. 3.

12. Ibid., p. 3.

13. Ibid., p. 3.

14. World Bank, 2001, p. 12.

15. Ibid., p. 13 para 3.18.

16. Ibid., p. 16.

17. IDA, the International Development Association, is the branch of the World Bank which provides low-interest loans to the poorest developing countries.

18. World Bank, 2001, p. 17.

19. The document itself is neither dated, nor signed, nor is its source identified.

20. Republic of Yemen, *Poverty Reduction Strategy Paper (PRSP) 2003–2005*, 2002,

pp. 26–7.

21.   Ibid., p. 60 ff.

22.   Ibid., p. 59.

23.   Republic of Yemen, Ministry of Planning and International Cooperation, *The Socio-Economic Development Plan for Poverty Reduction*, 2006, p. 3.

24.   Ibid., pp. 4–5.

25.   Ibid., p. 6.

26.   Republic of Yemen, Ministry of Planning and International Cooperation (MOPIC), *Report on the Mid-Term Review of the 3rd Socio-Economic Development Plan for Poverty Reduction 2006–2010*, 2009, p. 5.

27.   Ginny Hill et al, *Yemen*, p. 36.

28.   Ibid., p. 36.

29.   Republic of Yemen, MOPIC, *Progress Report on the Use of Pledged Resources*, quoted in Ginny Hill et al, *Yemen*, p. 37.

30.   UK, *FCO Fact Sheet on Friends of Yemen for meeting on 7 March 2013*, p. 2.

31.   Republic of Yemen, *Executive Bureau, Annual Report 2014, Status Report Mutual Accountability Framework* 2014, p. 18.

32.   Ibid., p. 20.

33.   World Bank, Republic of Yemen, *Unlocking the Potential for Economic Growth: A Country Economic Memorandum*, 2015, p. 65.

34.   Given this situation, the data of the two periods are not strictly comparable and this may contribute to explaining why the report makes no comparisons.

35.   World Bank indicators from website.

36.   World Bank, 2015, p. 63.

37.   Republic of Yemen, *Poverty Assessment*, 2007, vol. 1, p. 13.

38.   Interview with the Minister of Civil Service Ahmed al-Shami in *al-Araby al-Jadeed*, 26 December 2014.

39.   Republic of Yemen, Ministry of Planning and Economic Cooperation, *Second Five Year Plan (SFYP) 2001–2005*, p. 67.

40.   World Bank, 2015, p. 14, figure 9.

41.   Republic of Yemen, *Poverty Assessment 2007*, footnote 9 p. 12.

42.   World Bank, Republic of Yemen, 2015, p. 14, figure 9.

43.   Republic of Yemen, International Labour Organisation (ILO), *Yemen Labour Force Survey*, 2013–14, 2015, p. 64, table 8.

44.   SFYP p. 65.

45.   Republic of Yemen, ILO, 2015, p. 37.

46.   Republic of Yemen, PRSP, p. 11.

47.   Republic of Yemen, ILO, *Working Children in the Republic of Yemen: the Results of the 2010 National Child Labour Survey*, 2013, p. ix.

48.   Republic of Yemen, CSO, *Statistical Yearbook 2012*, p. 178 and 180.

49.   CSO, quoted in World Bank, 2015, p. 8.

50.   World Bank, *Unlocking the Potential for Economic Growth*, 2015, p. 6.

51.   Ibid., p. 27.

52.   Ibid., pp. 40–42.

53. Ibid., p. 77.

54. Ibid., p. 85.

55. World Bank, 2001, p. 11.

56. Republic of Yemen, *PRSP 2003–2005*, p. 48.

57. Republic of Yemen, SFYP, p. 73.

58. Republic of Yemen, *Poverty Assessment*, 2007, vol. 1 p. 16.

59. World Bank, *Background Note,* para 1.

60. Republic of Yemen, *Poverty Assessment*, p. 16.

61. T. Bagash, P. Pereznieto and K. Dubai, *Transforming Cash Transfers: Beneficiary and Community Perspectives on the Social Welfare Fund in Yemen*, Overseas Development Institute, London, 2013, p. 1.

62. Republic of Yemen, *PRSP*, p. 49.

63. World Bank, UN, EU, Islamic Development Bank, Joint Social and Economic Assessment for the Republic of Yemen, Washington DC, 2012, p.49.

64. Republic of Yemen, *Social Fund for Development Annual Report*, 2014, p. 7.

65. Ibid., p. 86.

66. Nora Ann Colton, 'Yemen: A Collapsed Economy', *Middle East Journal*, vol. 64, no 3, 2010, pp. 410–426.

67. World Bank, Republic of Yemen, *Poverty Assessment report 15158-YEM*, 1996, p. 2.

68. Ibid., p. 7.

69. Ibid., p. 12.

70. Ibid., p. 12.

71. Ibid., p. 13.

72. World Food Programme, Republic of Yemen, *Comprehensive Food Security Survey*, 2010, p. 25.

73. World Bank, UN, EU, Islamic Development Bank, Republic of Yemen, *Joint Social and Economic Assessment*, p. xxi.

74. World Bank, *Country Engagement Note for the Republic of Yemen for the Period FY 17-FY 18*, Washington DC, 2016, p. 6.

75. Mentioning these usually attract wry smiles from Yemenis who point out that appointing senior regime corrupt individuals to senior posts is unlikely to change the system. The participation of corrupt people in NACA is mentioned in April Longley Alley, *Shifting Light in the Qamariyya: the Reinvention of Patronage Networks in Contemporary Yemen*, Georgetown University, Washington, PhD Thesis, 2008, p. 171.

76. This information from the *Wall Street Journal*, quoted in Hill et al, *Yemen*, p. 22.

77. April Longley Alley, *Shifting Light in the Qamariyya*, pp. 157–160.

78. USAID, 2006, p. 4.

79. Ibid., pp. 42–3.

80. Ibid., p. 4.

81. UNDP, *Illicit Financial Flows from the Least Developed Countries, 1990–2008*, 2011, p. 14.

82. Ibid., p. 61.

83. Al-Masdar website, Baraqish, 21 December 2016.

84. The World Bank, 2015, p. 6.
85. Ibid., p. 7.
86. Ibid., p. 6.
87. Ibid., p. 17.
88. The World Bank, *Country Engagement*, 2016, p. 8.

Chapter Ten: The Rural-Urban Nexus

1. Republic of Yemen, Ministry of Planning and Development, Central Statistical Organization (ROY/MPD/CSO), *Statistical Yearbook 1994*, Sana'a, 1995, p. 35.
2. Yemen Arab Republic (YAR), Central Planning Organisation, Statistics Department, *Statistical Yearbook, 1979–1980*, Sana'a, 1981, p. 41. The figures provided are for the 1975 and 1981 censuses. The 1975 Census was the first real census in the YAR while that of 1981 was implemented by the Confederation of Yemeni Development Associations. Their figures are not exactly compatible as the methodology was somewhat different; however, these are given as an indication of the population situation.
3. ROY/MPD/CSO, 1995, p. 28.
4. Christopher Ward, *The Water Crisis in Yemen: Managing Extreme Water Scarcity in the Middle East*, I.B. Tauris, London, 2015, p. 198.
5. Ibid., p. 189.
6. Ibid., p. 184. Between 1984 and 1987, coverage dropped from 61 percent to 58 percent.
7. R. J. Gavin, *Aden Under British Rule, 1839–1967*, Hurst, London, 1975, p. 445.
8. All figures for 1955 and earlier are from appendix B, p. 445 of Gavin.
9. People's Democratic Republic of Yemen (PDRY), MPO, CSO, *Statistical Yearbook 1980*, Aden, 1980, p. 26.
10. PDRY Central Statistical Organisation, *1989 Statistical year book*, 1988, pp. 45–6.
11. ROY/MPD CSO., p. 28.
12. Farea al-Muslimi, 'Yemeni Ports see Traffic Decline Dramatically', *Al-Monitor*, 5 March 2014.
13. ROY/MPD/CSO, p. 35.
14. Vincent Planel, 'Le réveil des piémonts: Taez et la révolution yéménite', in L. Bonnefoy, F. Mermier and M. Poirier, eds, *Yémen: Le tournant révolutionnaire*, Kathala, Paris 2012, p. 126.
15. ROY/MPD/CSO, p. 35.
16. Roman Stadnicki, 'Le Yemen vers la transition urbaine', in Bonnefoy et al, p. 205.
17. PDRY, 1980, p. 26.
18. Stadnicki, 'Le Yemen vers la transition urbaine', p. 205.
19. ROY/MPD/CSO, p. 28.
20. Thomas Pritzkat, 'Land Distribution After Unification and its Consequences for Urban Development in Hadramawt', in K. Mahdi et al, *Yemen into the Twenty-First Century*.

21. Ibid., p. 354. This paper also illustrates the erratic nature and the corruption involved in these distributions.

22. Ward, *The Water Crisis in Yemen*, p. 133. At that time, 47 percent of urban people had similar access, a figure which has since dropped. It is worth noting that only 20 percent of rural and 27 percent of urban people had access to safe sanitation at that time. These are just estimates among a wide range of other figures that are given. The World Bank, for instance, gives a statistic of 59 percent rural coverage for 1990.

23. World Bank, *Project Appraisal Document: Rural Energy Access Project*, Sana'a, 2009, p. 9.

Select Bibliography and Further Reading

Abdelkarim Zeinab, Hodachok Eric, and Monaco Danielle, *Yemen's Transition: Electoral Challenges and Opportunities for Reform*, Centre on Democracy, Development and the Rule of Law, International Foundation for Electoral Systems, working paper 139, 2013.

Bonnefoy, Laurent, 'Violence in Contemporary Yemen: State, Society and Salafis' in *The Muslim World*, vol. 101, April 2011, pp. 324–346.

Bonnefoy, Laurent, *Salafism in Yemen: Transnationalism and Religious Identity* (London: Hurst & Co, 2011).

Bonnefoy, Laurent, Mermier, Franck and Poirier, Marine, eds, *Yémen, le tournant révolutionnaire* (Paris: Karthala/CEFAS, 2012).

Bonnefoy, Laurent, *Yemen: Par-delà les marges du monde* (Paris: Fayard, 2017).

Boucek, Christopher, *Yemen on the Brink: War in Saada – From Local Insurrection to National Challenge*, Carnegie Endowment for International Peace 2010.

Brandt, Marieke, *Tribes and Politics in Yemen: A History of the Houthi Conflict* (London: C. Hurst & Co, 2017).

Brehony, Noel, *Yemen Divided: the Story of a Failed State in South Arabia* (London: I.B. Tauris, 2011).

Brehony, Noel, and S. al-Sarhan, eds, *Rebuilding Yemen: Political, Economic and Social Challenges* (Berlin: Gerlach, 2015).

Brehony, Noel ed., *Hadhramaut and its Diaspora: Yemeni Politics, Identity and Migration* (London: I.B. Tauris, 2017).

Bujra, Abdalla, *The Politics of Stratification: A Study of Political Change in a South Arabian Town* (Oxford: Oxford University Press, 1971).

Burgat, François, *L'Islamisme à l'heure d'Al-Qaida* (Paris: La Découverte, 2005).

Burke, Jason, *Al-Qaeda: the True Story of Radical Islam* (London: Penguin, 2004).

Burrowes, Robert D., *Historical Dictionary of Yemen* (Lanham: Scarecrow Press, 2009).

Burrowes, Robert D., 'The Republic of Yemen: The Politics of Unification and Civil War, 1989–1995', in Michael C. Hudson, ed., *Middle East Dilemma: The Politics and Economics of Arab Integration* (London: I.B. Tauris, 1999).

Burrowes, Robert D., 'The Yemen Civil War of 1994: Impact on the Arab Gulf States', in Jamal S. al-Suwaida, ed., *The Yemeni War of 1994: Causes and Consequences*, Ch. 4, pp. 71–80 (London: Saqi Books, 1995).

Carapico, Sheila, ed., *Arabia Incognita: Dispatches from Yemen and the Gulf* (Charlottesville: Just World Books, 2016).

Carapico, Sheila, and R. Tutwiler, *Yemeni Agriculture and Economic Change: Case Studies of Two Highland Regions*, (Sanaʻa: American Institute for Yemeni Studies, 1981).

Carapico, Sheila, *The Political Economy of Self-help Development Cooperatives in the Yemen Arab Republic*, PhD thesis, State University of New York at Binghamton, 1984.

Chelhod, Joseph *L'Arabie du Sud : Histoire et civilisation, tome iii, Culture et institutions du Yemen* (Paris: Maisonneuve et Larose, 1985).

Clark, Victoria, *Yemen: Dancing on the Heads of Snakes* (New Haven: Yale University Press, 2010).

Colton, Nora Ann, 'Yemen: A Collapsed Economy' in *Middle East Journal*, vol. 64, number 3, pp. 410–426, 2010.

Corstange, Daniel, 'Tribes and the rule of law in Yemen', paper for the Annual Conference of MESA 2008.

Corstange, Daniel, *The Price of a Vote in the Middle East: Clientelism and Communal Politics in Lebanon and Yemen* (New York: Cambridge University Press, 2016).

Dawod, Hosham, *Tribus et pouvoirs en terre d'Islam* (Paris: Armand Colin, 2004).

Dawsari, Nadwa, *We Lived Days in Hell: Civilian Perspectives on the Conflict in Yemen* (USA: Centre for Civilians in Conflict, 2016).

Dawsari, Nadwa, 'The Enemy of My Enemy is al Qaeda', Mena Source, Atlantic Council, 9 February 2015.

Dostal, Walter, ed., 'On Social Evolution' in Vienna Contributions to Ethnology and Anthropology, 1984.

Dresch, Paul, *A History of Modern Yemen* (Cambridge: Cambridge

University Press, 2000).

El-Zein, Abbas et al. 'Health and Ecological Sustainability in the Arab World: A Matter of Survival' in *The Lancet*, vol 383, 1 February, 2014, pp. 458–476.

Firebrace, James, A. Saif, M. Saleh, A. Shoqi, R. Franceys, C. Coles and C. Handley, *Reducing Conflict Through the Provision of Affordable Water and Increased Employment in Taiz* (Woodbridge: James Firebrace Associates, 2014).

Gavin, R. J., *Aden Under British Rule 1839-1967* (London: C. Hurst & Co, 1975).

Halliday, Fred, *Arabia Without Sultans* (Harmondsworth: Penguin, 1974).

Halliday, Fred, *Revolution and Foreign Policy: The Case of South Yemen, 1967–1987* (Cambridge: Cambridge University Press, 1990).

Hart-Davis, Duff, *The War That Never Was* (London: Century, 2011).

Hill, Ginny, P. Salisbury, L. Northedge, and J. Kinninmont, *Yemen, Corruption, Capital Flight and Global Drivers of Conflict* (London: Chatham House, 2013).

Hill, Ginny, *Yemen Endures: Civil War, Saudi Adventurism and the Future of Arabia* (London: C. Hurst & Co, 2017).

Hull, Edmund, *High Value Target: Countering al-Qaeda in Yemen* (Washington DC: Potomac Books, 2011).

Human Rights Watch, *Unpunished Massacre: Yemen's Failed Response to the 'Friday of Dignity' Killings,* US 2013.

Human Rights Watch, *'No Safe Places', Yemen's Crackdown on Protests in Taiz,* USA, 2012.

International Crisis Group, *The Huthis: from Saada to Sana'a,* Brussels 2014.

International Crisis Group, *Yemen: Is Peace Possible?*, Brussels, 2016.

International Crisis Group, *Yemen's Southern Question: Avoiding a Breakdown,* Brussels 2013.

International Crisis Group, *Yemen's Military-Security Reform: Seeds of New Conflict?*, Brussels 2013.

International Crisis Group, *Yemen: Enduring Conflicts, Threatened Transition,* Brussels 2012.

Jabar, Faleh A. and Dawod, H. eds., *Tribes and Power: Nationalism and Ethnicity in the Middle East* (London: Saqi Books, 2002).

Jerrett, Martin and al-Haddar, M., *Al-Qaeda in the Arabian Peninsula: From Global Insurgent to State Enforcer,* Hate Speech International, 2017.

Johnsen, Gregory, *The Last Refuge: Yemen, Al-Qaeda, and America's War in*

Arabia (New York: Norton, 2012).

Kamrava, Mehran, ed., *Fragile Politics, Weak States in the Greater Middle East* (London: C. Hurst & Co, 2016).

Khoury, Nabeel, *Journal Essay, Yemen: In Search of a Coherent US Policy*, Middle East Policy Council, Summer 2014, vol. XXI, Number 2.

Khoury, Philip S. and Kostiner, J., eds., *Tribes and State Formation in the Middle East* (Los Angeles: University of California Press, 1990).

Lackner, Helen, *PDRY Yemen, Outpost of Socialist Development in Arabia* (London: Ithaca Press, 1985).

Lackner, Helen, ed., *Why Yemen Matters* (London, Saqi Books, 2014).

Lackner, Helen, *Yemen's 'Peaceful' Transition from Autocracy: Could It Have Succeeded?* (Stockholm: International Institute for Democracy and Electoral Assistance, 2016).

Lackner, Helen, 'The Change Squares of Yemen: civil Resistance in an Unlikely Context', in Roberts, Adam, Willis, M. J., McCarthy, R., and Garton Ash, T. eds., *Civil Resistance in the Arab Spring: Triumphs and Disasters* (Oxford: Oxford University Press, 2016).

Lackner, Helen, 'Climate change and Security: Major Challenges for Yemen's Future', in Sternberg, Troy, ed., *Climate Hazard Crises in Asian Societies and Environments* (London: Routledge, 2017).

Lackner, Helen and D. Varisco, eds., *Yemen and the Gulf States: The Making of a Crisis* (Berlin: Gerlach, 2017).

Leveau, Rémy, F. Mermier, U. Steinback, eds., *Le Yemen contemporain* (Paris: Karthala, 1999).

Luciani, Giacomo, *The Arab State* (Los Angeles: University of California Press, 1990).

Meissner, Jeffrey, *Tribes at the Core: Legitimacy, Structure and Power in Zaydi Yemen* PhD thesis, Columbia University, 1987.

Moench, Marcus, *Yemen: Local Water Management in Rural Areas: A Case Study*, Washington DC World Bank, 1999.

Moench, Marcus and H. Lackner, *Decentralized Management Study*, Sana'a, World Bank, 1997.

Nonneman, Gerd, 'Key issues in the Yemeni Economy' in E. G. H Joffé, M. H. Hachemi, E. W. Watkins, *Yemen Today: Crisis and Solutions* (London: Caravel Press, 1997).

O'Balance, Edgar, *The War in the Yemen,* (London: Faber & Faber, 1971).

Pelletiere, Stephen, *Yemen and Stability in the Persian Gulf: Confronting the*

Threat from Within Strategic Studies Institute, US Army War College, PA, 1996.

Peterson, J. E., *Tribes and Politics in Yemen*, Arabian Peninsula Background, note APBN 007. 2008.

Phillips, Sarah, *Yemen's Democracy Experiment in Regional Perspective, Patronage and Pluralized Authoritarianism* (New York: Palgrave Macmillan, 2008).

Phillips, Sarah, *Yemen and the Politics of Permanent Crisis* (London: International Institute for Strategic Studies, 2011).

Rodionov, Mikhail, 'Social re-stratification in modern Hadramawt', in *Quaderni di Studi Arabi*, Nuova Serie, Vol 1, 2006.

Salisbury, Peter, *Yemen: Stemming the Rise of the Chaos State* (London: Chatham House, 2016).

Salisbury, Peter, *Yemen's Economy: Oil, Imports and Elites* (London, Chatham House, 2011).

Schwedler, Jillian, *Faith in Moderation: Islamist Parties in Jordan and Yemen* (Cambridge: Cambridge University Press, 2006).

Terrill, W. Andrew, *The Struggle for Yemen and the Challenge of al-Qaeda on the Arabian Peninsula*, US Army War College, Strategic Studies Institute, 2013.

Tutwiler, Richard, *Tribe, Tribute and Trade: Social Class Formation in Highland Yemen*, PhD thesis, State University of New York at Binghamton, 1987.

Walters, Dolores, *Perceptions of Social Inequality in the Yemen Arab Republic*, PhD thesis, New York University, 1987.

Ward, Christopher and N. al-Aulaqi, *Yemen: Issues in Decentralized Water Management*, Republic of Yemen, a WaDImena Research Study, World Bank 2008.

Ward, Christopher, *The Water Crisis in Yemen: Managing Extreme Water Scarcity in the Middle East* (London: I.B. Tauris, 2015).

Weir, Shelagh, *A Tribal Order: Politics and Law in the Mountains of Yemen* (London: British Museum Press, 2007).

World Bank, Yemen, *Assessing the impacts of climate change and variability on the water and agricultural sectors and the policy implications* report no. 54196-YE, 2010.

Zimmerman, Katherine, *A New Model for Defeating al Qaeda in Yemen*, (USA: American Enterprise Institute, 2015).

Index